Contents

Focus on neglected crises

International Federation
of Red Cross and Red Crescent Societies

Annex

Putting an end to deadly neglect

The past two years have seen unprecedented attention lavished on disasters by the media, by the public and by aid organizations across the world. The record hurricane season in the Caribbean, the South Asia earthquake and the devastating Indian Ocean tsunami combined to catapult so-called 'natural' disasters into the limelight.

The response has also been unprecedented. Last year, the resources committed to humanitarian aid reached at least US$ 17 billion – outstripping any other year on record. Over US$ 5 billion of this was donated by private individuals to tsunami survivors. So it may seem a strange time to speak of disasters and humanitarian crises being 'neglected'. Yet for every crisis that takes centre stage, there are a dozen more waiting in the wings for a walk-on part.

Common sense would dictate that the larger the disaster, the greater the media attention and the more generous the response. That was certainly the case with the tsunami. But it is not, unfortunately, a universal rule. Research across a range of disasters reveals that there is no clear link between death tolls and media interest. Rather, Western self-interest gives journalists a stronger steer.

To take one example among many, Hurricanes Katrina and Stan – which hit America's Gulf Coast and Central America respectively last year – both led to the deaths of around 1,500 people. Yet Katrina generated 40 times more articles in newspapers across Europe, the US and Australia than Stan. The disparity in the financial response to each disaster was greater still.

Whether we like it or not, the media continue to exert a strong influence over where resources flow for humanitarian crises – and not just for the tsunami or Katrina. The South Asia earthquake attracted 86 minutes of TV coverage on US networks in 2005 and raised over US$ 300 per targeted beneficiary. Meanwhile, Somalia and Côte d'Ivoire attracted no TV coverage at all and raised respectively just US$ 53 and US$ 27 per beneficiary.

However, neglect is not just about headlines or appeal targets. The timing and appropriateness of aid are also vital. Over recent years we have witnessed slow-motion food shortages becoming full-blown humanitarian crises before our eyes. Niger, Malawi, the Horn of Africa. We have the early warning systems, we can assess when households shift from 'reversible' to 'irreversible' coping mechanisms, we have the expertise and experience to invest in reducing risks before they become disasters. So why do we still

International Federation
of Red Cross and Red Crescent Societies

see last-minute, ultra-expensive airlifts of food aid in response to graphic TV images of starving children?

In Malawi last year, a state of emergency wasn't declared until eight months after the first signs of crisis. When appeals were made, donors provided food aid but neglected calls for vital agricultural inputs – such as appropriate seeds and fertilizers – which could have helped reduce the risk of future food shortages. While food aid can play a key role in emergency response, there is an urgent need to commit more resources towards measures to secure people's recovery, such as agricultural inputs, healthcare, livelihood interventions, water and sanitation.

This year's report also looks at less likely candidates for the title of neglected crisis. In Nepal, a country racked by civil war for a decade, an estimated 35,000 women and new-born babies die each year due to unsafe childbirth and neonatal practices. Mountains, conflict and lack of money conspire to prevent their access to adequate healthcare. Discrimination against women in the highly traditional villages of rural Nepal adds to their burden. Yet this silent tragedy, which has claimed over 25 times more lives than the conflict, goes virtually unnoticed by the media and shows few signs of improving.

We devote a whole chapter to studying the gendered impacts of disasters, with a particular focus on the women of northern Pakistan who survived the earthquake but struggled to access their fair share of aid. And we analyse the plight of Africa's boat migrants, several thousand of whom are thought to die each year in desperate attempts to reach Europe by sea. Theirs is such a neglected crisis that no single organization is even collating data on casualties, let alone appealing for their aid.

Ideally, each situation would be judged according to priority humanitarian needs and funds would be allocated accordingly. However, several factors still prevent that from happening: poor access and security in the some of the world's more awkward countries, geopolitical preferences of donors, the effects of global media and the lack of common humanitarian criteria to compare needs objectively between continents.

The solutions to most of these neglected crises lie far beyond the mandate or capacity of humanitarian organizations. The best we can do is bear witness to what we see and alleviate suffering where we can – however temporarily. The long-term answers lie in greater political, security, developmental and economic engagement. To that end, I commend you to read this report and share it as widely as possible with your colleagues and friends beyond the humanitarian sphere.

Markku Niskala
Secretary General

International Federation
of Red Cross and Red Crescent Societies

Neglected crises: partial response perpetuates suffering

Global interest in humanitarian response is riding high – after a string of sudden, large-scale disasters triggered by the Indian Ocean tsunami, the South Asia earthquake and a record hurricane season along America's Gulf Coast last year. But the brighter the media spotlight shines on such high-visibility catastrophes, the deeper into shadow fall more chronic – and often more deadly – humanitarian crises.

Lists of forgotten disasters have multiplied as commentators seek to portray people and places that have missed out (see Table 1.1). Aid organizations and donors have reiterated their commitment to impartial humanitarian aid – according to need alone. But has this growing interest in neglected crises and equitable aid had much impact?

Table 1.1 Neglected crises of 2005–2006

No.	MSF, 2005[1]	AlertNet, 2005[2]	ECHO, 2006[3]	UNDPI, 2006[4]
1	Democratic Republic of Congo	Democratic Republic of Congo	Algeria (Western Sahara)	Liberia
2	Chechnya	Northern Uganda	India (Kashmir)	Asylum seekers and migrants
3	Haiti	Sudan/Darfur	Myanmar/Burma	Democratic Republic of Congo
4	AIDS drugs research and development	AIDS	Nepal	Nepal's children
5	North-eastern India	West Africa	Chechnya	Somalia
6	Southern Sudan	Colombia		Refugees
7	Somalia	Chechnya		South Asia earthquake reconstruction
8	Colombia	Haiti		Children behind bars
9	Northern Uganda	Nepal		Water wars/peace
10	Côte d'Ivoire	Infectious diseases		Côte d'Ivoire

[1] Médecins Sans Frontières (MSF): 'Top 10 most under-reported humanitarian stories', based on monitoring by the Tyndall Report of the nightly newscasts of the US's three major TV networks (CBS, NBC and ABC) in 2005.
[2] Reuters AlertNet: 'top 10 forgotten emergencies', based on a poll of over 100 humanitarians, media, academics and activists published in March 2005.
[3] European Commission's Humanitarian Aid department (ECHO): most 'forgotten crises', based on ECHO's nine-point methodology covering level of development, poverty, exposure to disasters, population movements, under-five health and donor contributions.
[4] United Nations Department of Public Information (UNDPI): list of '10 stories the world should hear more about'.

Photo opposite page: A mother carries her malnourished infant in Maradi, southern Niger. Poverty and the worst drought in years left 3.6 million people short of food during 2005. As G8 countries met in Scotland to discuss ways to help Africa, Niger's emaciated children provided a case study of rich world inaction.

© REUTERS/Finbarr O'Reilly, courtesy www.alertnet.org

In 2005, the world responded more generously to people's humanitarian needs than at any time in recent history – yet millions still missed out on vital, potentially life-saving aid. The tsunami attracted billions of dollars – 50 times more per affected person than was donated for Chad, Guyana or Côte d'Ivoire. The gap between the best- and worst-funded disasters remains unacceptably wide, as detailed in Chapter 7 of this year's report.

Why is humanitarian aid still unfairly distributed? Which communities languish in the shadows of emergency response and prevention – neglected by the media, aid organizations, donors, even by their own governments? Why do some crises rate news coverage, donor money, a place in international disaster databases, while others don't? What is the human impact of this neglect and what can be done about it?

This lead chapter seeks to provide some answers to these questions – focusing on humanitarian crises and natural disasters, both chronic and acute. It starts by briefly unpacking the meaning of neglect and then presents a typology which encompasses ways in which neglect of humanitarian needs is manifested and the underlying reasons why. It concludes by arguing that, while the acute symptoms of human suffering are often neglected, the critical need to address the underlying causes of that suffering is more neglected still.

Neglect or select? Of what and by whom?

Neglect signifies not being considered, incorporated or provided for. Neglect is wide-ranging in its causes and consequences and is therefore difficult to cover comprehensively in any short introduction to the topic. But distinguishing between neglect and select is one approach.

Neglect of humanitarian needs can arise from simple ignorance of a problem, due to lack of access to data or news. It may also be explained by forgetfulness or misunderstanding. But many cases of neglect relate more to conscious prioritization, bias (often geographical or strategic) and self-interest. Neglect thus becomes select and selection is exercised by donors (public and private), aid organizations and the media.

Neglect is not only about the relative attention and resources given to different humanitarian crises. It's also about the way the needs of different social groups are addressed within crises. Humanitarian response and recovery are often flawed by discrimination (deliberate or not) against the poorer, the ethnically marginal, women, children, the aged and the politically weak.

Underpinning the neglect of people's immediate needs is a wider neglect of root causes. The dominant assumption of aid organizations is that emergencies, disasters and crises are deviations from the 'normal' conditions of daily life. The alternative

International Federation
of Red Cross and Red Crescent Societies

view – that daily life for many people contains the seeds of crisis – is not often considered. So an unreal distinction arises between everyday life and crisis, when in reality vulnerable people are exposed to a wide spectrum of risk – as this year's chapters on Guatemala, Malawi and Nepal make clear.

Disaster and emergency managers are understandably reluctant or unable to tackle the thorny issue of root causes. However, the 17 members of the Good Humanitarian Donorship initiative agreed on a set of principles in 2003 which make clear that the objectives of humanitarian action are not only to save lives and reduce suffering, but also to "strengthen the capacity of affected countries and local communities to prevent, prepare for, mitigate and respond to humanitarian crises". They add that humanitarian action should "facilitate the return to normal lives and livelihoods".

Donor-led distinctions between humanitarian and development assistance, while convenient in terms of accounting, make it hard for organizations to meet the full range of people's life-threatening needs. This is particularly the case in situations of acute malnutrition found across sub-Saharan Africa, where the most appropriate response is urgent, large-scale support for livelihoods – an intervention which does not fit easily into either humanitarian or development boxes.

Typology of neglect

There are many types of neglect – and the same types can be both cause and effect. For example, lack of media coverage is a manifestation common to many neglected disasters, but the failure to report on such crises is equally a cause of their neglect. One way of grasping hold of this slippery issue and the challenges it presents is through the following typology:

1. **Unreported** – or under-reported, by global media.
2. **Unfunded** – or under-funded, by donors, aid organizations or host governments.
3. **Uncounted** – not registered by disaster databases or not assessed by aid organizations.
4. **Secondary** – disasters triggered by a secondary event not prepared for by governments, aid organizations or communities.
5. **Secret** – concealed by host governments for political reasons or by communities for cultural reasons.
6. **Awkward** – not addressed by governments or aid organizations for political, strategic, security or logistical reasons.
7. **Misunderstood** – complex crises whose causes and solutions may not be understood by experts or decision-makers.

The distinctions are somewhat artificial and some neglected crises will manifest several types of neglect at once. However, the advantage of this typology is that it reveals the roles of different players – whether journalists, donors, database managers, aid organizations, analysts, governments or affected communities – and how they could do more to highlight the plight of people whose needs are neglected. And behind these types of neglect there lies a common theme: neglecting the root causes of socially constructed vulnerability and chronic poverty.

1. Unreported

In 1998, the non-governmental organization (NGO) Médecins Sans Frontières (MSF) began publishing its 'top 10' most under-reported humanitarian stories of the year. Since then, Colombia, the Democratic Republic of Congo (DRC), Chechnya, Somalia and the issue of access to life-saving medicines have all featured six times or more.

MSF's source is the Tyndall Report, which monitors the amount of airtime devoted to disasters on the nightly newscasts of the three largest US television networks. Of the 14,000-plus minutes of news broadcast by these networks last year, Hurricane Katrina captured 1,153 minutes – making it the most covered news story of last year, after Iraq. The tsunami (250 minutes), Hurricanes Rita (136 minutes) and Wilma (122 minutes), and the South Asia earthquake (86 minutes) also featured in the top 20 news stories of 2005 – helping triple average annual coverage of natural disasters.

By contrast, DRC attracted just six minutes and Chechnya two minutes of coverage. The other eight stories highlighted by MSF were not covered at all. To help raise money for the people of DRC – and awareness of their plight – the Netherlands Red Cross launched a six-day media campaign with the help of local radio DJs (see Box 1.1).

In January 2006, media consultancy CARMA International published the results of a detailed survey of the coverage of six disasters, based on an analysis of news publications across Europe, the US and Australia. It concluded that: "Western self-interest is the pre-condition for significant coverage of a humanitarian crisis."

In particular, while there appeared to be no link between the scale of a disaster and media interest in the story, there was a clear correlation between the quantity of media coverage and the perceived economic impact of a disaster on Western markets.

Of the six disasters analysed, Hurricane Katrina, which hit America's Gulf Coast in August 2005, inflicted the fewest deaths (around 1,300) but generated the greatest number of articles (1,035) in the ten weeks following the disaster. This was 40 times more press coverage than the 25 articles generated by Hurricane Stan and the consequent rains and landslides that killed over 1,600 mainly Mayan people

Box 1.1 Netherlands Red Cross: "Save a Child in the Congo"

Just before Christmas 2005, the Netherlands Red Cross gave three well-known DJs the tastiest apple they had ever eaten. It was their first food after fasting for six days, shut in the Glass House in Utrecht from where they broadcast on the radio 24 hours a day to raise money for the Democratic Republic of Congo (DRC).

The public showed enormous interest. The appeal, 'Serious Request: Save a Child in the Congo', raised over EUR 2.2 million (US $ 2.7 m). One million of that was donated by the Dutch government.

In 1998, civil war broke out in DRC, during which 3.9 million people died of disease, hunger or violence. Children die mainly from preventable illnesses like diarrhoea.

A shortage of good food and safe water makes children more prone to disease. In the chaos of war, they lose their families. Some are abducted to become child soldiers.

The International Committee of the Red Cross (ICRC) is using the money raised to reunite children with their families and to train volunteers who search for families, as well as for transport, temporary shelter, food and medical assistance.

The Netherlands Red Cross has set up a special fund to provide aid in forgotten areas such as the Congo.

In 2004, the organization coordinated an appeal with Radio 3FM, which raised EUR 915,995 (US$ 1.1 m) to build a hospital in Darfur.

It's not enough to issue a press release to highlight forgotten disasters. A buzz has to be created, like in December 2005:

- Well-known Dutch personalities visited the Glass House. They gave performances or donated autographed items for the Internet auction organized by eBay.
- Listeners could request a record on payment of a donation. A total of 25,271 tracks were requested. One company donated EUR 15,000 (US$ 18,500) for one song.
- Students cycled alongside the house, covering the distance from Utrecht to Kinshasa and back. Listeners sponsored the bike ride.
- One couple even paid EUR 2,720 (US$ 3,300) to get married in the Glass House.
- The marathon broadcast was also carried on TV (90 hours live), cable and the Internet.
- The campaign was supported by advertising, posters on roadside hoardings and 3.3 million debit card payments. People could also make a donation by text message.

Subsequent research showed that 7.5 million people in the Netherlands followed the campaign, which reached 83 per cent of Dutch youth.

Eric Corton, a DJ with Radio 3FM, went to DRC to make radio and TV reports for the campaign. He met a four-year-old girl who was in a temporary shelter before being reunited with her family. "She was walking around in a ragged skirt, but when she saw me with my headphones and mike she ran away immediately, only to return in a pink dress, fit for a princess, that she had got from the people at the shelter. That child had always been used as a worker. And then suddenly adults turn up who are 'simply' kind to her. She was jumping and dancing around, hanging on my arm."

There are many more little girls like this who deserve a Serious Request. ■

Drought and locusts during 2004 led to harvest failure and the biggest shortfall of food for 20 years. By mid-2005, WFP reported 2.5m people on the brink of starvation, leading to what the UN described as "one of the most extreme examples of a neglected emergency".

2005

16 May UN launches US$16m appeal – raised in July to US$ 30m

6 July BBC web story: "No food aid as hungry flee Niger"

"Media attention has triggered donors' interest."
Gian Carlo Cirri, WFP representative in Niger

7 July UN appeal coverage: US$ 2.7m

7 July G8 conference starts at Gleneagles, UK – Africa high on agenda

14 July UN appeal coverage: US$ 3.6m

"The world wakes up when we see images on the TV and when we see children dying."
Jan Egeland, UN Under-Secretary-General for Humanitarian Affairs

19 July BBC's Hilary Andersson reports on TV and web: "Niger children starving to death"

21 July Niger's president visits famine zone

27 July US$ 17m committed inside and outside UN appeal

"The only reason aid efforts increased at all was the media attention at the peak of the crisis."
Nicolas de Torrente, MSF's executive director in the USA

Sources: BBC, IRIN, OCHA Financial Tracking Service, Reuters AlertNet, UN.

in Guatemala in October 2005. Stan caused an estimated US$ 1 billion in damage – far less than Katrina's bill (estimated at US$ 80 billion) – although the storm damage to Guatemala was about three times greater as a percentage of GNP than for the US.

According to CARMA: "The Hurricane Stanley emergency stands out as the worst indictment of the selfish Western approach to humanitarian disasters: here there is no obvious significant economic or political interest. Consequently, there is virtually no coverage." And the discrepancy in media interest between Stan and Katrina was mirrored by enormous differences in aid allocations (see Chapter 3).

Even the high-profile tsunami, which killed over 150 times more people than Katrina, attracted just half the media coverage. Meanwhile Darfur, with an estimated death toll of 180,000, generated only 73 articles in the 18 months after the crisis emerged – according to CARMA's survey.

Such deficiencies are all the more worrying because of the influence media appear to have on political decision-makers. Dennis McNamara, UN Special Adviser on Internal Displacement, told the BBC in April 2006 that: "Media support is critical... The influence on governments is much higher from the media than from the UN... There's no question once, I'm afraid, the babies are on screen." McNamara is not alone in thinking this – the donor response to Niger's neglected food crisis in 2005 was widely perceived as media-driven (see Figure 1.1).

The public are as swayed as the politicians by media coverage. The intense reporting on the tsunami had a major impact on the amount of money raised: 40 per cent of the US$ 14 billion pledged or committed to tsunami-affected countries was donated by private individuals. A more thorough analysis of available data on media and aid coverage of disasters during 2005 reveals a very close correlation between the two: from a selection of ten disasters, the coverage of UN appeals mirrors the extent of media coverage for all the crises except Darfur/Sudan. Meanwhile, total humanitarian aid per beneficiary decreases in line with lower media coverage (see Table 1.2).

The media, however, can only absorb so much at a time. Pouring huge resources into covering one disaster can cast other disasters into shadow. Overshadowing may also reflect the limited capacity of the global humanitarian system to respond, with the experts that might be in touch with the press preoccupied in one part of the world while another disaster occurs elsewhere.

Table 1.2 Links between media and funding, 2005 – sorted by appeal coverage

Crisis	Aid appeal coverage % (within UN appeal)[1]	Aid appeal coverage % (inside and outside UN appeal)	Aid per beneficiary US$[2]	Print media coverage – press citations (AlertNet/ Factiva)[3]	Print media coverage – number of articles (CARMA)[4]	TV media coverage – minutes of airtime (Tyndall)[5]
1 Tsunami	80	475	1,241	34,992	508	250
2 Uganda	76	105	86	5,209	n.a.	0
3 West Africa	69	125	50	4,804	n.a.	n.a.
4 South Asia/earthquake	68	196	310	n.a.	102	86
5 Chechnya	67	104	281	2,886	n.a.	2
6 Democratic Republic of Congo	66	122	213	3,119	n.a.	6
7 Guatemala/Stan	65	91	224	n.a.	25	n.a.
8 Somalia	59	87	53	n.a.	n.a.	0
9 Côte d'Ivoire	54	90	27	n.a.	n.a.	0
10 Darfur/Sudan	53	73	431	7,661	312	n.a.

The table reveals close correlations between aid appeal coverage and media exposure (with the exception of Darfur/Sudan) and between aid per beneficiary and media coverage.

n.a. denotes data not available.

[1] Source: UN Financial Tracking Service (OCHA FTS) for all aid appeal coverage – all appeals are for 2005.

[2] Source: Development Initiatives – total aid inside and outside UN appeals, sourced from OCHA FTS, using UN beneficiary estimates.

[3] Source: Reuters AlertNet – based on a Factiva survey of more than 200 global English-language newspapers, March 2004–February 2005.

[4] Source: CARMA International, January 2006 – based on survey of 1,967 print articles from 64 European, US and Australian newspapers published within ten weeks of the disaster (150 weeks for Sudan's Darfur region only, February 2003–December 2005).

[5] Source: The Tyndall Report – minutes of airtime on the US's three leading TV networks, 2005.

The tsunami cast a very long shadow over many very deadly humanitarian crises in Africa. Ruth Gidley of Reuters AlertNet commented that in 2005 the tsunami had "pushed hidden disasters off the map". And just as the tsunami overshadowed Darfur, so Darfur cast a shadow of neglect on the situation in Chad.

During the 2005 hurricane season, such shadows lengthened. Hurricane Rita was caught in the shadow of Katrina, despite packing winds of over 200 kilometres per hour and causing US$ 10 billion of damage. But Rita arrived in September 2005, late in the season, and was the tenth hurricane that year. After Rita came Wilma (affecting foreign tourists in Mexico), which in turn shadowed Stan.

Some of those affected by Rita believed the lack of media coverage translated into less assistance. According to an article in *The New York Times* dated 20 April 2006: "Texans… say the nation never really took notice of the 77,000 homes made uninhabitable by Hurricane Rita's force, 40,000 of which were not insured, or the piles of debris and garbage that still fester along the roads. 'Personally I am sick of hearing about Katrina,' said Ronda Authement, standing outside her trailer in Sabine Pass, where she will live until she can get the money and the workers to put her three-bedroom house back on its foundation."

However, despite clear reporting imbalances globally, there are some good media practices to report on (see Box 1.2).

2. Unfunded

While media coverage is certainly desirable in highlighting the plight of people in neglected crises, aid coverage is more important. Insufficient funding is a key cause – and symptom – of neglect.

Wealthy Western governments donated well over US$ 12 billion in humanitarian assistance last year – the highest figure since records began in 1970. In addition, private individuals gave at least US$ 5.5 billion in response to the tsunami – more than NGOs worldwide had ever collected in a whole year from all sources (see Chapter 7).

But how evenly were these considerable resources allocated? When the total amount of humanitarian funding per emergency is divided by the number of people targeted for that aid, some revealing statistics emerge. Chechnya, prominent in MSF's 'top ten' lists, received US$ 281 per beneficiary in 2005. The South Asia earthquake attracted US$ 310 and Sudan US$ 431 per head.

However, far and away the best-funded disaster was, not surprisingly, the tsunami, which raised at least US$ 1,241 per beneficiary in humanitarian aid alone – not including an extra US$ 8 billion for reconstruction. At the other end of the scale,

International Federation
of Red Cross and Red Crescent Societies

emergency appeals in 2005 for Chad, Guyana, Côte d'Ivoire, Malawi and Niger garnered an average of less than US$ 27 per person in need (see Figure 1.2 and Chapter 7, Figure 7.10).

To some extent, differences of funding between emergency appeals may reflect differing humanitarian needs and the costs of meeting those needs. But a comparison of the extent to which priority needs – as defined by the UN's Consolidated Appeals Process (CAP) – are met by total humanitarian funding (both inside and outside the appeal process) reveals a similarly warped picture. While appeals for the Republic of Congo, Djibouti and the Central African Republic were on average less than 40 per cent funded, the tsunami appeal was 475 per cent funded and the South Asia earthquake appeal was 196 per cent funded.

Timeliness of funding is vital during emergencies. Analysing UN appeals for 2005, nearly three-quarters of all contributions for flash appeals (for natural disasters) arrived within a month of the appeal launch. The comparable figure for consolidated appeals (for complex emergencies) was just 7 per cent (see Chapter 7, Figure 7.14).

The slowness of governments to respond to the food crisis in Niger, triggered by locusts and drought during 2003–2005, led not only to an avoidable loss of life and

Figure 1.2 Equitable aid? Humanitarian relief per beneficiary, 2005

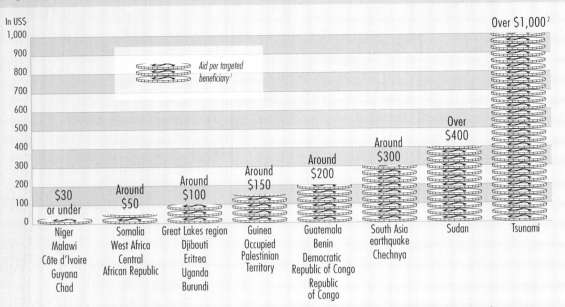

In US$

Over $1,000 [2]		(Tsunami)
Over $400		(Sudan)
Around $300		(South Asia earthquake, Chechnya)
Around $200		(Guatemala, Benin, Democratic Republic of Congo, Republic of Congo)
Around $150		(Guinea, Occupied Palestinian Territory)
Around $100		(Great Lakes region, Djibouti, Eritrea, Uganda, Burundi)
Around $50		(Somalia, West Africa, Central African Republic)
$30 or under		(Niger, Malawi, Côte d'Ivoire, Guyana, Chad)

Aid per targeted beneficiary [1]

1 Source: Development Initiatives – total aid received inside and outside UN appeals, sourced from OCHA FTS, using UN beneficiary estimates.
2 The multi-agency Tsunami Evaluation Coalition reports funding of "around US$ 8,000 allocated per survivor", based on a total funding figure which includes reconstruction over several years and using a smaller estimate of beneficiaries than that used by the UN.

livelihoods, but also increased the final cost of response a hundredfold (see *World Disasters Report 2005*, Chapter 3). However, it doesn't appear that the lessons of Niger have been learned. Analysing the donor response to 2006's drought in the Greater Horn of Africa, the Humanitarian Policy Group (HPG) at the UK-based Overseas Development Institute (ODI) highlights how "agencies, donors and national governments proved unable to address the crisis effectively in its early stages."

Despite warnings of "pervasive pre-famine conditions" in November 2005, the emergency response in the Horn did not reach capacity until April–May 2006 – missing the window of opportunity for preventative action. HPG blamed "inflexible funding mechanisms", among other factors, for the delays. When the aid did come, short-term food assistance predominated rather than livelihoods interventions which could have reduced future vulnerability.

In an interview with AlertNet in April 2006, Jan Egeland, UN Under-Secretary-General for Humanitarian Affairs, highlighted the under-funding of crises in Africa: "Sudan and Congo are the two worst wars of our generation… The accumulated death toll is several times that of Rwanda's genocide for each. We have to stay the marathon and we are not…We are not adequately able to finish the job, and that

International Federation of Red Cross and Red Crescent Societies

means funding the return of refugees and displaced people and demobilizing and giving jobs to the fighters." He went on to note that donors had only come up with one-fifth of the funding needed to bring peace and stability to these two countries, despite appeals launched four months earlier.

In March 2006, the UN launched an expanded Central Emergency Response Fund (CERF) to provide rapid funds for humanitarian response within days of a disaster or appeal. A third of its funds will go to neglected crises – and in its first month, the CERF allocated US$ 13 million to agencies in the Horn of Africa. By June, the fund had raised US$ 365 million towards its half-billion dollar target. The International Federation of Red Cross and Red Crescent Societies initiated a similar Disaster Relief Emergency Fund (DREF) 20 years ago, which dispersed over US$ 8.5 million of rapid-response funding in 2005 – half of it for minor or forgotten emergencies (see Chapter 7, Box 7.1).

Other forms of financing, beyond Western governments and publics, should not be neglected. Non-Western donor governments are playing a larger part in humanitarian aid, especially since the tsunami. Meanwhile, global remittances back to the developing world totalled around US$ 126 billion in 2004, according to the World Bank – 50 per cent more than all humanitarian and development aid from the West that year. In Guatemala, remittances received during 2005 in the municipalities affected by Hurricane Stan totalled US$ 413 million – 20 times more than the UN appeal had raised by early December (see Chapter 3).

3. Uncounted

Large, one-off, highly visible events that kill many people and cost a lot of money are generally less neglected than the many small, recurrent, cumulative and invisible events that happen every month. But are death and money the only losses that count?

There are two kinds of humanitarian crisis that are most commonly neglected:
- Small, recurrent, quick-onset (e.g., localized floods, landslides, fires).
- Large, recurrent or chronic, slow-onset (e.g., drought/food crisis, conflict, disease).

However, it is vital that humanitarian organizations and governments don't neglect such crises, for four reasons:
- The accumulated death toll from recurrent or chronic crises may equal or exceed that from big, quick-onset disasters.
- The impact on household livelihoods and national economies may equal or exceed that of high-profile disasters.
- Recurrent crises create a cumulative impact, ratcheting up vulnerability to larger hazards in the future.

■ Recurrent, small-scale crises provide an opportunity to intervene and mitigate the impact of future, larger hazards.

One reason why these types of crisis are neglected is because of a reluctance to think in terms of continuums and accumulations of risk – yet losses range along spectrums of kind and degree. Another reason is the lack of standardized methodologies for measuring their human and financial impact – either through real-time assessments or in retrospective databases. The chapter will now briefly examine different ways in which the impact of crises are measured.

Counting from above/counting from below

Various databases exist to capture the impact of disasters at a global level. The most well-known and widely used are: EM-DAT, an international database of natural and technological disasters managed by the Centre for Research on the Epidemiology of Disasters (CRED), based at the University of Louvain in Belgium; and the databases maintained by the reinsurance companies Munich Re and Swiss Re. These databases rely mainly on information from governments and international humanitarian organizations – counting from above.

Other systems, such as the DesInventar database, first developed in 1996 by the Latin American Network for the Social Study of Disaster Prevention (LA RED) count from the bottom up. Both types of database have their strengths and weaknesses, and finding ways in which they can complement each other is an important challenge.

Unlike DesInventar, EM-DAT provides global coverage, while its disaster data go back to at least 1970, enabling trends to be analysed over a number of decades. But while CRED plays a vital role in collecting much-used, impartial data on major disasters, it only includes disasters if ten or more people are reported killed, or over 100 people are reported affected, or if there is an emergency declaration or call for international assistance.

So, by definition, the smaller (or unreported) disasters don't make it into EM-DAT. Yet in these small, everyday events, that erode the already meagre livelihoods of millions of people, lie the roots of future harm – as well as opportunities to reduce vulnerability to tomorrow's catastrophes.

DesInventar's approach allows the registering of information on social and economic impacts associated with any type of hazard event at the most local scale for which information and cartography are available (usually district or municipal level). Data were originally built up using local press coverage but are now increasingly derived from official or aid agency sources.

Using DesInventar's data, local effects and conditions can be analysed and the relative losses between large and small events can be approximated. In general, up to 40 per cent of DesInventar's local registries of loss will correspond to the events that appear in EM-DAT. The remaining 60 per cent are usually independent, small-scale, localized events with cumulative effects on local vulnerability (see Box 1.3).

The DesInventar methodology has expanded over the last five years from 18 Latin American and Caribbean countries into various Asian countries and now exists in several language versions. Meanwhile, MANDISA, a similar kind of database pioneered in South Africa, records urban disasters such as shack fires, small floods and

Box 1.3 DesInventar: measuring impacts from the bottom up

In Latin America, the DesInventar method has been developed to register highly localized impacts of disruptive events, triggered by natural, technological or health-related hazards. Some examples illustrate the difference between top-down and bottom-up counting, and how they depend on definitions of what counts in the first place:

Pergamino municipality,
Buenos Aires province, Argentina.

- National level data sources for the period 1970–2002 revealed only 18 per cent of all flooding incidents registered in a local database for the same area, drawing on local publications and key informants.
- This suggests that four-fifths of flooding in the municipality is 'invisible' and hence neglected, when viewed from the top down.
- Although all larger-scale incidents appear in both databases, the great majority of events below the mean (in terms of impact) were not registered at the national level.

Peru earthquake, 23 June 2001.

- Analysis of the zone affected by the earthquake, using DesInventar data, reveals that in the previous 30 years the number of per-

sons affected by small-scale events (associated with a wide range of hazard types) was double that assigned to the 2001 quake.
- Compared to the quake, 30 years of smaller events had inflicted 20 per cent more housing loss, affected 13 per cent more houses, but affected 30 per cent less land.
- These data reveal that the cumulative impacts of smaller events are not insignificant, compared to one-off, large-scale disasters. Moreover, these small-scale events are likely to have increased the daily vulnerability of local people which the subsequent earthquake exposed.

Guatemala, 1988–2000.

- Analysing disaster data in Guatemala from 1988 to 2000, CRED's EM-DAT database reported 38 disasters which killed 1,617 and affected 225,644 people.
- Over the same period, DesInventar recorded 2,949 'adverse local impact events' which killed 1,848 and affected 557,820 people.
- DesInventar included 529 local records in Guatemala for the impact of 1998's Hurricane Mitch, compared to EM-DAT's single, global reference (see Chapter 3). ∎

building collapses which do not appear in other databases. And since 2005, a newly-formed African Urban Risk Analysis Network (AURAN) has been developing a bottom-up approach to quantifying urban risk across the continent.

Capturing the impact of slow-onset crises

Assessing the impact of recurrent or chronic slow-onset crises (e.g., drought/food crisis, disease/ill health, complex emergency) is fraught with methodological difficulties. While individual aid organizations have conducted mortality surveys over varying times, attributing a total death toll to a crisis is notoriously tricky. Figures for Darfur's death toll, for example, have ranged from 60,000 to 380,000, according to an article in *The Washington Post* newspaper, dated April 2005. And Darfur is arguably one of the more high-profile complex emergencies.

Surprisingly, no good global databases exist to track conflicts and collate their impact on civilians. CRED recently created CE-DAT – a database of mortality and malnutrition surveys from complex emergencies – but methodological differences prevent CRED from arriving at comparative death tolls per country or crisis (see Annex, Box 1).

While it is extremely difficult to measure the impact of complex emergencies in real time, survey work can play catch-up. For example, the International Rescue Committee (IRC), a US-based NGO, has conducted mortality surveys in DRC which estimate that 3.9 million people have died from conflict-related causes since 1998. Their surveys have played an important part in highlighting this most neglected of crises.

So-called natural, slow-onset disasters are not necessarily easier to quantify. Deaths arising in situations of chronic drought or acute malnutrition are often underestimated or attributed to disease.

For example, at the time of the Malawi famine in 2001–2002, fatalities from the disaster were widely estimated at around 1,000 (attributed mainly to a cholera outbreak). However, Stephen Devereux, a fellow of the Institute of Development Studies (IDS) at the University of Sussex, UK, contributing to a book called *The 'New Famines'* to be published in September 2006, presents four mortality estimates derived from three separate surveys conducted shortly after the crisis which put the death toll at between 46,000 and 85,000 (see Chapter 2).

However, mortality surveys remain contentious, according to Hisham Khogali, a senior disaster management officer at the International Federation. "For organizations on the ground, knowing the cause of excess mortality is vital, otherwise just knowing people are dying doesn't help you decide what to do. For example, a severely

International Federation of Red Cross and Red Crescent Societies

malnourished child may be dying because of lack of food or lack of clean water. By providing the community with food and not the latter, you may do nothing to prevent future deaths."

Comparative, participatory needs assessments remain elusive

Failure to measure the full impact of humanitarian crises not only occurs in retrospective databases, but in real-time needs assessments too. The capacity of the humanitarian system to assess global needs in a transparent and comparative way is vital to ensure that crises can be correctly understood and that adequate aid arrives in time to assist those who most need it.

In 2003, the HPG published the results of a year-long study into how humanitarian needs assessments influence allocations of aid – as part of a wider investigation into the equity of aid. They concluded that aid organizations' funding requests were often based less on an objective assessment of needs than on what the donor 'market' could bear for a given crisis (see *World Disasters Report 2003*, Box 1.3).

A woman sits with her child inside the hospital in the village of El Wok, three miles from the Kenyan border with Somalia. In this village that hasn't seen significant rainfall in more than two years, this hospital serves more than 42,000 people, but has no doctor.

Daniel Cima/
American Red Cross

Three years on, what's changed? According to James Darcy, the publication's lead author and now the head of HPG: "We've come some way since then." The Good Humanitarian Donorship (GHD) initiative has explicitly endorsed the principle that appeals should be based on sound needs assessments: "Donors are much more actively questioning the analysis that underlies UN flash and consolidated appeals."

However, argues Darcy, what's still lacking is a "comparative measure of severity gauged against certain agreed indicators". The CAP-related Needs Analysis Framework has enjoyed only "mixed success". National systems exist, such as the Integrated Food Security Phase Classification of the Somalia-based Food Security Analysis Unit (FSAU), which has the potential to be more widely adopted. But at an international level, "there is no consensus on how to measure the severity of humanitarian crises." Darcy identifies three key problems:

- **Funding for needs assessments.** "There is a gross underinvestment in diagnostics." Donors are increasingly realizing that they must help fund not only initial needs assessments, but continuous monitoring of humanitarian response.
- **Disconnect between needs assessments and decision-making.** Without a transparent link here, the best needs assessment in the world will have no impact.
- **Humanitarian storytelling.** "We tend to misrepresent situations in our need to portray them as life-threatening and our role as life-saving." Such a marketing approach to selected appeals can grotesquely underplay the severity of other situations, where response may be more difficult, as well as failing to highlight the capacities of local response.

Darcy's concerns reflect those of tsunami evaluators. The considerable resources available to aid organizations after the tsunami might have been expected to improve the quality of needs assessments. But according to an evaluation released in 2006 by the independent, multi-agency Tsunami Evaluation Coalition (TEC): "The slow moving humanitarian needs assessment did not drive the initial humanitarian response. The availability of enormous amounts of funds in search of activities was the driving force… As a result the international response was a poor match for the real aspirations of the people affected by the tsunami, who felt over-assessed but not consulted."

The TEC's evaluation of around 200 assessment reports prepared in the first months after the tsunami revealed several shortcomings: "the lack of a unique format for rapid assessments; the variable definition of who is affected and eligible for assistance; and the tendency of assessors to disregard local coping capacity". The neglect of aid organizations in failing to focus their response around the participation of affected people and their expressed priorities is a recurrent theme in the evaluation.

International Federation of Red Cross and Red Crescent Societies

Margareta Wahlstrom, UN's Deputy Emergency Relief Coordinator, suggests that the possibility (or not) of getting funding still plays a major part in guiding how much UN agencies appeal for: "You intuitively make an assessment of what you'll be able to mobilize," says Wahlstrom, adding: "We rarely have assessments that are the result of a joint effort – that is, including donor agencies. Implicitly, if you do them [needs assessments] you also create a mutual commitment to finance them." Factors other than humanitarian needs also affect the amount of money appealed for, including: the "ambition and focus" given to places, the capability of in-country humanitarian teams, the attitude of the host government and security considerations.

4. Secondary

Little attention is paid by media, researchers or donors to the secondary and tertiary disasters that often accompany a primary event. Oil spills from refineries along the US's Gulf Coast were secondary to 2005's record-breaking hurricane season, but caused considerable economic and health impacts.

Other little-noticed but massively life-changing 'secondary disasters' include: sexual or domestic violence and trafficking of women (see Chapter 6); problems with resettlement and land grabs (reported after the tsunami); and long-term disability from injuries (the South Asia earthquake resulted in several thousand amputations and permanent disabilities).

During hurricanes in the Americas, the greatest cause of death is not wind or storm surge but flooding and landslides. Yet these issues seldom receive direct analytical, programmatic or media attention. While they are secondary to the storm itself, they are also secondary to other drivers, such as decades of land degradation and deforestation.

When Hurricane Jeanne hit Haiti in 2004, floods and landslides down mountain slopes denuded of trees caused 2,000 deaths. But it was poverty and a lack of livelihood options that forced generations of Haitians to cut down their forests to make charcoal for sale. Where then is the disaster situated – in hurricanes, landslides, environmental degradation, poverty or poor governance?

Following the tsunami, the emergency response focused on coastal fishermen and their families but missed many communities living inland who suffered the secondary, 'invisible' impacts of the disaster: people whose livelihoods depended on the fishing industry – from boat-carpenters to *idli* sellers who provided rice cakes for returning fishermen (see *World Disasters Report 2005*, Chapter 5). Capturing such indirectly-affected people in needs assessments and disaster databases is an important first step in meeting their humanitarian needs.

A different kind of secondary disaster can arise from uncontrolled or illegal population movements. By the end of 2005, the world's 12 million refugees were greatly outnumbered by the 21 million people displaced within their own countries, according to the US Committee for Refugees and Immigrants (see Annex, Tables 14–16).

In recent years, an estimated 2 to 3 million Colombians (half of them children) have been displaced by conflict over land and drugs in their country, prompting the UN to describe it as the "worst humanitarian crisis in the western hemisphere". A study conducted by the World Food Programme (WFP) between December 2002 and April 2003 concluded that 80 per cent of Colombians displaced by violence lived in extreme poverty and lacked access to sufficient food. The secondary impacts of displacement include exploitation, rape, violence, land loss and urban profiteering. The Colombian government gives displaced populations just three months' emergency support (extendable in some cases), offering them few opportunities to stabilize their lives. And UNHCR's expenditure per 'person of concern' during 2003 was nine times lower in the Americas than in West Africa.

According to Gustavo Wilches-Chaux, a Latin American analyst, population movement in Colombia "generates new threats and vulnerabilities, because the influx of displaced people into the country's towns and cities makes it necessary to ignore all the town planning regulations… They occupy high-risk areas (or areas that become high-risk when they are overburdened) and put a severe strain on the ability of the state and society to provide public health and education services and to offer employment and other income-generating opportunities."

Meanwhile, hundreds of thousands of sub-Saharan African migrants attempt to reach Europe illegally each year. Most are fleeing destitution at home, caused by conflict, chronic crop failure or poverty. A minority attempt to enter Europe by sea, committing their lives to ruthless people-smugglers charging exorbitant prices for a passage in an overcrowded, often unseaworthy boat. At least 2,000 migrants lose their lives each year in the seas surrounding Europe – while the suffering of those crossing the Sahara en route to the smugglers' ships goes unrecorded (see Chapter 5).

Innumerably more migrants put themselves at great risk trying to cross from Mexico into the US or by boat from China, Korea, and even Bangladesh to Japan. The long-term solutions are deeply complex and political, involving a combination of more legal employment opportunities in destination countries, coupled with better development in sending countries. But the immediate, short-term imperative to save lives lost in transit has received little serious attention.

5. Secret

Some life-threatening situations may be kept secret by governments for political reasons, or by communities for cultural reasons. The result can be hidden humanitarian crises, whose full, horrifying impacts are learned by the outside world too late.

State secrecy can be a major factor. Emperor Haile Selassie hushed up the 1974 famine in Ethiopia, argues Alex de Waal in his 1991 book *Evil days: thirty years of war and famine in Ethiopia*. In China, local officials did not alert the central authorities when drought combined with a depletion of rural labour to produce the Great Leap famine in the late 1950s.

While there is generally more openness in the 21st century, some nation states still seek to limit investigations by the media or humanitarian organizations into disastrous conditions. In April 2006, Jan Egeland, the UN's humanitarian chief, was refused permission by the Sudanese government from visiting Darfur or from flying over Darfur to visit Sudanese refugees in neighbouring Chad, according to Reuters news agency.

In the same month, the government of Niger told a BBC team, which found evidence of continuing hunger, that their permission to report on the humanitarian situation had been withdrawn. Reporting on the ban, BBC Africa correspondent Orla Guerin said officials would not allow international or local media to report on the food situation as "they did not want that subject touched".

Contemporary state secrecy is not limited to Africa. Severe hunger and health problems for millions of citizens in the Democratic People's Republic of Korea (DPRK) were almost completely hidden for years, and humanitarian access is still tightly controlled. In a detailed analysis of the DPRK famine of the mid- to late 1990s, Andrew Natsios, the former administrator of the United States Agency for International Development (USAID), put the number of excess deaths at around 2.5 million, nearly ten times the government's official figures. Human Rights Watch, in a report dated May 2006, says: "It is DPRK government policy to keep conditions inside the country secret from the rest of the world, even when information would lead to desperately needed assistance."

The plight of ethnic Karen people, displaced internally in Myanmar, is another example of a humanitarian emergency a government would prefer to keep in the dark. Meanwhile, in June 2006, the Committee to Protect Journalists, a US-based NGO, expressed concern at a proposed Chinese law that would subject news outlets to fines for reporting on natural disasters, riots and other emergencies without official approval. And when David Loyn, the BBC's developing world correspondent, approached Iranian officials about the possibility of returning to Bam to report on recovery after December 2003's earthquake, he was "advised not even to bother applying for a visa".

Apart from state secrecy there is cultural secrecy, which can particularly exaggerate the impacts of humanitarian crises on women. After the South Asia earthquake of October 2005, many women from remote, highly traditional mountain areas were forbidden by their families from coming down to relief camps in the valleys, for fear of compromising their honour. As a result, women's specific needs were not fully met even six months after the disaster (see Chapter 6).

In the rural communities of Nepal, the plight of women in childbirth is exacerbated by the social and religious discrimination they suffer. Women cannot discuss pregnancy with anyone other than their husbands and mothers-in-law. They are considered polluted and impure for eleven days after giving birth. Male relatives, including husbands, are not permitted to go near them, so they often have to live in isolation with their newborn babies in a cowshed or hut.

Each year, it is estimated that between 5,000 and 6,000 Nepalese women die in childbirth, while an estimated 30,000 newborn babies die within their first month of life. Although this annual death toll is over 25 times higher than the number of deaths attributed to Nepal's ten-year conflict, the issue of maternal and neonatal mortality has received virtually no media attention (see Chapter 4).

6. Awkward

Some humanitarian crises are neglected for years because Western donors find it politically awkward to engage fully and address them. The restrictions placed on media and aid workers alike by countries such as Myanmar, DPRK and Zimbabwe make humanitarian interventions extremely difficult. Political and logistical factors can make deploying peacekeeping troops tricky.

In the case of Darfur, after three years of brutalization which has displaced 2 million people and claimed several hundred thousand lives, Western attempts to broker a peace agreement in May 2006 failed to win over all factions. Nor could the international community persuade the Sudanese government to allow the UN to deploy a more robust peacekeeping force than the 7,000 troops under the command of the African Union.

Without adequate security, aid organizations cannot operate effectively. But humanitarian crises of differing geostrategic significance attract widely varying numbers of peacekeepers. In Kosovo in 2001, NATO fielded 45,000 soldiers to keep the peace in a territory of 2 million people. The following year, international peacekeepers in Afghanistan, mandated by a UN Security Council resolution, numbered less than 5,000 among a population of around 25 million.

During 2006, the international peacekeeping force in DRC numbered 17,000 troops in a country of 62 million people, where, according to the IRC, 1,250 excess deaths still occurred every day. Over 70 per cent of these deaths were in the insecure eastern provinces, where armed gangs roamed unchecked. Most victims died from easily preventable and treatable diseases. "Less than two per cent of the deaths were directly due to violence," points out IRC's health director Rick Brennan. "However, if the effects of violence – such as the insecurity that limits access to healthcare facilities – were removed, mortality rates would fall to almost normal levels."

The HPG's James Darcy argues that aid organizations should do more to highlight the humanitarian imperative in such politically awkward situations. "For too long, the humanitarian situation in Darfur took backstage to [Sudan's] North–South peace process," he says, adding that humanitarians allowed the politically driven narrative of the peace process in DRC to overshadow the acute humanitarian crisis in the east of the country.

'Never again' risks becoming 'again and again'. Following a trip to Darfur in January 2005, Paul Rusesabegina, the real-life manager of the fictional Hotel Rwanda, likened the situation to the Rwandan genocide of 1994 and lamented: "We see, we look and we never learn from the past."

The UN's Margareta Wahlstrom cautions that "the risk is always that you reduce a political crisis to a humanitarian one and therefore you apply the wrong mix of internationally available instruments." In such cases, she adds: "We don't solve any problems, we mitigate them for a while. But they will always rebound on us: just look at Darfur over the past few years." She advises humanitarians to be more robust in advocating for the full range of actions needed to solve neglected crises – including political and security measures.

7. Misunderstood

In 1998, the analyst Mark Bradbury wrote an article entitled *Normalising the crisis in Africa*, in which he criticized donors and humanitarian organizations for concocting exit strategies from ongoing humanitarian operations, such as southern Sudan and Somalia, based on the twin myths of 'relief dependency' and the 'transition to development'. "In redefining them as opportunities for development," wrote Bradbury, "what we are seeing is a process of 'normalisation'. This normalisation is characterized by a creeping acceptance of higher levels of vulnerability, malnutrition and morbidity."

Revisiting those two countries in 2003, to research for an HPG report, Bradbury found little change – with high levels of malnutrition or epidemic levels of disease treated as the 'accepted' norm. If anything, the thresholds for triggering humanitarian response were increasing: "For example, in Sudan and Somalia, global acute malnutrition rates of 20 per cent or higher are commonplace and do not automatically generate a response, even though this is 10 per cent above what is considered acceptable by international standards and would be considered catastrophic elsewhere."

What exactly should trigger a humanitarian response, and when, remains a vexed and misunderstood issue – especially when chronic food insecurity transmutes into acute food crisis or famine. The International Federation's Hisham Khogali points out that, for slow-onset disasters, one trigger or threshold could be the point at which coping strategies become irreversible, rather than reversible. Once households start selling vital assets, such as livestock or possessions, simply to buy food, the point of no return may already have passed.

The problem is that humanitarian aid often doesn't arrive before coping strategies become irreversible. We have seen how the donor response to the food crisis in Niger was triggered not by months of expert warnings about shrinking household assets or distress migration, but by sensationalist media footage.

The risk is that, in simplifying and overdramatizing disaster, the nature of the crisis and how best to respond to it is misunderstood. The BBC's David Loyn wrote recently: "It is difficult to fit the full story of a complex emergency into the simple narrative demanded by TV news. There had been a drought, and harvests were reduced up to a point by locusts – the reasons usually given to explain the images of suffering – but the real reason for the emergency was high food prices caused by suppliers defaulting on deliveries to Niger."

Loyn added: "People were hungry because they were poor. Climate change and years of bad development policies were as much to blame as the locusts and short-term drought, but both the international response and the language of most TV reporting were framed as if a sudden disaster had hit Niger."

The result was an expensive, last-minute intervention dominated by airlifts of food aid, which saved lives but failed to reduce the risk of future crisis in a way that earlier, livelihoods-based interventions could have.

Malawi's recent food crisis was anticipated by the government as far back as February 2005. But the UN didn't launch a humanitarian appeal until late August and the government delayed declaring a state of emergency until October. Why? The government was desperate to regain credibility with the International Monetary Fund

(IMF) for prudent economic management, so as to complete the debt-relief process. Announcing an emergency earlier might have triggered panic buying and sent food prices soaring. Pride was another factor: "Must we go begging?" asked one of Malawi's senior civil servants at the time (see Chapter 2).

However, by late 2005, maize prices had soared anyway, 5 million people (nearly half the country) faced a severe food crisis and innumerable women were forced into potentially irreversible coping strategies by seeking sex in return for cash or food – putting themselves at risk of HIV/AIDS.

The UN's Malawi appeal embraced a 'smart' two-pronged strategy, which included food aid and support for agricultural inputs, to enable the government to distribute improved seeds and fertilizers free to all smallholder farmers. These inputs – aimed at enhancing recovery and reducing the risk of another food crisis the following season – were based on a similar government initiative which had boosted crop yields to record levels from 1998 to 2000. But donors provided just one-fifth of the funds for this smart part of the appeal, while food aid requirements were three-quarters covered.

Malawi's experience is replicated globally. Some sectors – notably those holding out the chance for recovery – are consistently more neglected than others. From 2000 to 2005, appeals for food aid within the CAP were on average 79 per cent covered, while economic recovery, shelter, protection, water and sanitation, health and agriculture were all less than 40 per cent funded (see Chapter 7, Figure 7.13).

Livelihoods interventions, such as free agricultural inputs for smallholders or restocking the animal herds of pastoralists in semi-arid zones, are vital measures to mitigate – or prevent – the impact of slow-onset disaster. Neglecting such measures allows the resilience of marginal communities to erode, leaving them more vulnerable to recurrent hazards.

Do such funding patterns arise because the lessons of the past have been neglected or misunderstood? The UN's Margareta Wahlstrom suggests several reasons: "There's lots of money and power in food aid," she says, adding: "The recurrent food security crises in Southern, East and West Africa have complex causes that require multi-institutional cooperation and a will to support institutions such as the Food and Agriculture Organization, which is not an emergency response agency but is often expected to act like one."

According to Wahlstrom: "It is clear that unless situations such as the one in Malawi are addressed with urgency, they will return with regularity as emergencies requiring humanitarian intervention. The donors' reaction was to some extent prejudiced by their opinion that flash appeals should only be for life-saving aid. We, the international community, still do not have adequate and appropriate financing instruments for the number of situations today that need to be dealt with as something 'between relief and development'. Our instruments still force a choice of 'either/or'. And we all know there are fewer and fewer such situations."

Social vulnerability: anticipating crises

Disasters and humanitarian crises share common root causes. It is social vulnerability that unites Mayan farmers who die on unstable slopes in Guatemala, destitute smallholders in Malawi and pastoralists in Niger, families displaced by conflict in Colombia, mothers who die in childbirth across the developing world, children who are trafficked or forced to be soldiers, irregular migrants who wash up on the beaches of southern Europe. Yet tackling the social vulnerability that underpins all crises (forgotten or not) is itself a neglected issue.

A large and growing research literature shows clearly that development, risk reduction and humanitarian response are intimately bound. Social vulnerability predisposes groups of people to the impact of a wide range of hazards. It also undermines their ability to cope and recover. Disasters are foreshadowed in the day-to-day vulnerability of people whose lives and livelihoods are blighted by failed development.

Neglect – no matter what type it falls under – betrays a failure, principally on the part of governments, to adequately analyse or address the root causes of chronic social vulnerability. The phrase 'forgotten crises' misleadingly suggests the problem is one of temporary oversight – when in fact the crisis will recur until the underlying failure of development that constructs social vulnerability is understood and tackled.

Following the World Conference on Disaster Reduction (WCDR) in 2005 and agreement by 168 nations to the Hyogo Framework for Action, a multi-hazard, comprehensive approach to disaster risk reduction is slowly becoming the norm. It is being institutionalized in many countries under new laws for civil protection and risk management. Official agencies, such as the UK's DFID and Germany's GTZ, are beginning to build disaster risk reduction into their development programmes. DFID, the World Bank and others are also exploring social protection structures which address widespread vulnerability.

Of course, not all manifestations of poverty and marginalization should be treated as disasters. But the commitment by the WCDR to bridge the gaps between disaster management, risk reduction and sustainable human development should be accompanied by broadening the category of disaster to include a wider range of humanitarian crises.

International Federation of Red Cross and Red Crescent Societies

A good example of social vulnerability is the silent, but avoidable death of 35,000 mothers and babies in Nepal each year. The reasons are rooted in the poverty, isolation, violence, poor governance and discrimination against women that prevent access to adequate healthcare. The solution is more than a medical one. It involves changing cultural attitudes, prioritizing health funding and improving infrastructure.

However, in Nepal as elsewhere, there aren't any coherent efforts to capture the full range of risks – disaster, conflict, technological hazards, health risks, livelihood instability – that vulnerable people face. Everyone, from researchers to aid organizations to donors, is compartmentalized along sectoral lines.

Any analysis of (or response to) neglected crises will be limited if it focuses solely on losses rather than on risks and capacities. What does this mean for humanitarian organizations, used to rapid, short-term interventions? The HPG's James Darcy is clear that humanitarian donors and agencies must "acknowledge risk factors and how to reduce them". Risk reduction is "hugely neglected", he says, yet it is "the language we must be talking to our development colleagues". Meanwhile, spending on disaster risk reduction remains low and poorly monitored (see Box 1.4).

Darcy suggests that "not just diagnosis but prognosis" is needed – so the probable outcomes of crises can be projected in time for preventative action. Such leading indicators of risk – ranging from dirty water to roaming militias – are as important for humanitarians as lagging indictors of impact such as acute malnutrition. By measuring and reducing such risk factors, humanitarians could reasonably argue they had also reduced unnecessary suffering. Measuring impact through a combination of leading and lagging indicators would then provide a fuller picture of the success of humanitarian action.

There is increasing recognition that humanitarian response must embrace not just short-term relief, but also vulnerability reduction, as made clear in 1994's widely-adopted *Code of Conduct for the International Red Cross and Red Crescent Movement and NGOs in Disaster Relief* and, more recently, by the Good Humanitarian Donorship initiative.

Where humanitarian organizations lack expertise in this area, then options for closer integration with other specialized agencies dealing with root causes need to be explored. Humanitarian and development agencies need to cooperate in plugging the gap of risk reduction – social vulnerability is not something that 'either side' can address alone. The gap is not only one of joint analysis of needs and capacities, but also one of financial and human resources, of adequate research into cost-effective interventions, and of understanding risk from the viewpoint of the vulnerable.

Box 1.4 **Neglected: funds for risk reduction**

Attempts to estimate how much is spent on disaster risk reduction (DRR) can quickly hit a brick wall. DRR is rarely a national priority of governments or aid organizations and is not defined or monitored as an economic sector. So it's seldom possible to establish total DRR spending from government or donor expenditure reports.

Trawling through detailed lists of individual projects and capital investments can also prove fruitless, without in-depth information on every item, as DRR expenditure is not always obvious. Construction of a sea dyke may be explicitly listed as such. However, incremental expenditure on, for example, the construction of a new hospital or school to ensure it is earthquake-proof, or on the time spent by an agricultural extension worker advising how to minimize drought losses, cannot be readily identified.

Aid organizations with separate DRR budgets can provide an exception to this rule. The European Commission's Humanitarian Aid department (ECHO) has a disaster preparedness programme (DIPECHO), which was launched in 1996. DIPECHO's share in the EC's annual humanitarian budget has gradually increased, from 0.9 per cent (EUR 7 million, US$ 7.5 million) in 1999 to 2.7 per cent (EUR 17.5 million, US$ 21.8 million) in 2005.

However, there is additional DRR spending under the EC's development budget and individual Directorates-General, which is not reported as such. In fact, there is an implicit danger in creating specific DRR budget lines solely under humanitarian departments, as it can perpetuate the belief, held by some development practitioners, that DRR is the responsibility of emergency aid managers alone.

The UK's Department for International Development (DFID) has deliberately sought to avoid such compartmentalization. Since 2004, DFID has formally linked DRR to its humanitarian aid programme, committing it to spend the equivalent of 10 per cent of disaster response funding to reduce the impact of related future disasters, where this can be done effectively. The money can come from the development or humanitarian budgets – opening opportunities for development staff to take more interest in DRR.

From the perspective of involving development practitioners in DRR, difficulties obtaining data on total DRR expenditure could be interpreted positively. The vulnerability of development to disasters has been demonstrated many times. This has made governments and aid organizations realize the need to 'mainstream' disaster risk – routinely addressing risks from natural hazards while designing development projects and strategies. These efforts towards mainstreaming may partly explain the invisibility of data on DRR spending, to the extent that mainstreaming has actually occurred.

However, it is important to ensure that expenditure on DRR can be monitored. Progress towards DRR is not simply about ensuring adequate funding. For instance, enforcing building codes and strengthening institutional capacity for disaster risk management are also important. Nevertheless, data on DRR expenditure are important in determining whether the level and nature of expenditure are commensurate with levels of risk.

One simple approach would be to tag all public projects that entail some element of disaster risk reduction as they are approved, at the same time estimating expenditure to be undertaken specifically on DRR. This information could be maintained in a central government database, to which ministries would have to report their data. It would be relatively straightforward and inexpensive to operate, generating comprehensive quantitative information for use in monitoring areas of progress in reducing risk and identifying critical remaining gaps that need to be addressed. ■

Interestingly, the process of planning the UN's first consolidated appeal for Nepal during 2005 led to humanitarian and development organizations discussing for the first time how to deal with chronic risks in a conflict setting.

Of course, a balance between longer-term, strategic prevention and shorter-term, tactical treatment must be struck – it is not a situation of either/or. In the case of HIV/AIDS, both are being pursued. For many years, care and treatment for people living with HIV and AIDS (PLWHA) lost out to prevention campaigns. But recent efforts to get cheap, generic anti-retroviral drugs onto the market mean more people can access drugs that greatly improve the length and quality of their lives. Furthermore, treatment is having a constructive effect on prevention. People who previously would not have admitted to being HIV-positive, or feared getting tested, are now coming forward to get the drugs. That should in turn slow the epidemic.

The same approach can be applied to disasters and humanitarian crises, generating a dynamic relationship between prevention and response. For example, good response and recovery can integrate risk reduction measures – such as stronger buildings, cleaner water supplies, diversified livelihoods, empowerment of socially vulnerable groups – showcasing such approaches to new audiences.

Conclusion

The problem with analysing neglected disasters is that it can quickly become a catalogue of everything that's wrong with the world – leading to an equally long and impossible list of recommendations. Innumerable different countries, peoples, sectors, needs and capacities could be identified as neglected, in different ways and by different people. In that sense, to describe a crisis as neglected conceals as much as it reveals.

This chapter has attempted to define seven types of neglect – along with the underlying and all-encompassing neglect of social vulnerability. This typology provides a structure for certain recommendations about ways forward for humanitarian organizations:

1. Unreported
■ Develop closer dialogue with media on neglected crises and connections with root causes.
■ Provide journalists with more objective data on crises and opportunities to collaborate.

2. Unfunded
■ Establish larger common, unearmarked emergency funds for neglected crises and sectors.
■ Commit at least 10 per cent of emergency funds to disaster risk reduction.

3. Uncounted

- Develop joint databases to capture the full spectrum of humanitarian risks and impacts.
- Invest more resources in creating and implementing a globally comparative measure of humanitarian needs, gauged against agreed indicators.

4. Secondary

- Improve analysis and mapping of secondary disasters, their impacts and root causes.
- Ensure minimum standards of care apply to those forced to flee their homes, regardless of legal status.

5. Secret

- Work with international and domestic media to reveal the reality of humanitarian needs in closed societies.
- Encourage governments to champion transparent analysis of humanitarian suffering and its root causes.

6. Awkward

- Avoid reducing a political crisis to a humanitarian one.
- Advocate for sufficient global political and security attention to enable humanitarian action to continue.

7. Misunderstood

- Improve analysis of appropriate responses to chronic, slow-onset crises – especially the nexus of drought/hunger/disease.
- Agree with donors and host governments on appropriate trigger points for action.

8. Social vulnerability

- Capture the perspectives, capacities and needs of vulnerable people.
- Explore options for integrated risk reduction with development organizations and governments.

Principal contributors to this chapter and Box 1.2 were Ben Wisner, an independent researcher affiliated with the Development Studies Institute at the London School of Economics, the Benfield Hazard Research Centre (University College London) and the UN University Institute for Environment and Human Security in Bonn; Allan Lavell, Coordinator, Programme for the Social Study of Risk and Disaster at the Secretariat General's office of the Latin American Social Science Faculty, San Jose, Costa Rica and founding member of the Latin American Network for the Social Study of Disaster Prevention-LA RED; and Jonathan Walter, editor of the World Disasters Report. *Box 1.1 was contributed by Marja Verbraak of The Netherlands Red Cross. Box 1.3 was contributed by Allan Lavell. Box 1.4 was contributed by Charlotte Benson, an economist with 15 years' experience of research on the economic aspects of natural disasters. All tables and figures were contributed by Jonathan Walter.*

International Federation
of Red Cross and Red Crescent Societies

Sources and further information

ActionAid International and PDHRE. *Tsunami Response: A Human Rights Assessment.* January 2006.

Becker, Jasper, *Hungry Ghosts: China's Secret Famine.* London: John Murray, 1996.

Borger, J. 'Katrina oil spills may be among the worst ever', *Guardian Online*, 16 September 2005.

Bradbury, M., Hofmann, C-A., Maxwell, S., Venekamp, D. and Montani, A. *Measuring humanitarian needs: Needs assessment and resource allocation in Southern Sudan and Somalia.* London: HPG, September 2003.

Bradbury, M. 'Normalising the Crisis in Africa' in *The Journal of Humanitarian Assistance,* London, February 1998. Available at http://www.jha.ac/articles/a043.htm

BBC. *Why 'Never Again' is not Enough*, BBC, 27 January 2005.

BBC. *Chad refugee crisis 'overlooked'*, BBC News, 10 May 2005.

Canadian Broadcasting Corporation (CBC). *Crisis Zone: Darfur, Sudan*, CBC Online, 5 May 2006.

CARMA International. *The CARMA Report on Western media coverage of Humanitarian Disasters.* CARMA International, January 2006.

Chaiban, T. and Ramiro, S. *Indifference is not an option in Darfur.* US Fund for UNICEF, 27 April 2006.

De Ville de Goyet, C. and Morinière, L. *The role of needs assessment in the tsunami response.* London: Tsunami Evaluation Coalition, 2006, forthcoming.

De Waal, A. *Evil days: thirty years of war and famine in Ethiopia.* New York: Africa Watch, 1991.

Guerin, O. *Niger halts BBC hunger coverage*, BBC News Online, 3 April 2006.

Human Rights Watch. *A Matter of Survival: The North Korean government's control of food and the risk of hunger*, ReliefWeb, 4 May 2006.

Humanitarian Policy Group (HPG). *Saving lives through livelihoods: critical gaps in the response to the drought in the Greater Horn of Africa.* Humanitarian Policy Group briefing note. London: Overseas Development Institute, May 2006.

Large, T. *Fickle donors ignore Africa's worst wars – UN*, Reuters AlertNet, 10 April 2006.

Loyn, D. 'No easy answers' in *Developments*. Department for International Development, London, June 2006.

Marcus, D. 'Famine Crimes in International Law' in *American Journal of International Law*, Vol. 97, pp. 245–281, 2003.

McDoom, O. *Sudan risks aid loss over Egeland ban – UN official*, Reuters AlertNet, 6 April 2006.

Médecins Sans Frontières (MSF). *Top 10 most under-reported humanitarian stories of 2005.* MSF, January 2006.

Natsios, A. *The Politics of Famine in North Korea*. Special Report No. 51. United States Institute of Peace, 2 August 1999.

Steinhauer, J. 'Storm Evacuees Strain Texas Hosts', *The New York Times*, 20 April 2006.

Renzaho, A. *Nutrition and Dietetics*, Vol. 60, pp. 85–91, Australia, 2003.

Ross, S. *Toward New Understandings: Journalists and Humanitarian Relief Coverage*. New York: Fritz Institute, Columbia School of Journalism, 2004.

Sackur, S. *IDPs: A world of misery*, HARDtalk, BBC World, 5 April 2006. Available at http://news.bbc.co.uk/1/hi/programmes/hardtalk/4879228.stm

UN Department of Public Information (UNDPI). *2006 list of '10 stories the world should hear more about'*. New York: UNDPI, 2006. Available at http://www.un.org/events/tenstories

The Washington Post, 'Darfur's Real Death Toll', 24 April 2005.

Web sites

ActionAid International **http://www.actionaid.org**

BBC News **http://news.bbc.co.uk/1/hi/world**

Canadian Broadcasting Corporation **http://www.cbc.ca/news**

CARMA International **http://www.carma.com**

CBS News Disaster Links
http://www.cbsnews.com/digitaldan/disaster/disasters.shtml

Center for Research on the Epidemiology of Disasters, the international disasters database **http://www.em-dat.net**

Department for International Development **http://www.dfid.gov.uk**

DesInventar **http://www.desinventar.org**

European Commission's Humanitarian Aid department **http://ec.europa.eu/echo**

Food Security Analysis Unit – Somalia **http://www.fsausomali.org**

Good Humanitarian Donorship **http://www.goodhumanitariandonorship.org**

Humanitarian Policy Group **http://www.odi.org.uk/HPG**

International Strategy for Disaster Reduction – Hyogo Framework for Action
http://www.unisdr.org/eng/hfa/hfa.htm

Médecins Sans Frontières **http://www.msf.org**

Reuters AlertNet **http://www.alertnet.org**

Tehelka **http://www.tehelka.com**

The Guardian – special reports on natural disasters
http://www.guardian.co.uk/naturaldisasters

The New York Times **http://www.nytimes.com**

The Tyndall Report **http://www.tyndallreport.com**

Tsunami Evaluation Coalition **http://www.tsunami-evaluation.org/home**

UN High Commissioner for Refugees **http://www.unhcr.org**

UN Office for the Coordination of Humanitarian Affairs **http://ochaonline.un.org**

International Federation
of Red Cross and Red Crescent Societies

Hunger in Malawi: a neglected emergency

Poverty indeed turns a man into nothing. A poor man is never listened to. He has nowhere to go to complain for nobody will take action on his story. This is the case because the people in the system know each other and they protect each other too. It feels bad to have a heavy heart and to have nowhere to go to express your concerns.

Joseph Graciano, Bangwe township, Blantyre

Malawi, one of the poorest countries in the world, faced a severe food crisis during 2005 and 2006, with 40 per cent of the population – nearly 5 million people – in need of food aid. A combination of poor rains and insufficient access to food, seeds and fertilizers brought Malawi's most vulnerable people to the brink of starvation. Underlying this crisis was a high prevalence of HIV/AIDS, poor health, very high maternal mortality, chronic poverty, rising maize prices and malnutrition – turning life for millions into a fight for survival.

As early as February 2005, the Ministry of Agriculture warned that the crisis could be as bad as the 2002 famine. On 30 August 2005, the United Nations (UN) launched a flash appeal, adopting a two-pronged 'smart' strategy of immediate food aid plus support for agricultural inputs, to prevent another food crisis recurring. But two months later, the US$ 98 million appeal was just 29 per cent covered, with huge shortfalls in the health, agriculture and food sectors. While the appeal eventually met three-quarters of its food requirements, donors provided just a fifth of the funds needed for agricultural inputs – the smart second prong.

Meanwhile, on 18 October 2005, the International Federation of Red Cross and Red Crescent Societies launched an emergency appeal for US$ 30 million, covering seven southern African countries including Malawi. By early December, this appeal was just 13 per cent covered.

This chapter considers the food crisis from the perspective of those directly affected. The first part presents the results of fieldwork conducted by the authors throughout Malawi in February 2006. Chronic hunger is familiar to Malawians – one-third of the population needed food aid in 2001–2002 and 2002–2003. Have people recovered from those crises? Is the latest crisis even worse? The chapter reveals the reality of people's lives as they struggle to cope with hunger and chronic poverty. It examines the targeting of food aid and the dynamics that evolve in communities with limited access to food. And it looks at the longer-term impacts on health, nutrition and vulnerable children.

CHAPTER 2

Photo opposite page: Providing smallholder farmers with appropriate, improved seeds and fertilizers is a far more cost-effective way of addressing recurrent food crises than appealing for emergency food aid.

Yoshi Shimizu/ International Federation

The second part of the chapter takes an institutional perspective. Why were there delays in declaring a state of emergency? Was the donor response commensurate with need? What can be done to break the recurrent and devastating cycle of food crises which typifies Malawi today? The chapter concludes with constructive recommendations for improving the agricultural production and diversification of smallholders, based on past experience.

Part 1: Fieldwork gives the vulnerable a voice

The fieldwork consisted of detailed focus group discussions in 18 communities across the country – mainly in the southern and central regions – using a structured questionnaire. Dominating the field evidence was the painfully slow recovery by poor households after the previous food crises in 2001–2002 and 2002–2003. Many had sold all their assets and few had been able to rebuild their reserves. The poorest households had consumed most of their next harvest prematurely (as green maize), leaving them with inadequate stores to last until the next harvest. So families, already suffering the after-effects of famine, fell desperately hungry the following season. Marriages broke up under the strain of severe food shortages. Early pregnancies and sexually transmitted infections (including HIV/AIDS) rose as the poor were driven into sex work to survive. Children, especially orphans, proved particularly vulnerable to malnutrition, disease and exploitation (see Box 2.1).

Most Malawians need access to land to grow food, but after the 2001–2002 famine, some households were forced to sell or lease their land. "Many people had rented their fields out for five years in exchange for food," said Peter Madeya from Dedza district, "so they had no fields left to cultivate and had to rely on piece-work only." Inequality in land ownership is resented. "There are big estates that are just standing idle when some people have no land to cultivate," said Edward Kamanga from Mzimba district. "Land distribution is a problem and it continues to contribute towards the ongoing hunger."

Hunger pervades every aspect of life. Malawians are desperately frustrated at their inability to break out of poverty. "There is no year in which we have rested from hunger," said Stephano Keyala from Chikwawa district. "Every year when we try to recover, the same problem comes back." Rainfall is both a blessing and a curse. Some farmers suffer from dry spells at critical periods, others nearby lose their houses and crops to floods. The most unfortunate face both disasters in a single planting season. "This year we thought that we would be blessed with some decent harvest, but the floods have swept away all our crops and we are left without much hope," said Justin Kankanyoza from Chikwawa. "After the floods, we had three weeks of scorching sun and this finished off the crops that had survived the floods."

Households have tried to adapt. People in the centre and north of Malawi reported a noticeable increase in households growing and consuming alternative food crops, especially

International Federation
of Red Cross and Red Crescent Societies

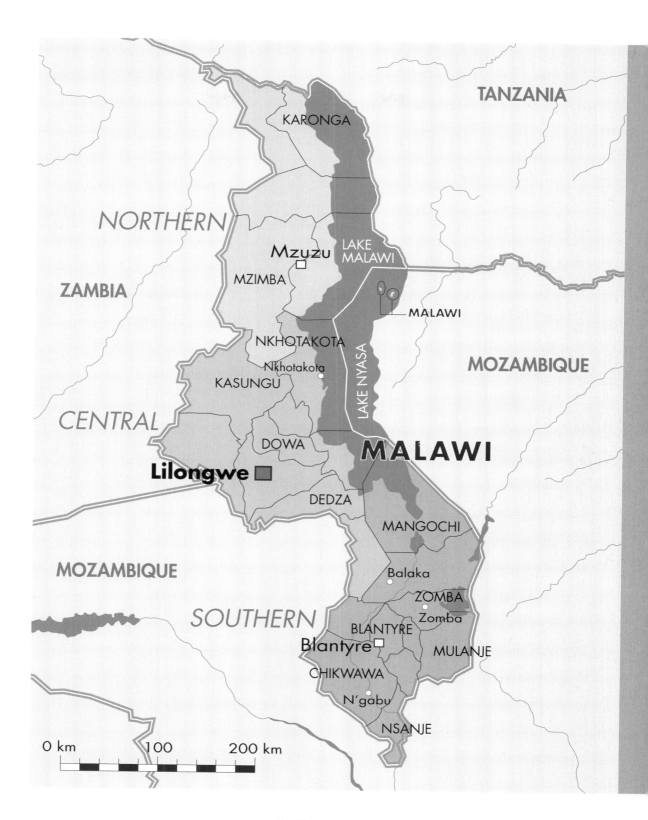

Box 2.1 Children pay hunger's heaviest price

Food crises target the most vulnerable groups in society, especially children, who are already under threat from poverty and the HIV/AIDS pandemic.

During 2005, the country's average glo-bal acute malnutrition rate was 7 per cent – affecting 144,000 children under the age of five, according to the UN's flash appeal for Malawi. Half the country's children were stunted (low height for age), nearly one-third were underweight and 50,000 were severely malnourished, according to Mary Shawa, secretary for HIV/AIDS and nutrition in the office of Malawi's President.

Children who are severely underweight may be up to eight times more likely to die of malnutrition than children of normal weight for height, while being mildly underweight doubles the risk. Malnutrition is implicated as a causal factor in over 60 per cent of child deaths, according to expert Majid Ezzati, and contributes significantly to Malawi's very high rates of infant mortality (110 per 1,000 live births) and child mortality (175 per 1,000 live births).

Even before the 2005–2006 hunger crisis, Malawi had very high rates of protein malnutrition, with 70 per cent of children admitted to nutritional rehabilitation units (NRUs) suffering kwashiorkor due to protein deficiency. Data from the NGO Action Against Hunger, in collaboration with UNICEF, showed that admissions to NRUs increased by 79 per cent in the central region and 48 per cent in the southern region in the year to December 2005.

Unless they are HIV-positive, children do well in NRUs. But the underlying drivers of malnutrition have not been addressed. "Children are taken into clinics and put under the feeding programme. They do well," said Simon Mchewerewatha from Zomba district,

"but once they are discharged, they go back home and there is no food. What happens? They go back to their former condition."

The humanitarian response should have ensured that sufficient protein-rich pulses were included as part of food aid. However, this component was underfunded. The impact on nutrition and recovery will inevitably be very serious, according to Roger Mattisen, nutritionist for UNICEF Malawi.

Meanwhile, malnutrition reduces immunity to disease. Life expectancy in Malawi has declined from an average of 41 years in 1975 to 37.5 years today. There is a huge burden of communicable diseases, the most important of which is malaria, the major cause of outpatient admissions and child deaths. "In the villages this time round, malarial infection is very high," said Antanasio Manyenga from Dedza district. "Children that have malnutrition are weak already and they are dying when they are attacked."

Malawi also has a devastating HIV/AIDS pandemic, with close to 15 per cent of the adult population (aged 15–49) infected with the virus. The pandemic has fuelled a major increase in the incidence of tuberculosis. Both HIV/AIDS itself and antiretroviral (ARV) therapy increase the body's overall nutrient demand by around 30 per cent in adults, according to Shawa.

People recognize the clear links between food crises and increased HIV transmission. "Due to famine, many women and girls go for casual sex to get money for food. It's a survival mechanism," said Edward Kamanga from Mzimba district. "The HIV infection rate is already high in this country and they get infected. The people who are positive move to full-blown AIDS because of the hunger. Even those on ARVs are dying quickly because of lack of food."

Father Nyantakanya from Ngabu district voiced the frustrations of many, when people are given good medical advice but lack the means to follow it: "When famine is rampant, it does not sound sensible to send sick people home when they are too weak to look after themselves. There is no food at home. People are given medications, but they cannot take them without food. The lack of nutritious food is a major problem. People are dying who could otherwise have been cured."

And the more adults who die, the more orphans are left behind – now numbering over a million in Malawi. This in turn puts more pressure on children to leave school early and earn whatever living they can: 1.2 million are involved in child labour.

Since the latest food crisis began in early 2005, the number of children living on the street has increased by 50–60 per cent in Malawi's two main cities, Lilongwe and Blantyre. Children leave their homes and come to town to work in maize mills or simply to beg for food. They are vulnerable to sexual abuse and cases of child trafficking have increased significantly, according to Linda Kabwila of UNICEF Malawi.

Girls are forced into early marriages, particularly in northern Malawi where they command a bride price. In early 2006, the media reported that six girls in Karonga district were exchanged for maize, cows, money, or used as collateral for a loan.

Severe hunger and poverty in childhood can have a lifelong impact. Malnutrition reduces a child's ability to learn, by reducing interaction and exploration. For the hungry, learning is almost impossible. "Usually there is nothing in the homes. Children go to sleep on an empty stomach, but they cannot sleep," said Mary Nangwale from Nsanje district. "The following day, they cannot even think of going to school because they cannot concentrate and feel dizzy."

Those that do go to school may drop out early. Over 81 per cent of Malawian children attend primary education, but less than 34 per cent complete five years of school. A mere 20 per cent go on to secondary school, as many parents simply can't afford the fees. Even for pupils who attend school, learning is impeded by a nationwide shortage of trained teachers and materials. "In some courses, there is only one book for five students. Our parents cannot afford to buy exercise books or pens. We go to school but have nowhere to write," said Susan Kachingwe from Mulanje district.

Hungry children may turn to theft. "Children would go and steal sugar cane or cassava from the fields," said Stephen Maluza Mua from Dedza district. "Some of them were severely beaten and others harmed with *panga* knives." Children caught stealing food have lost their hands after having them put in boiling water.

The effects of malnutrition span generations, as a malnourished girl becomes a malnourished mother. In Malawi, 78 per cent of expectant mothers are malnourished. Such mothers give birth to babies with low birth weight, who are more at risk of dying in infancy. Malnutrition also increases the risk of mothers dying in childbirth. The latest published data from UNICEF estimates maternal mortality at 1,800 per 100,000 live births – one of the highest rates in the world.

The Malawi Red Cross Society, with its international partners, has prioritized the protection of Malawi's most vulnerable citizens. Using emergency funds to supplement ongoing programmes, the Red Cross provides food and nutritional support for orphans and vulnerable children, as well as vital home-based care for those suffering from communicable diseases such as HIV/AIDS. ■

cassava and potatoes. Progress on diversification is, however, limited by the scarcity of planting materials (e.g., cassava cuttings and sweet potato vines). Irrigated vegetable production works where opportunities and markets exist (primarily near urban centres). Traditional *dimba* (wetland) gardens are used more intensively, both for staple foods and for horticulture. But for the majority of smallholders, who don't produce enough to feed themselves most years, diversification is difficult, because they can't generate enough surplus to invest in new assets, replenish livestock or diversify their income base.

Agricultural recovery is constrained by other major factors. Environmental degradation is spreading alarmingly, reducing the land's productivity. Better inputs (appropriate seeds and fertilizers) are too expensive. Nearly half of Malawi's 2.8 million smallholder households own less land than the bare minimum (0.5 hectares) needed to grow enough food to survive.

Investment in increasing agricultural productivity and reducing the vulnerability of livelihoods is a vital part of the fight against hunger and poverty. But the interactions of health, poverty and gender inequality must also be understood. UN special envoys Stephen Lewis and James Morris clearly warned that the food crisis of 2001–2002 would exacerbate poverty and the HIV/AIDS pandemic in southern Africa.

Malawi finds itself today in a recurring food crisis situation, where short-term survival – at household and national levels – is derailing investment in education, health and governance. The development policy community, both national and international, has been slow to act on these conclusions.

Chronic food crisis strikes twice in four years

Poor rains and insufficient access to agricultural inputs during the 2004–2005 season led to "the worst critical food crisis since 1994", according to the UN appeal. Production of maize, Malawi's most important staple crop, fell to just 55 per cent of the 2.1 million tonnes needed each year to sustain the nation. In August 2005, the UN estimated that at least 4.2 million people were at risk of serious food shortages between June 2005 and March 2006 – with the southern part of the country worst affected. The shortfall was calculated as equivalent to 269,000 tonnes of maize.

Towards the end of 2005, the estimated number of people in need of food aid rose to nearly 5 million. This compared with 3.2 million in need of food during the 2001–2002 crisis. But communities were divided over which crisis was worse. Speaking of 2002, Hannock Phiri of Kasungu district said: "During that hunger, the whole village was so quiet – one could not even hear someone who is drunk make noise in the village." Some noted that more people died of hunger in 2001–2002. But deaths due to hunger tend to be under-reported in Malawi as elsewhere (partly because it is very difficult to separate hunger from other causes of mortality, e.g., communicable diseases).

Others felt the situation was far worse in 2005–2006 because of the cumulative impact of the failure to recover from 2001–2002 and 2002–2003, plus the poor harvest in 2005–2006. "We had already sold our livestock, our bicycles, our radios and even our wrist-watches", said the headman of Chibothera village, Nkhotakota district, "so this time we started with nothing."

The main difference between the two crises has been the availability of maize on the commercial market. In 2002, the Malawian government imported 250,000 tonnes of maize. It was sold at subsidized rates through the Agricultural Development and Marketing Corporation (ADMARC), the parastatal marketing network. People who had cash could access maize at affordable prices, since the presence of large quantities of subsidized maize pushed down prices in informal markets, thus helping the poor.

However, the importing and subsidizing of commercial maize proved very costly for the government. Some of the maize remained unsold and was exported at a loss. Domestic debt swelled to unsustainable levels and the exchange rate sank, plunging the country into a fiscal crisis.

To avoid this debt trap, the government imported a modest 70,000 tonnes of maize in 2005, utilizing futures options on the South African market. The effect on prices was equally modest. In January 2006, the Famine Early Warning Systems Network (FEWS NET) reported: "Maize prices continue to increase at an unprecedented rate. Many ADMARC markets sold little or no maize in January due to the fact that government commercial stocks are exhausted. This comes at a time when maize demand is at its peak… Maize prices this January are much higher than during the 2001 food crisis or any other year in the past four seasons."

The shortage of subsidized maize this year has had a major impact on the poor. Simon Mcherewatha described the situation during early 2006 in his home district of Zomba: "When maize does arrive at the ADMARC depots, people line up for two to three days before they are able to buy anything. Many things happen at ADMARC depots. Some women have to sleep with the ADMARC staff so that they can have the possibility of buying some food. The maize comes in very little amounts so people scramble on the line. They push each other and fight over positions. Sometimes security people beat up people in the name of bringing order, yet these are people trying to get food when they are weak and hungry."

In an attempt to share limited supplies fairly, ADMARC initially restricted sales of maize to 20kg per person. In February 2006, they reduced this to 9kg per person (where maize was available at all). Those interviewed during the fieldwork were concerned about the transparency of maize sales behind closed doors. Some said that ADMARC staff overcharged or demanded a tip. "They tell us that *uyikepo ya panwamba* – literally meaning 'put something on top'," said MacCloud Banda from Kasungu. "As a result, we end up buying at double the normal ADMARC price."

The UN's September 2005 figure of 4.2 million people in need of food aid was based on the assumption that maize would remain at between 19 and 23 Malawi kwacha (MWK) per kilogram – around 15 to 18 US cents. However, by February 2006, maize prices on the informal market had soared to around MWK 60 per kilogram in much of Malawi. In the south, a 50kg bag of maize (which would last an average family a month) would sell for MWK 3,000–3,500.

By comparison, the average monthly minimum wage in Malawi is under MWK 2,000. People knew they were being ripped off, with reports of cut-down buckets being used to measure out the maize. But for most, the main problem was that they couldn't access maize anywhere. "You cannot find maize now – not even a single grain," said Lyness Yohane from Dowa district in January 2006.

Food aid and fertilizers fail to feed all

Efforts were made to target food aid on the basis of objective criteria through a participatory field-based process developed by the Vulnerability Assessment Committee (VAC), which comprises government, UN and non-governmental organization (NGO) players. The VAC made detailed recommendations in May 2005 about how food aid should be phased by district – but not all recommendations were followed or effectively communicated.

The chair of the Parliamentary Committee on Agriculture, Dzoole Mwale, commented: "This time around I am completely in the dark. I don't understand the basis for targeting. The Vulnerability Assessment Committee has not briefed parliament on their report. I am not invited to meetings of the food security task force. There has been no communication with us. How can we inform our constituents when we don't know anything?"

Outside the food security joint task force – dominated by government officials, donors and NGOs – very few people had access to, or an understanding of, the VAC report. Key players in parliament, civil society and the faith communities were not informed about the VAC's basis for food distribution. They had limited input into the policy, design or implementation of the humanitarian response. Parliamentarians felt sidelined from decision-making. Faith communities, with their detailed knowledge of the local situation, were not given the opportunity to participate.

This created a perception that all decisions were being made by the government in consultation with donors, to the exclusion of civil society and parliament. "Donors have their own policies and come and impose them on NGOs or partners, even

International Federation
of Red Cross and Red Crescent Societies

though the people on the ground understand the local situation," said Father Nyantakanya from Ngabu district. "The beneficiaries may have some queries, but they are afraid of losing out on the much-needed food. They simply accept everything that they are told."

In areas targeted for food aid, people reported that things were better than during 2001–2002. "Though the food is not enough, we are getting something. People are receiving maize, cooking oil and beans. Many people would have died were it not for the help we are getting," said Peter Sofoliano from Nsanje district.

But in a desperately poor country like Malawi, for targeting to be accepted, the rationale behind targeting needs to be clearly understood. Few outside senior government circles and donor agencies understand how beneficiaries are identified. Although the criteria are objective, the majority of those not targeted for food aid failed to meet their basic nutritional requirements. In 2006, over 80 per cent of Malawi's population reduced their already unsatisfactory food intake due to hunger, but only 40 per cent were targeted for food aid under VAC guidelines.

During fieldwork for this chapter, some respondents were concerned at how the targeting of food aid was affecting community relationships. "People are very bitter with the chiefs who have been instrumental in determining aid," said Enoch Phiri. "This has resulted in violence. There is chaos in the villages because some chiefs are seen as corrupt and unfair."

There were problems when only the most vulnerable were targeted. While most of them shared the food with their relatives, as is customary in extended families, they risked discrimination if they didn't share. "In some cases, those targeted are old people who cannot help themselves," said Peter Madeya from Dedza district. "If they do not share, they are left on their own and life becomes hard for them. The community spirit is threatened."

There was also widespread criticism of the way fertilizer was subsidized. The government's aim was to provide each smallholder with coupons to reduce the cost of one 50kg bag of fertilizer from MWK 2,300 to MWK 950 (US$ 7.50). The UN had appealed for donors to cover the remaining cost so smallholders could access the fertilizer completely free. But this part of the appeal failed to raise sufficient funds.

"We were promised that we would get coupons for fertilizer and seed but very few people received coupons. We don't know how they decided who should get the coupons," said Grace Umali from Mangochi district. "Anyway, we cannot buy fertilizers – we don't have the money. I have never seen MWK 950 at the same time."

Martin Naluso of Blantyre district added: "The coupons were given out through chiefs or village headmen. Most of the chiefs were selling them to people rather than giving them free. In some places a coupon was going for MWK 300, in others MWK 500. Those who had the money, especially businessmen, bought these coupons and sold them back to poor people at a very high price."

However, despite these problems, the fertilizer subsidy programme helped increase maize production and reduced the likelihood of another food crisis in 2006. The government acknowledged problems with the distribution of fertilizer vouchers and commissioned an evaluation to inform programme design in future.

"Imagine having to become a thief because of hunger"

In areas not targeted for food aid, the situation could be desperate. In Ngabu district, Peter Nzonda said: "People are now eating the seeds of grass known as *nkhoka*. Birds feed on these seeds and now human beings and birds are competing for them. Many have stomach problems and pain." The same was happening in Balaka district.

There was despair where communities were excluded. "It is terribly bad not to be targeted for food relief when you don't have food. It's a matter of life and death. Denying you food is like killing you and whoever tries to kill you is not a friend," said Glades Fatchi in Chikwawa district. "The people involved in choosing face a challenge in presenting themselves as good to the whole suffering community." This sense of exclusion will persist after the crisis has passed and undermines scope for future collaboration in community development.

Households survived the way they did during the 2001–2002 food crisis (see Box 2.2). Those not getting food aid cut back their meals to one a day – in the evening. Their diet was limited to green vegetables and dried okra leaves, eaten with fresh leaves as a relish. Some households bought commercial maize seed as food as it's cheaper than maize grain in local markets.

Eating patterns changed. In Kasungu district, families used to eat from the same pot, which wasted food and made young children vulnerable. "With the present hunger, they eat once a day and food is measured out in individual portions," said McCloud Banda. "This is to ensure that children get adequate food."

However, hunger also led to widespread exploitation. "In some places you find unscrupulous people who employ others and take advantage of their being hungry and their desperation for food. They make them do hard labour and give them very little pay in return," reported Vincent Morson from Mulanje district.

International Federation of Red Cross and Red Crescent Societies

Box 2.2 How Malawians have survived recent food crises

Selling belongings

They've sold goats, chickens, bicycles, roofing sheets, even plates, blankets and clothing. The poorest households have sold virtually all they own to feed their families.

Cutting meals

Many households have reduced meals to one a day. They eat grass seed, banana stems, wild yams and roots, the bitter tubers of water lilies, cassava and *chisoko* leaves, maize husks and unripe mangoes. Consuming some of these 'non-traditional' foods can be fatal, especially for children. The media have reported a number of deaths from eating poisonous roots and water lilies.

Piece-work

Piece-work, or *ganyu* labour, is when members of the family work on another farm for money or a plate of food. This diverts labour from their own gardens, reducing their own harvest and pushing them deeper into poverty. *Ganyu* labour rates are very low and variable, as the supply of labour outstrips demand. Hungry people can't bargain and take any wage offered. While better employers pay around MWK 100 per half day, others openly exploit casual labourers by paying them in maize bran, non-traditional foods or, in some cases, refusing to pay at all. Some Malawians have worked for up to ten days anticipating wages that never materialize.

Taking children out of school

Primary education is free in Malawi, but some parents have sent their daughters to work in the homes of richer families to earn money for food. "This is not a thing that parents were pleased to do, but they felt forced to sacrifice their children in this manner for the sake of survival," said Vincent Morson from Mulanje district. Many children have been withdrawn from secondary school as parents can't afford the fees. "Their families preferred to use the little money they could for getting food rather than paying school fees," explained Peter Madeya from Dedza district.

Transactional sex

This has increased due to recent food crises. "Many young girls went with men who would help them with soap, clothes and some of their needs which their parents could not afford," said Sofoliano Kungaecha from Nsanje district. "Women and girls who lived near towns would flock into the town in the evenings as sex workers for survival," added Vincent Morson. "Married women and single women would do this out of desperation in order to feed their families." The wages for commercial sex work vary according to circumstances and the extent of desperation. Young girls go with businessmen to pay for school fees, while their mothers have casual sex to feed the family.

Theft

There's been an increase in people stealing to survive. Those with sugar cane or cassava gardens are usually the victims. People also steal unripe 'green' maize. If caught, thieves have been subjected to mob justice, including severe beatings and attacks with *panga* knives. Between May 2002 and May 2003, the theft of crops and livestock accounted respectively for 17.2 and 8.5 per cent of all crimes, according to authors Pelser, Burton and Gondwe, who termed such theft 'crimes of need'. ■

Most communities in the worst affected southern region confirmed an increase in high-risk sexual practices, including transactional sex, forcing young girls into prostitution, forced early marriages, domestic violence and child abuse. "With the present hunger, women who have children and whose families cannot get any food go to the extent of selling their bodies to those who have food or money," said John Lockie in Nsanje district.

Families and marriages broke down. "The husbands know what is happening, but since they have failed to provide the food themselves they just look on in pain," said Peter Sofoliano from Nsanje. Some communities in central and northern regions said people had lost interest in sex, as their only priority was to survive. The spirit of community cooperation was strained, as people struggling to survive neglected the chronically sick and elderly.

Hunger has undermined human dignity and shattered self-esteem. Robert Mchunju spoke for many when describing the situation in his home district of Ngabu: "Ordinary people have been reduced to beggars relying on hand-outs. It is really degrading not to be able to feed your family. You feel a failure," he said, adding: "The dignity of the family has been shaken due to all the quarrels that have arisen between husband and wife. The dignity of women is gone because they have to go for men with money. They become the second or third wife of a man who can provide food. They could not tolerate this if it were not for the hunger. The dignity of people is affected because now they have even turned to stealing food from other people's gardens. Imagine having to become a thief because of hunger."

People became angry. They lost hope in their future and faith in their god. Many communities believed the government had betrayed them. "It is difficult to understand our politicians," said Robert Mchunju. "They promise a lot but do very little." Some, like Joseph Graciano from Blantyre district, pointed the finger at the opposition: "Government has done its best – only that this year the famine is very bad. The politicians in the opposition have not helped. They did not support the government's efforts. Instead, they wasted their time on im-peachment and gave little time to those issues that matter for the people of the country."

At the root of many people's anger was the sense that this crisis could have been prevented. In the words of J. Banda from Blantyre: "This hunger was known long before and all of us knew that it was going to be very, very serious. But no proper mechanisms were put in place to avert it. We blame our politicians for this. We are disappointed in them. Even the president was very hesitant to declare a state of disaster for political reasons, which was very bad. When he did declare it, it was rather late."

International Federation
of Red Cross and Red Crescent Societies

Part 2: Analysing the response

When was it clear that the food shortages would become a humanitarian emergency? The parliament's agriculture committee warned on 7 February 2005 that if the current dry spell were to persist for the next two weeks, Malawi would be hit by a devastating food shortage. The next day, the *Daily News* newspaper reported the committee as saying: "The magnitude would be similar to the 2002 famine which killed several hundreds of people." Their concerns were echoed by the government's agriculture minister, Andrew Daudi, who told the *Nation* newspaper on 16 February that he was concerned that the dry spell would adversely affect the maize harvest. Civil society groups also sounded warnings.

Almost immediately, others in government and the donor community sought to allay these fears. A number of resident donors said that the scale of the crisis was exaggerated and that the predicted national maize harvest of 1.3 million tonnes did not represent a food crisis (even though the country needs 2.1 million tonnes a year to feed itself).

Two major donors, the UK's Department for International Development (DFID) and the European Commission, were the first to respond to the food crisis in March 2005, providing money to restock the country's strategic grain reserve of 60,000 tonnes of maize. As the scale of the crisis became evident, donors increased their support through regular programmed resources and in response to the UN's flash appeal in September. But, as the evidence from the markets has shown, this was insufficient to stop food prices escalating.

Financial and political fears delay declaration of emergency

"A consensus has emerged that we have a serious food shortage affecting many people in Malawi and accordingly... I declare all districts in Malawi disaster areas with effect from today," said President Mutharika in a statement issued on 15 October 2005, according to Reuters. Why did it take over eight months from the first signs of crisis for the government to declare a state of emergency?

When Mutharika's government was elected in May 2004, Malawi's international financial reputation had been destroyed under the previous administration. Domestic debt had exploded sixfold to MWK 60 billion since 2002, due to serious macroeconomic mismanagement and the cost of importing maize in response to the crises of 2001–2002 and 2002–2003. Aid from the International Monetary Fund (IMF), balance of payments support from international donors (worth US$ 70m per annum), and the Heavily Indebted Poor Countries (HIPC) debt-relief process had all been suspended.

Meanwhile, Malawi had to continue servicing its external debt of US$ 3.1 billion, costing over US$ 110 million in 2004 alone – around 15 per cent of total government expenditure – according to data from the Reserve Bank of Malawi. As a result, debt repayments crowded out spending on essential social services.

One of the major factors, therefore, lying behind the government's decision to delay declaring a state of emergency was the need to re-establish its credibility for prudent economic management. This was vital to get back on track with the IMF and complete the debt-relief process. Other factors also contributed to the delay:

- **Fear of panic and hoarding.** Declaring an emergency might trigger exactly the rise in food prices the government was desperate to avoid, as those with cash rush to buy up whatever maize supplies remain. The government couldn't afford to buy sufficient reserves to influence market prices.
- **Political vulnerability.** The new president was under threat of impeachment. Opposition parties could exploit a state of emergency as a failure of government policy and derail economic reforms.
- **National pride.** One of Malawi's senior civil servants reflected the views of many when he said: "Why should we declare a state of disaster? Do you want to humiliate us? Must we go begging? Right from the beginning in February, the president called the donor community – he told them that there would be a food crisis. He asked for help. The donors live here; they are not blind. They know that this will be a food crisis. They should increase aid for this crisis now. They should not ask us to declare a state of disaster as this will only cause more problems."

It is not clear whether a declaration of a state of emergency is actually required for donors to increase aid. Those with existing programmes can reallocate budgets to respond to an emergency. But to get significant additional humanitarian funds in the absence of a state of emergency or UN appeal or significant press coverage is difficult, especially for a slow-onset disaster.

Response saved lives but failed to reduce vulnerability

In May 2005, Malawi's Vulnerability Assessment Committee presented donors with two scenarios: the first assumed that maize prices would range between MWK 19 and MWK 23 per kilogram. On this basis, an estimated 4.2 million people were at risk and the missing food entitlement was 269,000 tonnes. The second scenario, based on maize prices of MWK 33–40 per kilogram, predicted that 330,000–400,000 tonnes of maize equivalent would be needed as relief for those unable to access food in the market.

Donors planned their response around the first scenario, even though the government revised the numbers at risk to 4.8 million – a missing food entitlement of

335,400 tonnes – in November 2005. Meanwhile, during early 2006, maize prices throughout Malawi continued to soar above scenario two levels.

The decision to plan around scenario one was unrealistic from the outset. It was probably driven by resource considerations and the recognition that congestion on transport routes into landlocked Malawi would limit the amount of food aid that could be imported on time. As the situation deteriorated, the UN flash appeal September 2005–March 2006 called for US$ 51 million in humanitarian relief and US$ 36.5 million for agricultural inputs. The total appeal was later revised to US$ 98 million. "Food aid must be prepositioned in many areas before the rains start in November," said the appeal.

The aim of the agricultural inputs support was to help the government provide 2 million smallholder farming households with access to 50kg of free fertilizer and 5kg of free maize seed – in time for the next growing season (January to March 2006). The expected impact was to improve agricultural production and reduce the "prospect of another food shortage and costly humanitarian operation in 2006–2007". It made the appeal "forward-looking", in the words of Jan Egeland, the UN's humanitarian chief.

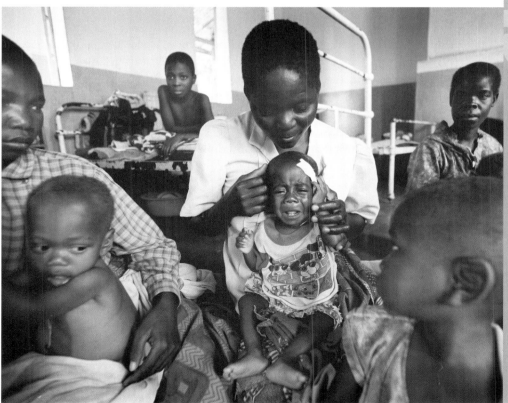

Hospitals in Malawi are receiving a rising number of malnourished children. Mashina Haudi is one year and four months old. Her weight has been improving since she came to the nutritional rehabilitation unit at Nkhotakota district hospital in Malawi.

Bo Mathisen/ International Federation

The timing of aid was clearly as important as the overall quantity delivered. However, by late October 2005, the UN appeal was less than one-third covered. Food had attracted US$ 18m of the US$ 49m needed, while just US$ 7.5m was given for the vital agricultural inputs – covering 21 per cent of original requirements. In February 2006, emergency food relief had to be scaled back, at the height of the hunger crisis.

By late April 2006, the appeal had garnered US$ 56 million, just over half the US$ 98 million requested. Donations for food, health, water and sanitation had all increased since October – but not for agriculture. According to the UN's financial tracking system, a further US$ 61 million was contributed outside the UN appeal. This included programmes by NGOs and the International Federation, but the bulk of the money was a reallocation of US$ 37 million of World Bank funds to help the government cover the cost of maize and fertilizer imports.

To put this response into perspective, for every dollar of aid Malawi received for its food crisis – whether inside or outside the UN appeal – it paid a dollar back in debt repayments. Malawi is one of the world's poorest countries – an estimated 65 per cent of its people live below the poverty line. It is difficult to understand how its external debt could not have been reviewed at a time when the country was facing a humanitarian emergency affecting 5 million people.

The failure to finance the true scale of the humanitarian crisis (the VAC's second scenario), combined with delays in the arrival of aid-bearing ships, overloaded transport corridors and the poor performance of some suppliers, compromised the food distribution pipeline. As a consequence, the UN World Food Programme (WFP) was forced to reduce planned food aid distributions.

However, while the humanitarian response prevented widespread hunger-related deaths, it was insufficient to ensure agricultural recovery, prevent escalating malnutrition among children or help households avoid destructive coping mechanisms that have forced them ever deeper into poverty.

Neglected solution: subsidies for agricultural recovery

The inclusion of support for agricultural inputs in the UN appeal was designed to promote recovery in a desperately poor agriculture-based economy where the majority of the population fails to meet basic nutritional requirements, even in non-crisis years.

To break the vicious cycle of poverty and food insecurity in which many smallholders are trapped requires long-term, carefully implemented policies to transform the agricultural sector – plus effective programmes to alleviate the immediate impacts of

International Federation
of Red Cross and Red Crescent Societies

food insecurity. Both are essential if Malawi's development is not to be continually disrupted by recurring food crises. Such an approach constitutes three main elements:

- Ensuring effective, evidence-based subsidies for agricultural inputs which clearly benefit the poor.
- Enhancing market access for inputs and outputs – with explicit recognition of the cash constraints of the poor.
- Strengthening the linkages between science and policy.

Direct subsidies on fertilizer prices are politically appealing, but exclude the poorest smallholders who can't afford to buy inputs even at subsidized rates. The costs can quickly spiral out of control, since the government doesn't control the international price of fertilizer, the exchange rate or fertilizer demand.

A better option is an 'area-based subsidy', similar to the universal 'starter pack' programme designed and implemented by the Malawian government in 1998–2000 to increase smallholder maize productivity. The starter pack provided *all* smallholder households with sufficient free seed and fertilizer for 0.1 hectares. It led to record maize production of around 2.5 million tonnes, averted recurrent food crises and brought down the price of food for the poor. At around US$ 45 million per year in 1998–1999, its cost compares favourably with the cost of emergency responses, which totalled US$ 117 million in 2005–2006 (see Box 2.3).

The starter pack planners used the 'common sense' criterion of providing sufficient inputs to put one extra bag of maize in every household's granary – ensuring the inputs were big enough to make a difference, but small enough not to be diverted or sold.

The intention with area-based subsidies is to provide all farmers with the resources they need to start the long haul out of poverty. In the first year, the focus would be on inputs to produce the staple food (e.g., maize). As farmers improve their food security, subsidized inputs could be varied to promote crop diversification. By year three, for example, the maize component could be reduced and inputs for other important food or cash crops (e.g., groundnuts, beans, pigeonpea) might form the bulk of the pack. Inputs could be adjusted according to agro-ecological and market conditions. Key principles include:

- Sufficiently comprehensive to address rural and urban hunger without building debt – benefiting all smallholder households.
- Sustained for the medium term – 10 to15 years' guaranteed funding.
- Incorporating 'best-bet' technologies – high-quality seed designed for local conditions, early maturing varieties to reduce vulnerability to drought.
- Sound advice in: early planting, timely and efficient fertilizer application, correct husbandry and weeding practices.
- Improving soil fertility and environmental sustainability through economically viable biological technologies.

Box 2.3 Subsidized seeds and fertilizer save lives and money

Past experience shows that it is far more cost-effective to address recurrent food crises by providing universal subsidies to support agricultural production rather than through emergency food imports and appeals for food aid.

Malawi has a chronic food deficit, with a national maize requirement of around 2.1 million tonnes and production levels averaging around 1.6–1.7 million tonnes. So, in the absence of a significant intervention by government, Malawi has a maize production deficit of 500,000 tonnes.

But when the government, facing a food crisis, implemented its own programme to promote food security, the results were remarkable. In the 1998–1999 and 1999–2000 agricultural seasons, the government implemented a universal 'starter pack' programme. Under this, all 2.8 million of Malawi's smallholder households were given 2.5 kilograms of improved hybrid maize seed, 15 kilograms of fertilizer and 1 kilogram of legume seed. For two years, maize production increased by an average of 125–150kg per household. Nationwide production reached around 2.5 million tonnes – half a million tonnes higher than before or since, and 67 per cent above the 21-year average.

The evaluation of the programme concluded the universal starter packs were capable of producing between 280,000 and 420,000 tonnes of maize, according to Sarah Levy, the editor of a recent book on the subject. The key requirements were that the programme promoted 'best-bet' technologies (seeds and fertilizer best suited to local environmental and economic circumstances) and that inputs were delivered in advance of the planting rains. When these requirements were met, the programme was capable of closing the gap between production and consumption requirements.

The universal starter pack programme, which cost around US$ 45 million per annum, proved very cost-effective compared with the alternatives of subsidizing commercial maize imports or appealing for emergency aid (in 2005, the UN alone appealed for US$ 98 million for Malawi). In addition, compared to food aid, starter packs encouraged development rather than dependence.

Following Malawi's devastating food crisis in 2005, the government implemented a fertilizer subsidy programme focused on increasing maize productivity. The government subsidized 147,000 tonnes of fertilizer at a cost of around US$ 60 million. Donors contributed US$ 7.5 million, through the UN appeal, to support the distribution of 4,000 tonnes of improved maize seed, logistics and agricultural extension. An external evaluation will calculate the total incremental production under the fertilizer subsidy programme, but initial indications were that production in 2006 would hit 2.4 million tonnes.

According to a report tracking soil health from 1980 to 2004, published recently by the International Center for Soil Fertility and Agricultural Development, more than 80 per cent of farmland in sub-Saharan Africa is plagued by severe degradation. Major factors include a soaring population, erosion by wind and water and, crucially, farmers' inability to afford fertilizer. Fertilizer use in Africa is the lowest in the world – less than 10 per cent of the global average – resulting in the world's lowest crop yields.

The lesson for African governments struggling with recurrent food crises and chronic hunger is clear. It is better to subsidize agricultural production than be forced to deal with food crises which divert scarce foreign exchange for maize imports, undermine growth, fuel inflation and lead to incalculable human misery. ■

International Federation
of Red Cross and Red Crescent Societies

- Promoting crop and livelihood diversification.
- Active collaboration with the private sector, local government and NGOs.

The advantage of area-based subsidies is that they reach and benefit all farmers, although the evidence suggests that the better-off will, unsurprisingly, make more of the opportunities provided. This is integral to the approach. Farming leaders must be actively involved in promoting and improving new technologies. There are clear rewards for good husbandry and the effective use of inputs, as well as a direct impact on poverty through improving food security and nutrition.

Such subsidies are a mechanism for driving the nation out of poverty and into profitable agriculture and other associated businesses. They can be adjusted to changing national priorities by altering the mix of subsidized inputs. The costs are known largely in advance. If the programme is properly planned and implemented, it complements commercial input supply and doesn't disrupt trade.

The model could be varied according to the specific priorities of different farmers and regions of the country, with inputs adjusted from the start. One package could be free and targeted at very poor farmers; another could comprise partially subsidized inputs for more diverse crops – appropriate for better-off farmers. The explicit development of crop diversification was a major gap in the original starter pack initiative. A revised programme should include the evaluation (with farmers' full participation) of various diversification options. These are vital to recovery and should be introduced at the earliest opportunity, so that smallholders are no longer tied to their food crop as an income source.

But careful attention needs to be paid to the market price of farm outputs. One of the benefits of such a programme is its effect in keeping down food prices. This benefits the poor as well as schools and hospitals, which could buy up food at reasonable rates to feed vulnerable groups.

To succeed, area-based subsidies need to be implemented with adequate lead time, plus a 10–15 year commitment. There is little international experience in executing this type of programme. Importantly, it depends on the availability of reliable, high-yield technologies suitable for the poor as well as for better-resourced farmers. Inputs must be provided on time – before the planting rains – and supported by public awareness and advice through radio messages and focused extension efforts. To have a significant impact on reducing vulnerability, the programme has to engage all smallholders.

For the majority of Malawi's population – as in most of Africa – agriculture is the most important livelihood activity and agricultural constraints are immediate and critical. Transforming agriculture must form a significant part of the solution to Malawi's poverty and vulnerability.

CHAPTER 2

That transformation will come, as it has elsewhere, from the development and adoption of productive, profitable new technologies. A participatory 'Green Evolution' in agricultural development is needed, which builds on an evolving partnership of scientists, farming communities and development agencies, and harnesses the best available skills in a collaborative, 'learning-by-doing' manner in which all feel ownership and pride.

Conclusion: listen to locals, invest in agriculture

This chapter has outlined the human impact of Malawi's recent and recurrent food crises from the perspective of the people affected. Hunger has forced people to 'cope' in the most destructive ways imaginable: selling precious possessions and vital assets, taking children out of school and forcing young girls and their mothers into exploitative sexual relationships. It has led to the break-up of families and forced children onto the street. It has exacerbated domestic tensions leading to grief, hurt and a sense of betrayal. It has eroded the spirit of community cooperation and aggravated relationships with traditional leaders.

The failure to ensure that a strong public awareness campaign accompanied the humanitarian relief operation has left large swathes of the population, especially those not targeted for food or fertilizer, feeling betrayed, confused and angry. Trust in national governance has been badly damaged. Too few decision-makers within the government and aid community have appreciated the true extent of poverty in Malawi. Too few have listened to people who live in vulnerable communities, even though it is a small country. None of this augurs well for Malawi's long-term development.

Yet, in the face of chronic hunger and grinding poverty, the spirit of resilience and hope remains alive. People understand their situation and are articulate about their priorities. They want their most basic needs met: access to seeds and fertilizers so they can grow sufficient food and not have to rely on food aid; access to quality healthcare, good education and clean water. They want stability in their family lives rather than being torn apart by poverty and premature death from disease and hunger. People want to be consulted about their needs – listened to, not talked down to. They would like to see their elected representatives outside of election campaigns. They want transparency, rather than watching the maize vanish through the back door when they've been waiting for days in line for their fair share. They want equal access to subsidized fertilizer without being forced to pay bribes.

Malawi is in a recurrent and devastating sequence of food crises – which need a development as well as a relief component if the cycle is to be broken. But the humanitarian response was underfunded from the outset and donors provided very

International Federation
of Red Cross and Red Crescent Societies

little support for the agricultural inputs envisaged by the UN appeal. The only way to avoid food crises in future is through increasing investment in agriculture, led by national authorities and supported by international donors. Otherwise, this deadly cycle of crisis and short-term response will continue.

Some names have been changed to protect the identities of respondents. We would like to acknowledge the assistance of Mary Shawa in the Office of the Malawi President and Cabinet, and Michael Keating, the United Nations resident representative, in preparing this chapter.

This chapter was contributed by Anne Conroy, who has lived in Malawi for over 15 years, working on research, policy analysis and advocacy in the areas of agriculture, food security, health and HIV/AIDS; Malcolm Blackie, a Zimbabwean agricultural economist who has worked in sub-Saharan Africa for four decades and is director of bT Associates, a small network of African development experts; Father Boniface Tamani, Chair of the Malawi-based Public Affairs Committee (PAC), an inter-faith advocacy and civic education agency; and Austin Ngwira, an agriculture and rural development specialist, who has worked extensively on rural food economies in Malawi and Zimbabwe.

Sources and further information

Bationo, A., Kimetu, J., Ikerra, S., Kimani, S., Mugendi, D., Odendo, M., Silver, M., Swift, M.J. and Sanginga, N. *The African Network for Soil Biology and Fertility: New Challenges and Opportunities.* Scaling soil nutrient balances workshop proceedings. Nairobi, 2003.

Esser, K., Oygard, R., Chibwana, C. and Blackie, M. *Opportunities for Norwegian Support to Agricultural Development in Malawi.* Noragric Report No. 27. Aas, Norway: Norwegian University of Life Sciences, 2005.

Ezzati, M., Lopez, A.D., Rodgers, A., Vander Hoorn, S., Murray, C.J.L. and the Comparative Risk Assessment Collaborating Group. 'Selected major risk factors and global and regional burden of disease' in *The Lancet*, Volume 360, Issue 9343, pp. 1–14, 2002.

Famine Early Warning System Network (FEWS NET). *January Food Security Update*, 2006.

Gillespie, S. and Haddad, L. *The Relationship between Nutrition and the Millennium Development Goals: a Strategic Review of the Scope for the Department for International Development's Influencing Role.* Washington DC: International Food Policy Research Institute, 2003.

Harrigan, J. *Agricultural Diversification Options.* Paper presented to the Malawi After Gleneagles Conference, Scottish Parliament, Edinburgh, November 2005.

Levy, Sarah. 'Production, Prices and Food Security' in Sarah Levy (ed.), *Starter Packs: A Strategy to Fight Hunger in Developing Countries?* CABI Publishing, 2005.

Malawi Government. *Food Security Assessment Update.* Paper presented to the Vulnerability Assessment Committee of the National Food Crisis Task Force, November 2005.

Malawi Ministry of Health and UNICEF. *Nutrition Survey.* Paper presented to all stakeholders in the National Food Crisis Task Force, December 2005.

Pelser, E., Burton, P. and Gondwe, L. *Crimes of Need: Results of the Malawi National Crime Victimisation Survey.* Institute for Security Studies, 2004. Available at http://www.iss.org.za/pubs/Books/CrimesOfNeed/Contents.htm

Reuters. *Malawi leader declares disaster over food crisis.* London, 15 October 2005.

Shawa, M., Secretary for HIV/AIDS and Nutrition, Office of the President and Cabinet. *National Overview Nutrition and HIV/AIDS.* PowerPoint presentation to Malawi's cabinet ministers, November 2005.

Thangata, P.H. and Nkedi-Kizza, P. *Fertilizer Subsidy: the need for a pluralistic policy approach to combating hunger and poverty in Malawi.* Paper presented to the Presidential Parliamentary Committee on Agricultural Policies (Malawi Government), 1998.

United Nations (UN). *Malawi 2005: Flash Appeal.* UN Consolidated Appeals Process, 30 August 2005.

UN Children's Fund (UNICEF). *Humanitarian Situation Update.* Paper presented to the National Food Crisis Task Force, Lilongwe, April 2006.

UN Development Programme (UNDP). *Humanitarian Situation Reports.* Papers presented to the National Food Crisis Task Force, Lilongwe, January and February 2006.

Zamba, C. *Malawi's Debt Situation.* Paper presented to the Malawi After Gleneagles Conference, Scottish Parliament, Edinburgh, November 2005.

International Federation
of Red Cross and Red Crescent Societies

Web sites

Demographic Health Survey 2004, Malawi
   http://www.measuredhs.com/pubs/pdf/SR113/SR113.pdf
National Statistical Office of Malawi **http://www.nso.malawi.net**
UN Children's Fund (information on Malawi)
   http://www.unicef.org/infobycountry/malawi_statistics.html
UN Malawi 2005 Flash Appeal
   http://ochaonline.un.org/cap2005/webpage.asp?Page=1249
UN Population Fund (information on Malawi)
   http://www.unfpa.org/profile/malawi.cfm
World Bank Group in Malawi **www.worldbank.org/mw**
World Food Programme (information on Malawi)
   http://www.wfp.org/country_brief/indexcountry.asp?country=454

Hurricane Stan lifts the lid on Guatemala's vulnerability

Doña Petronila doesn't understand how rain – a divine gift for the harvest and the life it provides – can have become a punishment. Like her neighbours, Doña, a Guatemalan woman and a Maya Indian, survived the country's long civil war from 1960 to 1996, only to see her community devastated by Hurricane Stan in October 2005. Homes, friends and family vanished – washed away by the mud and water.

The mountains that surround these communities were stripped by rain and erosion. Underground streams and floods brought terror to the small homes on the river's edge. The inhabitants had settled here while on the run from the war, ten years ago, because no one else lived here. They rented land on the slopes of the mountains and cultivated maize. It was an uninhabitable wasteland when they arrived. Now it is again.

This scene, described by Costa Rican journalist María Suárez in *A Personal Account of a National Disaster*, provides an insight into understanding the vulnerabilities of present-day Guatemala: the long and bloody civil war, which displaced hundreds of

Photo opposite page: Volunteers prepare to search for the victims of a deadly mudslide near the village of Panabaj, Guatemala, 8 October 2005. Around 1,400 people died under the mudslide, which was triggered by torrential rains from Hurricane Stan.

© REUTERS/Daniel LeClair, courtesy www.alertnet.org

thousands of poor people; a peace process that has failed to deliver more equitable, sustainable, secure development; and disasters of all kinds that lay bare the deep-rooted marginalization affecting mainly the Maya population.

According to CONRED, the national disaster reduction agency, the torrential rains that accompanied Stan affected 1,156 communities: over a third of Guatemala's total area. Hardest hit were the western and central highlands, inhabited largely by indigenous people living in extreme poverty (see Box 3.1). This disaster reconfirmed what 1976's devastating earthquake and 1998's Hurricane Mitch had previously revealed: the neglected, marginalized poor are much more likely to be killed or affected by disaster (see Box 3.2).

This fresh tragedy brought to the fore many frustrations about the perilous conditions in which millions of Guatemalans live today. The impact of Stan and attempts to recover from it reveal the enormous complexity of factors determining people's vulnerability to environmental and social hazards.

Box 3.1 Guatemala: vulnerability statistics

Poverty
56 per cent of Guatemalans (6.4 million) live in poverty.
76 per cent of indigenous people are poor.
41 per cent of non-indigenous people are poor.
21.9 per cent of Guatemalans live in extreme poverty.
93 per cent of the extreme poor live in the countryside.
38 per cent of rural indigenous people live in extreme poverty.

Inequality
The top 20 per cent account for 54 per cent of total consumption.
Indigenous people comprise 43 per cent of the population, but claim less than 25 per cent of total income and consumption.

Malnutrition
Chronic child malnutrition is amongst the highest in the world (only higher in Yemen and Bangladesh).

50 per cent of children under five years of age are stunted.
70 per cent of stunted children are indigenous.
Acute malnutrition levels have increased.
Over 15,000 children under five years of age die every year.
People suffering malnutrition: 16 per cent (1992) rising to 25 per cent (2001).
People without access to adequate food: 1.4 million (1992) rising to 2.9 million (2001).

Illiteracy
31 per cent – only Nicaragua and Haiti rank worse in the region.

Lack of access to land
56 per cent of agricultural land is owned by 1.8 per cent of the population.
There are 47 farms of 3,700 hectares or more.
90 per cent of producers survive with an average of 1 hectare.

Sources: World Bank, 2003; UN Special Rapporteur on the Right to Food, 2006; FAO, 2003; IV Censo nacional agropecuario, 2003; UNDP, 2005. ■

International Federation
of Red Cross and Red Crescent Societies

The chapter does not intend to review progress made in risk reduction since Mitch, but provides an insight into the more neglected aspects of Guatemalan vulnerability exposed by Stan and reports on how the disaster has led to some surprising changes. The text is divided into four sections:

- **Stan – a disaster foretold.** How small, recurrent disasters reflect and increase everyday vulnerability and prefigure larger disasters in the future.
- **Contexts determining disaster risk.** This section examines some of the contexts and processes specific to Guatemala, which construct and maintain disaster risk.
- **Recovery boosts community cohesion.** The response to and recovery from Stan has led to greater bottom-up community organization, which could contribute to better governance with the right support from the top down.
- **Future risks demand sustained action.** This section assesses the dangers of addressing disaster risk reduction as an occasional and intermittent problem, rather than as an urgent and permanent commitment.

Stan – a disaster foretold

Stan was reported in the media as a disaster foretold – not just in the light of Hurricane Mitch in 1998, but also because in Guatemala, as in the rest of Central America, the number of small-scale disasters has been increasing in recent years, particularly those caused by torrential rains, mudslides and floods.

Stan was a repetition on a wider scale of what had been happening year after year in Guatemala – even in the months running up to the 'big disaster'. For example, three months before Stan, a mudslide in Senahú village, Alta Verapaz (in the north-east), left 22 people dead and 57 homes destroyed. Five years earlier, a mudslide killed 13 in the same place. There are similar stories of flooding on the south coast, where many communities are subjected to the same disaster year after year.

Although not as common as floods and mudslides, earthquakes are also regarded as a disaster waiting to happen. As more people move into weak buildings in high-risk areas, so vulnerability to seismic hazards is growing. In 1991, an earthquake measuring 5.3 on the Richter scale, triggered along a minor fault line beneath the town of Pochuta, Chimaltenango, left 25 people dead and 2,300 homes in ruins.

Evidence of risk patterns and insights into potential disasters can be found in the DesInventar database for Guatemala (see Chapter 1). DesInventar does not define disaster in quantitative terms, but records all the events that have an adverse effect on lives, property and infrastructure. The information, derived from secondary sources and disaggregated by community, provides a picture of the very varied daily risk scenarios existing at local level. It is a powerful tool for raising risk awareness at all levels and provides useful guidelines for making risk management an integral part of development.

Box 3.2 Guatemala: windstorms and seismic hazards

The historical memory of disasters in Guatemala revolves around major earthquakes and dangerous volcanoes, which destroyed the capital city three times: in 1541, 1773 and 1917–1918. In 1902, the country was shaken by an earthquake measuring 8.2 on the Richter scale and the dormant Santa Maria volcano awakened with one of the largest eruptions in history.

This year is the 30th anniversary of the great 1976 earthquake that shook a fifth of Guatemala's territory, leaving over 23,000 dead and 233,000 homes destroyed. Described by American journalist Alan Riding as a 'class-quake', this disaster exposed the hardship and misery enveloping the country and highlighted the extreme vulnerability of both the urban poor and rural Maya people living in the western highlands.

As Wisner et al have observed in their book *At Risk: Natural Hazards, People's Vulnerability and Disasters*: "What makes Guatemala unusual is the high degree of awareness of these social weaknesses on the part of a large proportion of the population, so that post-disaster relief and rehabilitation became a political battleground." However, the growing awareness and local organization that emerged as reconstruction got under way were among the factors that led the state to unleash a wave of repression in 1978, marking the start of the most violent period of internal armed conflict.

Nowadays, the word disaster more often conjures up images of windstorms – epitomized by Hurricanes Mitch (October 1998) and Stan (October 2005). However, neither of these storms struck Guatemala directly. It received fringe effects in the form of prolonged heavy rain coming at the end of rainy seasons that had already recorded above-average rainfall.

Mitch, a category 5 hurricane at its peak, moved across the Caribbean and made landfall on the Honduran coast, causing torrential rains and the biggest disaster recorded in the region in the 20th century, with thousands of floods and mudslides. By the time it passed through Guatemala, Mitch had weakened to a tropical depression, although it caused considerable impact, with continuous rains causing 529 local disasters throughout the country, mainly in the north-east and central parts, including the metropolitan area, where the highest number of deaths was recorded in the slum areas. Overall, the disaster killed 268 people, affected a further 110,758, destroyed 2,293 homes and caused direct and indirect damage totalling US$ 747.8 million, according to figures provided by CONRED, the national disaster reduction agency, and ECLAC, the Economic Commission for Latin America and the Caribbean.

Stan developed mainly as a tropical storm, reaching category 1 hurricane status for a few hours only. It passed over Mexico but did not come near Guatemala. However, Stan's outer bands of humid air gave rise to heavy rains over the mountains of Guatemala's western highlands, causing countless mudslides and river flooding. In the lower part of the southern coast, there was extensive flooding. According to CONRED, the disaster affected 1,158 communities in 15 of the country's 22 departments, leaving 669 people dead, 844 missing and 9,136 homes destroyed. Estimates put the total number of directly affected people at 474,928 (4 per cent of Guatemala's population) and the total number of people directly or indirectly affected at 3.5 million. ECLAC estimated that losses amounted to over US$ 920 million.

In addition, the years 2001–2002 will be remembered as a period of chronic food crisis – which caused numerous deaths as well as prompting solidarity in response. ■

International Federation
of Red Cross and Red Crescent Societies

During the 13-year period from January 1988 to December 2000, DesInventar recorded 2,949 adverse events in Guatemala (see Figure 3.1). The annual average number of adverse events doubled from 130 in the period 1988–1995 to 275 in the period 1996–2000, excluding Mitch-related incidents.

Most of these events can be classified as low- or medium-impact incidents, which are not included in official statistics. As a result, the people affected receive little, if any, assistance. In the period 1988–2000, the only disaster recorded by DesInventar with a major, regional impact was Hurricane Mitch (for which 529 adverse incidents were registered). The remaining 2,420 events were local disasters, although many of them caused considerable damage and loss.

According to Xavier Castellanos, senior officer for disaster preparedness and response at the International Federation of Red Cross and Red Crescent Societies, these everyday, recurring disasters are "common problems in the most vulnerable sectors of the population. They are considered one-off problems and therefore accorded little importance in the national context, even though hundreds, perhaps thousands, of families are affected by such disasters year after year. This tends to weaken the economic capacity of families and communities and results in a permanent increase in their levels of vulnerability."

In Guatemala, the 2,949 events recorded by DesInventar correspond to 25 different types of hazards (natural, technological and disease-related). Although some recur

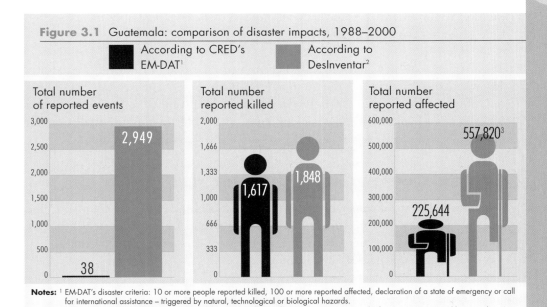

Figure 3.1 Guatemala: comparison of disaster impacts, 1988–2000

According to CRED's EM-DAT[1]   According to DesInventar[2]

Total number of reported events
2,949
38

Total number reported killed
1,617   1,848

Total number reported affected
557,820[3]
225,644

Notes: [1] EM-DAT's disaster criteria: 10 or more people reported killed, 100 or more reported affected, declaration of a state of emergency or call for international assistance – triggered by natural, technological or biological hazards.
[2] DesInventar's 'disaster' criteria: all events that have an 'adverse effect' on lives, property and infrastructure – triggered by natural, technological or biological hazards.
[3] Refers to victims who have suffered direct material losses, e.g., destruction of homes, workplaces, livelihoods.

more than others, they must all be taken into account when formulating risk-reduction policies. Six categories of hazard accounted for 87 per cent of all recorded events: fires (822 events), heavy rains (524), mudslides (469), floods (440), forest fires (186) and epidemics (132).

Only 15 per cent of the events involved deaths, killing a total of 1,848 people. The deadliest hazard was epidemics (702 deaths, mainly cholera), followed by mudslides (336), heavy rains (204) and fires (144). The database recorded 557,820 direct victims *(damnificados)*, most of whom were affected by floods (400,982 persons), heavy rains (85,471), epidemics (35,000), earthquakes (10,660), fires (9,384) and mudslides (4,433). It should be added that, in many cases, there are no accurate figures for disaster victims, suggesting the real figures could be higher.

Many manifestations of risk – particularly those caused by man-made hazards – are not considered disasters, so they receive little attention from state institutions. Yet they have serious, sometimes deadly, consequences. The most common type of adverse event in Guatemala is fires, particularly in urban areas. Fires often kill children and the elderly. They destroy dozens of homes in overcrowded shanty towns, fuelled by highly inflammable construction materials such as wood, cardboard and plastic. Fires in market-places are also very common.

The causes are always the same: candles or, where there is electricity, faulty installations that short-circuit; cooking on an open fire or, where gas is used, defective cylinders. Guatemala's rural and urban poor are caught in a risk trap – they face a multiplicity of hazards because they are poor and their vulnerability increases each time a hazard becomes a disaster.

The frequency of fires highlights another problem: the lack of rules and regulations, and where they do exist, the failure to enforce them. DesInventar reveals that 84 per cent of loss and damage in the industrial sector can be attributed to fires and a further 8 per cent to explosions and toxic gas leaks, as a result of unsafe installations or technology and negligence in handling materials and hazardous substances.

Contexts determining disaster risk

While many aspects of vulnerability are common to all situations, each country, region or community has its own specific dimensions of risk which must be identified. Five contexts or processes encompass any consideration of disaster risk in Guatemala:

- The struggle for democracy and peace.
- Ongoing social violence.
- Social, ethnic and gender discrimination.
- Population dispersal to rural hamlets.
- Migration to the United States.

Democracy and peace: progress... but challenges remain

Democracy and peace are basic conditions which must be fulfilled if disaster risk reduction is to become a sustained policy rather than an intermittent concern in the wake of major disasters – as happened after Mitch in 1998 and now with Stan.

These conditions are only just beginning to be met in Guatemala. Furthermore, there is a real risk that the incipient process of democratization and transformation may suffer set-backs from growing political instability if post-Stan recovery does not address the survival crisis faced by the 1,000-plus storm-affected communities.

In 1986, after a long succession of military regimes, democratic elections were held in Guatemala and a civilian government was voted into power. Although progress has been made towards democracy, interrupted in 1993 by a short-lived coup d'état, the risk of political instability remains high. Increasingly, new social actors – peasants, the young, women and indigenous people – are making themselves heard. But the process of building participatory citizenship is very fragile.

The country's new institutions are very weak, suffer continuous changes and have failed to achieve reforms contributing towards establishing the rule of law. The historical mutual distrust between civil society and the state remains, while the business sector continues to use its political clout to assert its private interests over the common good. Political and social conflicts, particularly at the local level, often culminate in violent acts, including lynching in extreme cases.

This year was declared National Peace Year, marking the tenth anniversary of the Peace Accords. According to a report issued in 1999 after years of research by the Guatemalan Comision de Esclarecimiento Historico (CEH, or 'truth commission'), Guatemala's civil war was one of the bloodiest in Latin America, resulting in over 200,000 people killed or disappeared and another million displaced. A scorched earth policy led to the complete destruction of over 600 villages, often leaving no inhabitants alive. The investigation found that 93 per cent of the violence was attributable to agents of the state (particularly the military) and that 53 per cent of the victims were Mayan, 11 per cent were Ladino and 30 per cent were of unregistered ethnicity.

The World Bank's 2003 report on poverty in Guatemala suggested that "the Peace Accords represented a turning point for Guatemala's development path, paving the way for a transformation to a more prosperous and inclusive nation. Progress has occurred… but challenges remain. However, changing the course of history in such a short time span is not easy in any country. The hierarchical relations, attitudes, and institutional forces that have pervaded for centuries do not disappear overnight.

Furthermore, recent events (including Hurricane Mitch and political instability) have delayed the implementation of the Peace Agenda."

There is a long way to go in fulfilling the commitments made in the Peace Accords, particularly those requiring structural changes, such as agrarian reform, access to land as a means of livelihood and the rights of indigenous peoples. Social exclusion, racism and discrimination are still commonplace.

Social violence: problem number one

Today in Guatemala, the risk of losing one's life or property is most people's biggest worry. The risk of disaster pales in comparison, particularly since disaster affects poor, socially excluded sectors of the population. The issue of violence is a major priority on the government's agenda, but it is struggling to reduce it.

The 2006 report of the United Nations High Commissioner for Human Rights on the situation in Guatemala concluded that: "Violence, arising from various causes such as organized crime, common crime, gangs of youths and illegal, clandestine security bodies and units, has become a national priority owing to its effects on public security and the creation of a state of public alarm. The phenomenon of gangs of youths (*maras*) is at the forefront of the social agenda, but the absence of any reliable analysis makes it difficult to assess its real impact on the security situation."

Homicides have soared. The Guatemalan human rights prosecutor, Sergio Morales, quoting the National Civilian Police (PNC), declared that 3,230 people were killed in 2001, rising to 5,338 in 2005. The number of violent deaths registered over the last five years equals the death toll of the great earthquake of 1976. Guatemala's homicide rate (44 per 100,000 inhabitants) is one of the highest in Latin America, itself one of the most violent regions in the world. In the capital, however, the homicide rate rises to 109 and in some municipalities, such as Nueva Concepción (Escuintla) on the south coast, it is as high as 199, according to a report published in June 2006 by the UN Development Programme (UNDP). According to the World Health Organization (WHO), in 2000, the world's average homicide rate was 8.8 per 100,000 inhabitants.

Guatemala is also one of the countries with the highest number of violent deaths among women: 1,729 were killed between 2001 and 2005, according to the PNC. Congresswoman Alba Maldonado, interviewed by the Inter Press Service in June 2005, said the methods used are reminiscent of those employed against the guerrillas and residents of rural indigenous villages during the civil war. A report released at the same time by the London-based human rights group Amnesty International said the alarming increase in murders of women was compounded by impunity, weak laws and a firmly entrenched *machista* or sexist mind-set.

Discrimination: root cause of vulnerability

Exclusion and racism drive much of Guatemala's poverty and inequality and lie at the root of people's vulnerability to disaster. Such discrimination has deep-seated historic causes in Guatemala, making it very difficult to overcome.

The World Bank's poverty report said that:"Past policies greatly contributed to an exclusionary pattern of development in Guatemala, particularly for land, labour, and education. All of these spheres were intertwined with each other, and with the development of coffee, Guatemala's primary export crop. Policies such as massive land expropriations, forced labour, and exclusion from the education system (as part of a broader political strategy), all sought to promote economic growth, but to the exclusion and detriment of the indigenous population. Women were also excluded from these spheres."

It is therefore indigenous women who are most seriously affected by discrimination, which perpetuates the invisibility of the many needs and risks affecting their day-to-day existence and their fight for survival. The UN High Commissioner for Human Rights, writing in 2006, expressed particular concern at the dual discrimination against indigenous women, reflected in rejection of their costumes, their limited access to education, basic public services and land, and the lack of opportunities in the workplace.

Guatemala, with a population of 13 million, has the largest number of indigenous people in Central America. They speak 23 languages (21 Mayan languages, Xinca and Garifuna) and they account for 41 per cent of the total population, according to the 2002 national census (other estimates put the figure at over 50 per cent).

The UN's 2005 National Human Development Report maintained that: "Racism is still very much alive and deeply rooted in the attitudes and practices of common people and of institutions – public and private – as well. However, it is worthwhile noting that most of the time, racism is not explicit. After the colonial times, there have never been official 'apartheid' policies applied in Guatemala. One of the main outcomes of racism is discrimination in the access to human development opportunities for the indigenous – Maya – population. There is no sphere contained in the human development paradigm (economic, social, political or cultural) where the Maya people have equal conditions and opportunities when compared to the non-indigenous population. This situation also affects the Garifuna and Xinca people."

Meeylyn Lorena Mejia Lopez, a researcher and writer with extensive experience in indigenous rights, says that history shows indigenous peoples themselves have not escaped the male chauvinist vision at the root of colonial and modern societies. Within indigenous communities there is a belief that the man is the "boss, the head of the family", the one who takes decisions at household and community level.

CHAPTER 3

Exclusion and discrimination are also evident in the response to Hurricane Stan. The Economic Commission for Latin America and the Caribbean (ECLAC), in its 2005 report on the impact of the disaster, highlighted the "evident lack of information disaggregated by gender and ethnicity. The latter is of crucial importance, because it is necessary to harness and mobilize the cultural values of the indigenous communities expressed in organization, cooperation, solidarity, spiritual strength and social cohesion, important in the care of orphaned children." This lack of disaggregated information is particularly significant, because those most seriously affected by the disaster are indigenous communities, from which many of the men have emigrated to the US, leaving a high proportion of households headed by women.

There is much evidence to show that the vulnerability of women has increased dramatically since Stan, as has the incidence of domestic violence, already high before the disaster. As ECLAC pointed out: "Men are more likely to resort to violence when they are cut off from the familiar routines of daily life and lose their position as head of the household because they no longer have a job or source of income. When women lose their economic resources, their negotiating power within the household is seriously weakened. In the case of women, disaster therefore increases poverty and social vulnerability."

Population dispersal to rural hamlets

High population density, particularly in urban slums, is frequently cited as one of the most important factors determining disaster risk in Central America. But, according to Jacobo Dardón and Cecilia Morales of the Tzuk Kim-Pop Movement, the region hardest hit by Hurricane Stan was the western highlands, where there are 5,000 widely dispersed rural communities. Around 60 per cent of these communities are located on mountain slopes and at least 20 per cent are at high risk of disaster.

The dispersal of the rural population creates two types of vulnerability to disaster in Guatemala's highland areas. Lacking other options, people increasingly inhabit places that are dangerous because of their rugged terrain and deforestation, as the mountainsides are stripped to grow subsistence crops. The physical vulnerability of these communities to the growing threats of landslides and erosion is therefore high.

Secondly, for many communities, dispersal means 'territorial exclusion' or isolation. Geographic isolation – due to a complex topography and an inadequate road network – limits opportunities, constrains social networks and fosters vulnerability. Overall, 13 per cent of Guatemalan households lack any form of adequate motorized road access, while the poorest quintiles and the indigenous are even more isolated.

The problems of isolation became glaringly apparent during Hurricane Stan. It was extremely difficult to reach survivors in order to assist them, as the following

International Federation
of Red Cross and Red Crescent Societies

testimonies illustrate: "The list of names of the affected communities was endless. Most of them were communities, forgotten and excluded, about which very little is known" (Father Helio, Comitancillo, San Marcos); "The living conditions of the people affected are appalling; many live in geographically dispersed communities and are very isolated" (Francisco Díaz, Médecins Sans Frontières).

This pattern of settlement has historical roots in Guatemala. It was used by indigenous people as a strategy during colonial times to escape the control of the Spanish and, later, to avoid forced labour on the coffee plantations. Since the 1950s, Guatemala has experienced an intense process of land colonization, in which rural people have searched for land to farm in the absence of other livelihood options. So the agricultural frontier is being pushed back, mainly haphazardly, but also through organized projects.

The number of settlements in Guatemala increased from 13,375 in 1946 to 20,485 in 1993 and still further to 23,340 in 1998, according to the National Institute for Statistics. That means in just five years, 2,855 new settlements were formed – often very small villages in rural areas. There are now 12,200 localities with fewer than 500 inhabitants and around 500 localities with fewer than 50 inhabitants.

New rural settlements have also formed as a result of the displacement of people by the conflict, the creation of 'development poles' by the army and the resettlement of people returning from Mexico after the signing of the Peace Accords. Indigenous women, who resettled in Pochuta municipality on their return from Mexico, were so fearful of this year's rainy season that they appealed to the media to be relocated somewhere safer.

Survivors of Stan staying in high-risk areas must now find a new place to live – 87 communities need relocating and the homes of over 8,000 families need rebuilding. But it's extremely difficult for the government to find safe areas for relocation, as the best land is privately owned and prices have soared in anticipation of post-disaster resettlement. Eight months after Stan, none of the relocation plans announced in the government programme *Nuevo Hábitat Comunitario* was under way.

Migration to the US: a double-edged sword

"In Guatemala, migration to the United States has marked the economic, social, political and cultural dynamics of the country over the past two decades," says Irene Palma, an expert on this subject. But what are the links between the dramatic increase in migration to the US and disaster risk, specifically Hurricane Stan?

The impact of recent migratory trends is revealed in the value of remittances sent from the US back to Guatemala: US$ 11.3 million in 1987, soaring to US$ 563 million in 2000 and US$ 2,993 million in 2005, according to the Banco de Guatemala. The

International Organization for Migration (IOM) estimated that in 2004, almost a million Guatemalan migrants were sending remittances to their families, helping support 31 per cent of the country's households. In 2005, remittances accounted for an estimated 9.5 per cent of gross domestic product (GDP), according to IOM.

It is significant that 58 per cent of Guatemalans in the US who send remittances are from rural communities, while 22 per cent speak one of the Mayan languages. According to the UN's National Human Development Report 2005, 15 per cent of Maya Indians (around 712,000) have a family member working abroad. This is a strategy prompted by the total lack of opportunities in their own country and often adopted as the only means of survival in times of crisis, as after Mitch and Stan. In a survey of the plans of people affected by Hurricane Stan, conducted by the UN's Food and Agriculture Organization (FAO) in November 2005, emigration to the US was consistently mentioned as one of the few options open to them.

Remittances have helped avoid a greater deterioration in per capita income in Guatemala and reduced poverty among remittance-receiving families. According to Víctor Lozano, an IOM consultant, remittances helped 450,000 people to overcome

A man carries his son after he was injured by a mudslide in Sololá, Guatemala, 6 October 2005.

© REUTERS/Carlos Duarte, courtesy www.alertnet.org

poverty in the three years to 2005. Remittances also increase employment in rural areas, through more house-building, more business and a greater demand for services, private health facilities and schools.

In rural communities with a high level of emigration, pressure on land and forest resources falls, as other sources of income become available. Migrants' families enjoy a higher standard of living and better access to healthcare and education, reducing their vulnerability. Many communities can implement basic services and improvements with the help of their countrymen working in the US.

For many families affected by Stan with relatives in the US, the extra money sent to them has contributed decisively to their swift recovery. Field research carried out in affected areas by INCEDES, the Central American Institute for Social Studies and Development, showed that, since Stan, remittances sent to Guatemala have increased significantly. IOM, in a study presented in October 2005, revealed that remittances sent in 2005 to 43 municipalities affected by Stan totalled US$ 413 million, benefiting 107,379 families. This compared with US$ 21 million of international aid pledged through the UN's emergency appeal, as at 7 December 2005.

However, migrants face serious risks, as immigration restrictions in the US and Mexico force them to work without visas or permits and they receive no protection from the Guatemalan government. Risks in transit include death, accidents, rape, theft, hunger, disease, abuse, deception and, last but not least, deportation.

Emigration also leads to new forms of vulnerability back home. Social structures disintegrate in rural communities, particularly indigenous ones. Among families, women are left without husbands and children without fathers. Among communities, the divide grows between more prosperous families of emigrants and the rest, while a whole generation of younger migrants may be lost. The result is a growing individualization and lack of interest in preserving common resources, such as communal forests in the western highlands. It also leads to the emergence of new risks, such as HIV/AIDS and the *maras* (highly dangerous youth gangs).

Jacobo Dardón observes that: "Women who are heads of household as a result of internal labour migration or emigration to the United States were the population sector hardest hit by Hurricane Stan. In municipalities suffering severe damage, such as San Martín Sacatepéquez, it is estimated that 40 per cent of men aged between 18 and 35 are in the United States, many with wives and children living in Guatemala. Based on my own research, migrants need to work abroad for at least three years in order to earn enough to build a basic house, and in some cases homes were lost without the migrant husband ever having seen them." In such cases, the psychological price paid in terms of separation, loneliness and pressure to rebuild the family home and ensure economic survival is very high.

For the government, the problem of female-headed households receives little attention. But migrants' families are now beginning to organize themselves to address pressing issues, particularly the new migratory policies to be implemented by the US government. In December 2005, they founded the Regional Council of Development and Migration Community Committees in the western highlands, with the support of the Tzuk Kim-Pop Movement.

Recovery boosts community cohesion

Guatemala faces serious governance problems in terms of the integration, cohesion and capacity of the political and institutional system and, most importantly, in terms of citizen participation, which is key to ensuring the viability of any political project, in this case, risk reduction.

The political and socio-economic system in Guatemala has been highly exclusionary and bipolar since colonial times. The divisions are between the indigenous peoples and the *ladinos*, between *minifundios* (small landholdings) and *latifundios* (large agricultural estates), between urban and rural life, between the capital and the 'provinces' and, at the municipal level, between the main town and surrounding rural areas. The gap between rich and poor is one of the widest in Latin America. Following a visit to Guatemala, Jeffrey Sachs, director of the US-based Earth Institute, announced to the newspaper *El Periódico* on 17 April 2006: "I see two Guatemalas, which are not united. A divided Guatemala leads to instability."

However, one of the conclusions of the 2005 evaluation of the civil society participation programme by UNDP is that: "Guatemala is undoubtedly witnessing a silent movement and the seeds of change are growing at the local level."

This silent movement, which scarcely extends beyond community level, has been consolidated in the wake of Stan and during the recovery process. It is driven by two trends: the increased presence of local actors and a growing capacity for community organization. This process only became possible in Guatemala after the Peace Accords. Even now, community leaders run serious risks if they stand up against local power groups in conflicts over land, drug trafficking or illegal logging.

Experts agree that the most effective work in risk reduction is being achieved by organizations with a strong local presence. These include not only humanitarian organizations such as the Red Cross, but a wide variety of agencies involved in different development projects (see Box 3.3).

Meanwhile, those communities and regions that were already well organized and where non-governmental organizations (NGOs) were operating received humanitarian aid faster. Trócaire, an international NGO, worked through local

Since 1993, the Guatemalan Red Cross has adopted a community-based approach to disaster risk reduction. From three initial modules (community-based disaster preparedness, healthy home and community shelter management), the disaster risk-reduction programme has expanded to more than 11 community-based training modules, each of them using vulnerability and capacity assessments, which offer more possibilities for communities to understand their own strengths and how to reduce their vulnerabilities.

When Hurricane Stan hit, the National Society mobilized over 200 flights of emergency supplies to affected areas within the first week. The society opened a donation centre and deployed volunteers from the capital to support local volunteers during the emergency response. The International Federation, through the Pan American Disaster Response Unit (PADRU), assisted in the response.

Compared to Mitch in 1998, there is evidence to suggest a higher level of resilience among communities which have benefited from disaster risk reduction and community development initiatives. Since Mitch, the government has also increased its capacity to operate early warning systems, respond to emergency situations and coordinate disaster response.

The Guatemalan Red Cross and the Netherlands Red Cross have implemented a disaster risk-reduction education project, adapting expert knowledge for local languages. Meanwhile, the International Federation has helped develop a board-game called Riskland and a community first-aid training module, which have both been translated and culturally adapted for use among two different indigenous ethnic groups in Guatemala. ■

organizations, acknowledging that those who live the reality of under-development and poverty are best placed to propose solutions to their problems. "Local expertise helps the organization to identify the most needy members of the community, and aid recipients trust them more because they know them already," says Helga Gonzalez, Trócaire's project leader in Sololá.

The link between local NGOs and disaster risk reduction stems from the post-Mitch period. Civil society associations have been formed, such as COCIGER (Citizen Convergence for Risk Mitigation) in September 2001, with 14 member organizations, which recently launched a process to build local capacities through departmental and municipal task teams. One example is an integrated risk management project implemented – before Stan hit – by ASDENA, a founding member of COCIGER, in Pastores municipality, near Antigua Guatemala. The storm damaged or destroyed 150 homes but no one lost their lives, showing the value of risk-reduction training and community coordination (see Box 3.4).

The growing role of local NGOs has been accompanied by an increase in the capacity of communities to cope with the post-Stan crisis. Alfredo Puac, a consultant with

Miguel Antonio López, mayor of Pastores, speaks about his experiences two weeks after Stan had struck the municipality.

"Although we were aware that living near the Guacalate river was a risk, we never imagined that it could cause a disaster on this scale. Fortunately, we had received risk and vulnerability management training from ASDENA. I think that the training increased awareness about the issue and meant that the disaster caused no deaths in our municipality.

"A few days earlier, we had set up a disaster committee within the municipal council. The idea was to begin with the municipal council and then extend the same model to all the community development councils. We also decided to create an emergency telephone directory and planned to set up an information centre to gather all the data necessary to provide immediate solutions. We organized a disaster relief brigade to work with municipal personnel, which was also trained by ASDENA.

"An important aspect of the training was what we learned about land planning, which is the basis of disaster prevention. We began by identifying the places facing the greatest risks. We are particularly concerned about the people who live in the mountain areas, because the previous authorities gave them land in exchange for votes, but there was no planning. These people live in settlements with no proper roads, services or amenities, and we fear that there could be landslides...

"The training included a week in Honduras for a number of people to give them an insight into the community prevention work being implemented in this country in the wake of Mitch, mainly by community committees, although the town councils are also involved." ■

extensive experience in community work, confirms that communities at risk are at the forefront of dealing with disasters and usually provide the first emergency response. Meanwhile, the leading role in ensuring disasters are not ignored is taken by the communities themselves, argues Xavier Castellanos.

Community development councils flourish

Post-Stan recovery has seen the community development councils (COCODES) flourish, thanks to the involvement of affected communities. Salvador Casado, from the NGO CARE-Guatemala, observes that the formation of COCODES from 2002 onwards created a very favourable context for the post-Mitch project CAMI (Central American Initiative for Disaster Mitigation) in Guatemala. They proved their effectiveness once again in the response to Stan.

The COCODES are the most local units of the National System of Urban and Rural Development Councils. Although the system was established by law in 1986, it had remained virtually unused until 2002, when it was reformed and extended to the local level, as a participatory space open to all citizens in all the country's communities.

International Federation
of Red Cross and Red Crescent Societies

The Municipal Urban and Rural Development Councils (COMUDES), a higher local-level authority, were also reformed, so that they included representatives from public and private organizations and civil society. In addition to the Development Council Act, two relevant legal instruments (the new Municipal Code and the Decentralization Act, both passed in 2002) contribute to achieving this goal.

The World Bank's 2003 report stressed that: "The recent passage of three laws on decentralization and participation is an important step towards creating a legal framework for the empowerment of local communities. The implementation of these laws should seek to reverse the traditional exclusion of women, the poor, and uneducated from community-level participation."

Meeylyn Lorena Mejia Lopez, in her 2006 document *Indigenous Women and Governance in Guatemala*, wrote that many Maya women leaders now chair the community councils. The challenge of occupying these positions has allowed women to prove their capacities and commitment to community interests.

However, the blooming of the COCODES following Hurricane Stan is still a very fragile process, bound up with all the conflict, vulnerability and exclusion that characterize Guatemala's mainly rural communities. Many council members are illiterate and some only speak a Mayan language. Even in less adverse conditions, they would lack the expertise and experience necessary to draw up well-planned community development proposals; the work required involves much more than just submitting lists of projects to the COMUDES for financing. So the COCODES badly need support with training.

The big advantage of the COCODES is that they are permanent and represent the entire community. They present an opportunity to break with the detrimental practice of creating ad hoc, grass-roots organizations associated with certain projects, which disappear once the financing ends, often causing conflict and rivalry among different organizations within the same community. Training for the COCODES is a means of investing in the future and developing leadership skills (see Box 3.5).

Challenges and progress at national level

The government now faces the enormous challenge of responding to local management, made all the more pressing after Stan. Since the days of the military regimes, Guatemala's central government has implemented top-down systems, first with a view to maintaining territorial control and later to show its willingness to move towards decentralization.

Such systems are traditionally based on the established administrative structure: from the central authority to department level and then municipal level. None of these

Box 3.5 Panabaj: hope after so much suffering

Panabaj is a Tzutujil Mayan community on the shores of Lake Atitlán in western Guatemala. During the conflict of the 1980s, many Tzutujil men were killed by the Guatemalan military, leaving a disjointed community of widows and orphans. The community finally expelled the army in 1990, six years before the Peace Accords. The 5,000 people of Panabaj live in extreme poverty, struggling to survive through agriculture and the sale of handicrafts.

In the early morning of 5 October 2005, strong rains caused by Hurricane Stan resulted in tremendous flooding and landslides from the nearby volcano. Over 150 houses were completely buried under mud and rock. Others were swept away by the flood. Many more were left seriously damaged.

The disaster was so sudden that many people could not escape and were either buried by mud or swept away by it. Seven months later, the community had given formal burial to 100 people, while 600 remained unaccounted for. The disaster was so overwhelming that recovery efforts were abandoned. For survivors, the pain of lost loved ones is exacerbated by the inability to give them a traditional Mayan burial. The disaster zone has been declared a cemetery, closed to public access.

Many families were destroyed: 25 children lost both parents, around 50 lost one parent and 77 women were widowed. All members of the community suffered psychologically. More than 600 families were moved to temporary shelters or tents. The amount of land and crops lost had yet to be quantified, seven months after the disaster.

The magnitude of the tragedy left the community scarred and fearful. But, as it did during the armed conflict, the community transformed the pain of its loss into a united search for survival.

In the days following the tragedy, a group of neighbours helping to rescue survivors and clear bodies formed an emergency committee to organize the aid arriving for their community. They took a census of affected families, distributed food and tried to answer the many questions and concerns posed by the community.

The emergency committee soon realized that once the immediate emergency phase was over, the community had to think of sustainable medium- and long-term projects to contribute towards reconstruction and improving people's quality of life. In response to this need, the Association for Community Development in Panabaj (ADECCAP) was formed, with the support of international volunteers. Based on mutual respect and the will to participate, ADECCAP is working for disaster relief and the development of Panabaj, through community participation, gender equality and the recognition of human rights. The association has just founded a community centre to promote psychosocial rehabilitation, economic revitalization, youth education and professional training for adults.

The most important short-term project in the reconstruction phase, however, is the discussion of community problems mediated through the community and municipal development councils, regarding the security of land for permanent housing and the search for alternative land for 300 or more families who do not want to live in the designated zone. In a study conducted by CONRED, the national disaster reduction agency, in April 2006, the whole Panabaj area was declared a high-risk zone unsuitable for reconstruction. The temporary shelters and the government project to construct permanent housing (already under way), are in this high-risk area. No solution has been found to this problem as yet. ∎

systems has been effective so far, because of the lack of administrative capacity and financial support for departmental and local levels.

In the specific case of the CONRED (national disaster reduction agency) system, in which departmental, municipal and even local coordination offices are established by law, it was observed that the failure to work from the top down was not due to a lack of motivation, but to a lack of logistics and human resources.

The UN's Disaster Assessment and Coordination (UNDAC) team report of October 2005 said that CONRED's coordination and response were good at the national level, but this was not always mirrored at the departmental, municipal and community levels. Teresa Marroquín, from the Guatemalan Red Cross Society's national disaster department, observed that the system did not work because it failed at the local level. On the rare occasions when local coordinators were in place, it did work.

In its post-Stan report, ECLAC recommended that, as a priority medium-term measure, the budget allocated to CONRED in 2006 should be increased to strengthen decentralization, which would initially benefit the departmental authorities. However, this did not happen and additional funds were earmarked specifically for post-Stan recovery efforts, for example to re-establish early warning systems. The amount budgeted for 2005 was GTQ 20 million (US$ 2.6 million). Meanwhile, the national institute for seismology, volcanology, meteorology and hydrology (CONRED's scientific and monitoring body) has an annual budget of scarcely US$ 1.5 million, which drastically limits its ability to evaluate risk scenarios for the whole country.

Since Stan, it has become clear that the two systems – the development councils and CONRED – must work in an integrated manner rather than in parallel. As a first step, an agreement was signed on 17 March 2006 between CONRED and the President's Office, specifically to integrate disaster risk reduction and promote sustainable local development. The aim is to strengthen inter-institutional relations, on the basis of the National Disaster Risk Reduction System and the National System of Urban and Rural Development Councils.

The system of development councils not only permits effective, sustained community organization and participation in local and regional planning, it also provides a framework for better coordination among the actors involved in disaster risk reduction – between NGOs and development agencies, between civil society and government, and among government departments.

The Planning and Programming Secretariat of the President's Office (SEGEPLAN) has proposed several new planning and investment instruments to increase the effectiveness of development councils' work in disaster risk management.

SEGEPLAN's Susana Palma is enthusiastic: "We are confident that if we begin at the top of these systems, we will be able to work down to the implementing units, development councils and municipalities. For the first time in 2006, the regulations published by SNIP [National Public Investment System] include risk prevention and mitigation measures and a risk identification bulletin (developed in conjunction with CONRED), to be used in the process of analysing programmes and projects to assess how they will reduce or increase vulnerability and danger. An international cooperation policy has also been formulated, including integral security conditions in the guidelines for projects to be financed through international cooperation. Work has also begun on making risk reduction more specific."

In May 2006, seven months after Stan, Carmen Salguerro from UNDP Guatemala summarizes the current situation in these words: "The opportunity to rebuild and transform is there, but unless words are put into action in the next few months, time will run out. Evidently, Hurricane Stan exposed a weak state, the reconstruction process is taking shape during the run-up to elections and, added to all this, there is an oppressive climate of violence and public insecurity. These factors make advancing towards construction with transformation a complicated matter."

Future risks demand sustained action

When a major disaster strikes a country like Guatemala, where a large proportion of the population is highly vulnerable and the institutional capacity to ensure rapid recovery is very weak, development prospects can be seriously undermined. The chances of fulfilling priority objectives, such as reducing poverty, increasing job opportunities and improving health, education, housing, food security and environmental sustainability, are greatly reduced.

This is particularly true in the case of disasters that occur when risks constructed as the result of unsustainable socio-environmental processes materialize and when the detonating factor is a weather event that can recur every rainy or hurricane season. The impact of local disasters caused by Stan in Guatemala exacerbated vulnerability and environmental degradation in affected communities, increasing the risk of even normal rainfall unleashing another disaster. The capacity of rivers to drain away water has been significantly reduced and the mountainsides of the western and central highlands are highly eroded and unstable.

Extreme poverty in Guatemala, which had fallen from 20 per cent in 1989 to 16 per cent in 2000, climbed back in 2004 to 21.9 per cent, owing partly to falling coffee prices and the drought, which mainly affected the eastern part of the country in 2001. The general poverty rate, on the other hand, fell slightly to 56 per cent (about 6.4 million people) in 2000, thanks to remittances sent from abroad. In view of Stan's impact and the risk of future intense rainy seasons, poverty rates may well increase further and the mortality rate, particularly infant mortality, is very likely to rise.

With windstorms and rainstorms recurring each year, the Guatemalan government, aid agencies and community-based organizations are in a very difficult situation. While engaged in the slow process of recovering from one major disaster, they must also prepare at community and national levels for the possibility of more intense cyclone seasons in the near future. In this context, which could become a vicious circle of destruction and partial recovery, it may be difficult to achieve any real progress in wider risk reduction at a time when it is more necessary than ever.

Apply what we know, a little at a time

When Stan hit, Guatemala, like other Central American countries, had already experienced the impacts and lessons learned from Mitch, seven years earlier. Since then, new concepts, analytical and planning documents, commitments and proposals for disaster risk reduction in the region have been formulated and disseminated on an unprecedented scale.

As a result, a growing number of international cooperation organizations operating in Guatemala and national NGOs include risk management in their policies, programmes and projects, while various education and training initiatives have been launched in this area. The current challenge is to generalize and strengthen these initiatives and ensure that they are institutionalized and adopted by the government in a way that cuts across its sector-specific agencies.

The first step on the path to solving complex problems, such as disaster risk reduction, is a clear-cut policy establishing strategies with specific, achievable tasks, starting with priority or basic concerns. For example, the most pressing needs currently facing Guatemala in general terms are, among others:

- Acknowledgement of disaster risk reduction as a day-to-day, cross-cutting issue and not just a problem for a specific government agency or NGOs specializing in this area.
- Inclusion of risk reduction in school curricula at all levels.
- Incorporation of the disaster risk perspective in all development programmes and projects. Risk reduction should be accorded the same priority as gender or environmental considerations.
- Availability of information on risks at the local level and the capacity to produce such information, transfer it to local actors and disseminate it among people at risk.
- Better land-use management at the municipal level, based on the situations faced by different communities, taking into account the areas and types of risk involved.

- Promotion of relevant, accessible technology for communities to monitor growing risk factors (e.g., waste, mountainside erosion, vulnerable housing).
- Creation and application of legal frameworks, key to achieving risk reduction.

Principal contributor to this chapter and Boxes 3.1 and 3.2 was Gisela Gellert, a Guatemala-based geographer, independent researcher and member of the Latin American Network for the Social Study of Disaster Prevention-LA RED. Box 3.3 was contributed by Xavier Castellanos, the International Federation's senior officer for Disaster Preparedness and Response. Box 3.4 is sourced from an interview by Eddie Fernández, dated 15 October 2005 and published on the website of Inforpress Centroamericana, Guatemala: http://www.inforpressca.com. Box 3.5 is sourced from the web site of La Semilla, a Panabaj community-based foundation: http://www.fundacionlasemilla.net. We would also like to acknowledge the invaluable assistance and advice of Ben Wisner, an independent researcher affiliated with the Development Studies Institute at the London School of Economics, the Benfield Hazard Research Centre (University College London) and the UN University Institute for Environment and Human Security in Bonn, and Allan Lavell, Coordinator, Programme for the Social Study of Risk and Disaster at the Secretariat General's office of the Latin American Social Science Faculty, San Jose, Costa Rica and founding member of the Latin American Network for the Social Study of Disaster Prevention-LA RED, in preparing this chapter.

Sources and further information

Amnesty International. *Guatemala: No protection, no justice: Killings of women in Guatemala*. London: Amnesty International, June 2005.

Blaikie, P., Cannon, T., Davis, I. and Wisner, B. *Vulnerabilidad: El entorno social, político y económico de los desastres*. ITDG-LA RED, 1994.

Castellanos, Xavier. *Desastres Olvidados – Información para desastres*. Federación Internacional de Sociedades de la Cruz Roja y de la Media Luna Roja. Available at http://www.cruzroja.org/desastres/redcamp/docs/materiales/Desastres Olvidados.pdf

CEH (Truth Commission). *Guatemala, Memoria del Silencio*. Conclusiones y Recomendaciones del Informe de la Comisión para el Esclarecimiento Histórico. Guatemala: CEH, 1999.

Comisión Económica para America Latina y el Caribe (CEPAL). *El Desastre de Octubre de 2005 en Guatemala: Estimación preliminar de su Impacto Socio-Económico y Ambiental*. Guatemala: November 2005.

CEPAL, Secretaría de Planificación y Programación de la Presidencia (SEGEPLAN). *Efectos en Guatemala de las lluvias torrenciales y la tormenta tropical Stan, octubre de 2005*. Guatemala: November 2005.

Coordinadora Nacional para la Reducción de Desastres (CONRED). *Informe de la Secretaría Ejecutiva: Efectos de la Tormenta Tropical STAN en Guatemala y las acciones realizadas durante y post emergencia*. Guatemala: 3 December 2005.

Dardón, Jacobo and Morales, Cecilia (coord.). *¿Por qué tanta destrucción? Las amenazas naturales y estructurales: sistematización de la vulnerabilidad, la negligencia y la exclusión regional del altiplano occidental en la tormenta asociada Stan*. Guatemala: Editorial de Ciencias Sociales, 2006.

FAO. *Evaluación de los efectos de la tormenta tropical Stan en los medios de vida de la familias vulnerables de Guatemala*. Guatemala: December 2005.

Gellert, Gisela. *De desastre en desastre… ¿cuánto hemos aprendido?* Guatemala: FLACSO, Diálogo, año 5, No. 46, January 2006. Available at http://www.flacso.edu.gt/dialogo/46/46.htm#1

Gellert, Gisela and Gamarra, Luis. *La trama y el drama de los riesgos a desastres: Dos estudios a diferente escala sobre la problemática en Guatemala*. Guatemala: FLACSO, 2003.

Gobierno de Guatemala. *Reconstrucción con transformación: Obras necesarias para estabilizar las cuencas de mayor riesgo afectadas por la tormenta Stan. Parte I*. República de Guatemala, March 2006.

Instituto Nacional De Sismologia, Vulcanología, Meteorología E Hidrologia (INSIVUMEH). *Resumen del impacto asociado al huracán Stan en Guatemala*. Guatemala: INSIVUMEH, October 2005.

Lavell, Allan. *After Hurricane Mitch: Vulnerability and Risk Reduction in Central America*. Latin American Social Science Faculty-FLACSO and the Latin American Network for the Social Study of Disaster Prevention-LA RED, August 2002.

Mejia Lopez, Meeylyn Lorena. *Indigenous Women and Governance in Guatemala*. FOCAL (Canadian Foundation for the Americas), March 2006. Available at http://www.focal.ca

Programa de las Naciones Unidas para el Desarrollo (PNUD). *Diversidad étnico-cultural y desarrollo humano: La ciudadanía en un Estado plural: Informe de Desarrollo Humano 2005*. Guatemala: PNUD, 2006.

PNUD and Centro de Coordinación para la prevención de los Desastres Naturales en América Central (CEPREDENAC). *Memoria Foro Regional Mitch+5: ¿Dónde estamos y para dónde vamos?* Panama: PNUD, CEPREDENAC, 2004.

PNUD-Programa Participación de la Sociedad Civil. *Civil Society Participation Program. Closing report external evaluation*. Guatemala: December 2005. Available at http://www.pasoc.org.gt

Santa Cruz, Wendy. *La tormenta Stan: Impacto, acciones sociales, estatales y de la cooperación internacional*. Guatemala: FLACSO, Observatorio de Movimientos Sociales, March 2006. Available at http://www.sociedadcivil.tk

SEGEPLAN. *Plan de Reconstrucción, Tormenta Tropical Stan*. Guatemala: SEGEPLAN, March 2006.

SEGEPLAN-Banco de Guatemala. *Evaluación de los daños causados por el terremoto, su impacto sobre el desarrollo económico social y lineamientos para un programa inmediato de reconstrucción*. Guatemala: 1976.

Suárez, María. *Hurricane Stan: A Personal Account of a National Disaster.* October 2005. Available at http://www.globalfundforwomen.org/work/programs/stan-personal-account.html

UN Disaster Assessment and Coordination (UNDAC). *Informe de Misión: Inundación y deslizamientos ocasionados por la tormenta Stan.* Guatemala: October 2005.

UN High Commissioner for Human Rights (UNHCHR). *Report of the High Commissioner for Human Rights on the situation of human rights in Guatemala.* UNHCHR, February 2006. Available at http://www.ohchr.org/english/bodies/chr/sessions/62/listdocs.htm

Wiese, Anja Kristina and Wolpold-Bosien, Martin. *The Human Right to Food in Guatemala.* Heidelberg: ActionAid and Fian International, February 2005. Available at http://www.fian.org

World Bank. *Guatemala: Poverty in Guatemala.* Report of the Poverty Reduction and Economic Management Unit, February 2003. Available at http://www.worldbank.org/guatemalapoverty

World Health Organization (WHO). *Global Burden of Disease Project for 2000.* Geneva: WHO, 2000.

Zapata Marti, Ricardo. *CEPAL: Los efectos del huracán Stan en El Salvador y Guatemala.* Revista EIRD, 12, 2006.

Web sites

Centro de Coordinación para la prevención de los Desastres Naturales en América Central **http://www.cepredenac.org**

Coordinadora Nacional para la Reducción de Desastres **http://www.conred.org**

La Semilla foundation **http://www.fundacionlasemilla.net**

Médicos Sin Fronteras **http://www.msf.es**

Programa de las Naciones Unidas para el Desarrollo **http://www.pnudguatemala.org/stan**

Programa de las Naciones Unidas para el Desarrollo Guatemala Informe de Desarrollo Humano **http://www.desarrollohumano.org.g**t

ReliefWeb **http://www.reliefweb.int**

Santiago Relief Fund **http://www.santiagorelief.com**

Secretaría de Planificación y Programación de la Presidencia **http://www.segeplan.gob.gt/stan/index.htm**

Trócaire **http://www.trocaire.org**

CHAPTER 3

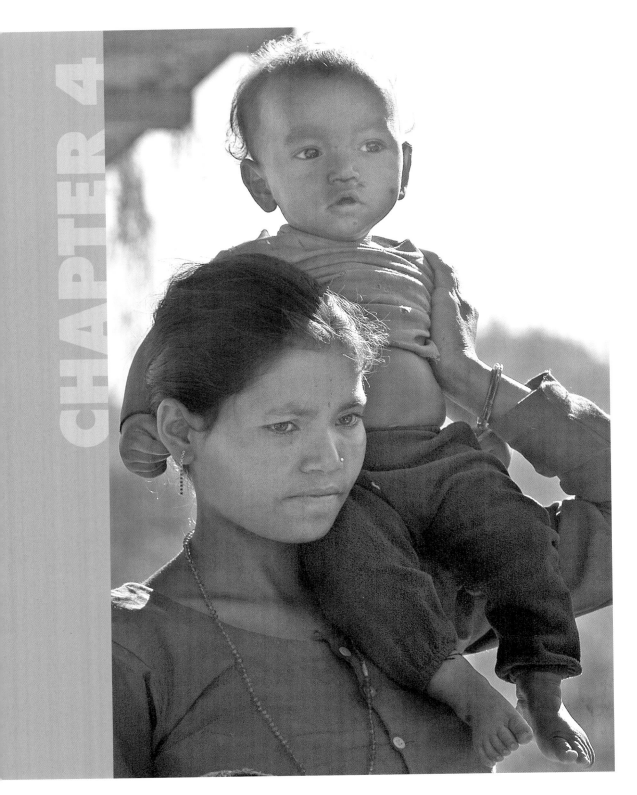

International Federation
of Red Cross and Red Crescent Societies

Unsafe motherhood: Nepal's hidden crisis

Maili Chettri's portrait hangs on the wall of her family's small wooden house – a mute reminder of their failure to find medical help for her, following complications delivering her first child.

In Maili's remote village of Pipal, in the mountainous Rukum district of Nepal, women with pregnancy-related problems do not have access to skilled birth attendants (SBAs) or to health centres equipped with emergency obstetric care (EmOC). So Maili's mother-in-law and female neighbours had little choice but to carry out the delivery themselves. However, due to a prolonged labour, her baby had already died in the womb. In an attempt to save Maili's life, the women tried to pull the baby out, but this ruptured her uterus, leading to excessive bleeding and shock.

Desperate to save her, some young villagers carried her on a stretcher for two hours over a rocky trail to the district hospital. The medical staff helped control the bleeding, but since their hospital lacked surgical and EmOC facilities, the family was asked to take Maili to a larger hospital in Nepalganj, a major city 150 kilometres away on the *terai* plains bordering India.

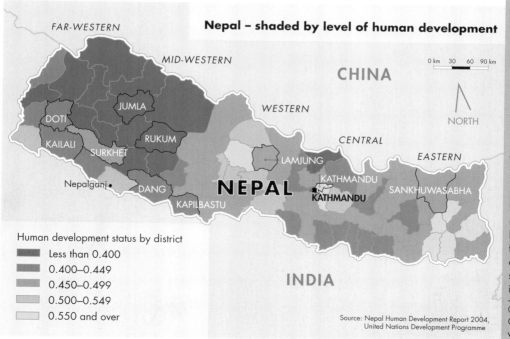

Nepal – shaded by level of human development

FAR-WESTERN
MID-WESTERN
CHINA
JUMLA
WESTERN
DOTI
RUKUM
CENTRAL
KAILALI
SURKHET
EASTERN
LAMJUNG
KATHMANDU
Nepalganj
DANG
NEPAL
KATHMANDU
SANKHUWASABHA
KAPILBASTU

0 km 30 60 90 km

NORTH

INDIA

Human development status by district
- Less than 0.400
- 0.400–0.449
- 0.450–0.499
- 0.500–0.549
- 0.550 and over

Source: Nepal Human Development Report 2004, United Nations Development Programme

Photo opposite page: A Nepali mother holds her child in the remote village of Dadeldhura, 500 km west of Kathmandu, in January 2006. One of the biggest-selling items in a tiny, nearby pharmacy is condoms. People are starting to realize they can no longer afford the large families once considered vital for supporting parents in old age.

© REUTERS/ Gopal Chitrakar, courtesy www.alertnet.org

As in most of Nepal's underdeveloped hill and mountain districts, there are few driveable roads in Rukum. The only way to reach Nepalganj quickly is by a 30-minute flight from Rukum's dirt airstrip. But since there were no flights that day, her family and friends gave up hope. Maili died four hours later. She was just 25 years old.

Such stories are all too common across Nepal, where between 5,000 and 6,000 mothers die each year in childbirth, according to data from Nepal's Ministry of Health and the United Nations. This maternal death toll of one woman every 90 minutes makes Nepal the deadliest place in the world to give birth, outside Afghanistan and a clutch of countries in sub-Saharan Africa. Meanwhile, the likelihood of a newborn baby surviving is greatly reduced if its mother dies in childbirth. In Nepal, an estimated 30,000 babies die before they are a month old – one of the highest neonatal mortality rates in the world (see Figure 4.1).

This chapter analyses maternal mortality in Nepal, within the context of a global tragedy of unsafe motherhood that silently steals over half a million lives a year. While Nepal has made progress in reducing child mortality, its maternal and neonatal mortality rates remain stubbornly high. What are the root causes lying behind the terrible statistics? Can these deaths – which have claimed at least 25 times more lives than Nepal's decade-long conflict – be termed a 'neglected disaster'? The chapter examines the impact of the conflict on maternal health and explores possible solutions.

Figure 4.1 Nepal fact file

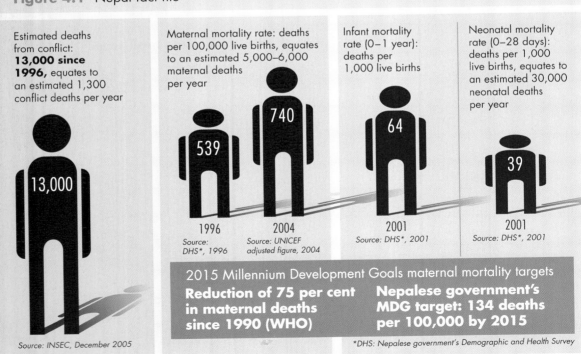

Estimated deaths from conflict: **13,000 since 1996,** equates to an estimated 1,300 conflict deaths per year

13,000

Source: INSEC, December 2005

Maternal mortality rate: deaths per 100,000 live births, equates to an estimated 5,000–6,000 maternal deaths per year

539 — 1996 — Source: DHS*, 1996

740 — 2004 — Source: UNICEF adjusted figure, 2004

Infant mortality rate (0–1 year): deaths per 1,000 live births

64 — 2001 — Source: DHS*, 2001

Neonatal mortality rate (0–28 days): deaths per 1,000 live births, equates to an estimated 30,000 neonatal deaths per year

39 — 2001 — Source: DHS*, 2001

2015 Millennium Development Goals maternal mortality targets
Reduction of 75 per cent in maternal deaths since 1990 (WHO)
Nepalese government's MDG target: 134 deaths per 100,000 by 2015

*DHS: Nepalese government's Demographic and Health Survey

International Federation of Red Cross and Red Crescent Societies

Why is childbirth so deadly?

As in many countries with a high maternal mortality rate, most mothers who lose their lives in childbirth in Nepal die from a lack of emergency obstetric care or assistance from a skilled birth attendant, following birth complications. According to Adik Wibowo, representative for the World Health Organization (WHO) in Nepal, 71 per cent of the country's maternal deaths are due to direct obstetric causes, most of which could be effectively managed and prevented.

Of these causes, post-partum haemorrhage is the deadliest – accounting for 46 per cent of all maternal deaths in Nepal. Put simply, each year nearly 3,000 women in Nepal bleed to death – usually within two or three hours of giving birth. Heavy bleeding requires swift emergency care. Delays can prove fatal. Over 20 years ago, international experts identified three kinds of delay, known as the '3Ds', which are particularly applicable in Nepal:

- Delay in deciding to seek care.
- Delay in reaching a healthcare facility.
- Delay in accessing adequate treatment at the facility.

There are many reasons for these delays – cultural, topographical, financial or a simple lack of awareness (see Box 4.1). Ten years of conflict, between government security forces and Maoist rebels, have made a bad situation worse.

Culture and superstition conspire against seeking care

Women living in traditional Nepalese societies suffer social and religious discrimination. A woman is treated as 'untouchable' during her first menstruation. She is not allowed to see the sun, her husband or her brother due to a superstition that her male relatives would die. Women are not allowed to discuss pregnancy with anyone other than their husbands and mothers-in-law.

For the first 11 days after giving birth, a woman is regarded as polluted and impure. Male relatives, including the husband, cannot go near her, so she is forced to live in isolation – often in a cowshed or makeshift hut. She sleeps with her newborn on a cold floor in unhygienic conditions, increasing her chances of septicaemia and risking the infant's health. Male relatives don't want to touch women who bleed after giving birth, while private and public vehicles alike may refuse to transport them.

Traditionally, women must defer to their husbands for all important decisions. Peeyoosh Kumar Rajendra, director of the family health division at Nepal's Ministry of Health, says: "It's really a disturbing fact that in most villages women cannot seek medical help on their own without sole permission of the husband and her in-laws. Despite awareness among women about taking help from trained health workers, they can't do anything."

Box 4.1 Delay nearly proves deadly

Sarada Lamichhane, 21, lives in Bhangsangwa, a village in Kapilbastu district in the western *terai* plains. In early October 2005, she entrusted the safe delivery of her first infant to her family. Despite being overdue, female relatives said she just had to wait patiently. So she continued doing household chores until two hours before giving birth. After giving bed tea to everyone in the house at 7am, she collapsed.

Her mother-in-law sought help from a female neighbour. The room where Sarada lay was dirty and unhygienic. After 90 minutes, they managed to deliver the infant alive. Sarada gave her new baby a hot bath and started breastfeeding. The next day, around noon, she began to bleed heavily and fainted.

Sarada's husband Dhundiraj, a tractor driver, was not at home when she passed out, even though he had seen his wife in great pain the previous night. "I was busy with work and came back around late afternoon," he says. On his return, he called for an ambulance to take Sarada to the nearest major hospital, which fortunately was just an hour away. After receiving five pints of transfused blood, she regained consciousness. Five days later she was discharged.

Shocked by the whole incident, her illiterate mother-in-law says they will never repeat their mistake of delaying delivery or failing to call a health worker in time. "She is like my own daughter," she said with tears in her eyes. "Thank you God, for saving her life."

But money also played its part in saving Sarada. Her husband spent Rs 16,800 (US$ 227) in transport and hospital expenses – a fortune for a tractor driver. "I have yet to pay for the cost of medicine and for the local health worker", he says, "as I had no money at home to afford her treatment." ■

In many districts, it's been mandatory for every household to send a male member to join the Maoist 'people's liberation army'. Those who have remained in the countryside have risked being arrested by the state security forces on suspicion of being Maoist collaborators. Tens of thousands of Nepalese men have emigrated in search of work – leaving grandparents, wives and children to cope alone. According to a World Food Programme (WFP) survey of 1,676 households conducted in September 2005 across 43 rural districts, nearly half the households reported that one or more members had left – mostly men aged 18–30.

"There has been severe indirect impact on girls reaching the age of giving birth, because there is now work overload on them as men are migrating more. There is mental pressure and the priority is less among them to seek healthcare," says Pinky Singh Rana, coordinator of the Safe Motherhood Network Federation Nepal.

In the absence of her husband, it's hard for a woman to seek healthcare, because of the travel expenses and hospital bills. In-laws are unlikely to give permission without discussing it with their son. Even when the wife has cash in hand, she may lack the courage to spend it without her husband's permission.

International Federation
of Red Cross and Red Crescent Societies

Furthermore, husbands and in-laws may not be aware of the risks involved in childbirth. "Most families think pregnancy is not a special condition. They believe it can be managed in a traditional way; but this is a dangerous notion, because deliveries always require special and skilled care," explains Indira Basnett, from the nationwide Support for Safe Motherhood Programme (SSMP), which is funded by the UK's Department for International Development (DFID) and run collaboratively with the government.

Health workers report that most rural families seek help too late. "Women and girls can be saved if the family members call us on time," says Mumkala Bhusal, a government nurse in Kapilbastu, 320 kilometres west of Kathmandu in the *terai*. But her health workers in hill areas are informed only after four or five hours of complications. The problem is worse among low-caste communities of the *terai*, where illiteracy can reach 90 per cent and discrimination against women is rife. "The problem is the level of ignorance and the attitude of the family towards women," says Bhusal.

Conflict, poverty and topography prevent access to facilities

Even if the poorest families decide to seek care, the barriers they face in getting the patient to a well-equipped health facility are considerable. Mountains, money and Maoists may all get in the way.

Nepal has suffered a decade of violence since February 1996, when the Communist Party of Nepal (Maoist) launched its 'people's war'. At least 13,000 Nepalese have lost their lives due to the conflict, leaving behind thousands of orphans and widows. Hundreds of thousands have been forced to flee their homes.

While access to healthcare in Nepal has always been difficult, the conflict has made it worse. During 2005 and early 2006, the Maoists reportedly controlled around 80 per cent of Nepal. Travelling from areas that Maoists control (rural and remote) to areas the government controls (district capitals, where the medical facilities are) has often required written permission in advance.

A survey carried out in 2003 by the Nepal Safer Motherhood Project (NSMP – the forerunner of SSMP), found that "the reduced availability of transportation and curfew [due to the conflict] have had most impact on the process of accessing services once the decision had been made to seek care." NSMP added that the conflict has scared people from travelling beyond the village, especially at night. Curfews and security checks have added around 20 per cent to journey times in moderately-affected areas and 40 per cent in the worst-affected areas, according to the report.

CHAPTER 4

Meanwhile, despite the conflict, the poorest families can't afford transport. For Maili Chettri, it would have cost around US$ 250 to fly from Rukum to Nepalganj, catch a bus to the hospital and find accommodation – before considering the price of surgery and medicine. Such an expense is unthinkable to many Nepalese. In Maili's region, the average agricultural wage is 54 rupees (75 US cents) a day, according to the World Bank. Nationwide, over 80 per cent of Nepalese subsist on less than US$ 2 a day.

The conflict has made people poorer, as tourism has plummeted, jobs are scarcer and markets for farm produce have been fragmented by constant *bandhs* (strikes) and blockades. Neighbours are less inclined to lend money. With their men abroad, women have to earn for the family on top of doing household chores. Rather than seeking proper antenatal and postnatal care, many women work hard either side of giving birth – greatly increasing the risks of complications, bleeding and prolapse of the uterus.

The United Nations Human Development Report noted that Nepal's human poverty index fell five places globally to 74th in 2005. During the report's launch in September, the UN said that Nepal's conflict had deepened poverty in affected areas and nationally, stunted development, increased internally displaced populations, reduced agricultural production and affected food security.

Another delay to accessing healthcare is the travel time involved. Most rural villages are days', sometimes weeks', walk from the nearest roadhead, airstrip or major town. The journey may mean crossing mountain passes 2,000–3,000 metres high. Women may have to be carried for hours on a stretcher by local porters or relatives. WFP's September 2005 survey found that only 40 per cent of households were within 45 minutes' walk of a driveable road.

"There is often hesitation among poor communities for a woman to visit health centres, as they know it would be useless travelling all the way and fear losing her life or the infant's," says Baburam Marasini from the Ministry of Health, which estimates that 11 per cent of maternal deaths occur on the way to health centres.

Most mothers who survive prolonged labour end up losing their newborns. "I could not get the bus on time as it was a long walk from my village to the bus stop," says Phulmati Kumari. By the time she reached Dang district hospital in western Nepal, it was too late to save her infant. The baby of another young woman who arrived the same day suffered a similar fate.

Lack of adequate facilities keeps death toll high

Even if, against the odds, a woman suffering labour complications succeeds in reaching a health facility, there is no guarantee she will receive adequate care.

In principle, there are around 3,200 sub-health posts across the country – one for every village development committee (comprising several villages). Each post is staffed by a nurse, serving 1,500–4,500 people. In practice, however, most have poor facilities and comprise one or two rooms. A separate room for maternal care is out of the question and none of them has emergency obstetric facilities.

Most sub-health posts don't function effectively, due to a shortage of medical supplies and trained staff. Re-supplies from the government often never make it beyond the district capital, as the security forces have been unwilling to support health posts in Maoist territory. "There is little financial support in the districts from the government budget and many health centres cannot even afford to store medicines for the whole year," says Baburam Acharya, health assistant at the Hasutha village health post in the western *terai*.

Out of an estimated 900,000 pregnancies in Nepal each year, the UN estimates that around 129,000 develop life-threatening complications and will require EmOC services. To access these services, women must travel to the district centre. However, of Nepal's 75 districts, only 25 have comprehensive EmOC facilities, while there are just 17 basic EmOC facilities in other locations. Surgery and blood transfusion services are limited (see Box 4.2). As a result, 95 per cent of women who develop birth complications receive no emergency care, according to the United Nations Children's Fund (UNICEF) in a report dated 2000.

Bishnu Jaiswal is public health director for Kapilbastu district hospital. Each month, 25–85 women come here for pregnancy tests, of whom 20–30 give birth. But for those with complications, "we have no choice but to refer the patients to a city hospital with surgical facilities [four hours away by bus]. We have no provision of blood bank, obstetricians and necessary equipments," she says. The hospital even lacks a separate room for maternal health services. Although UNICEF helped construct a new hospital building, the post of medical doctor (general practitioner) – usually skilled in obstetrics and surgery, among other things – has yet to be filled by the government.

The story is similar elsewhere. In Jumla, one of the poorest mountain districts in Nepal's far west, DFID helped build a maternity ward in the main hospital. But by spring 2006, the hospital still lacked resident doctors skilled in EmOC. As a result, the hospital's maternity facilities remained underused – in a district where Johns Hopkins University recorded a maternal mortality rate of 859 per 100,000 live births in 2000.

While recent government statistics suggest the public health system functions reasonably well, not all experts are convinced. "The data are sourced from village health posts, but are not verified by teams from the district health office, because of the conflict," says SSMP's Indira Basnett. Improving the quality of the health service monitoring system is an important priority.

Box 4.2 **Blood: a neglected priority**

Nearly half of Nepal's maternal mortality is due to post-partum haemorrhage – in simple terms, that means almost 3,000 Nepalese women bleed to death after childbirth, every year. A rapid transfusion of blood is often the only way to save them. But safe blood is in short supply in Nepal.

The government has given the Nepal Red Cross Society the mandate for blood services across the country. But although there is a system in place for 100 per cent voluntary blood donation, maintaining blood services is very expensive and requires a dedicated government budget. According to the Nepal Red Cross Society's health director, Pitamber Aryal, "there is a huge need to intensify support from the government side."

To ensure that blood is safe, it has to be screened for HIV and other infections. Voluntary donors from low-risk populations are usually the safest source of blood. But to build the public confidence needed to ensure a regular commitment from voluntary blood donors requires a well-organized blood service with quality systems in all areas. This is vital for donor retention and for the safe and effective use of blood – but it's a major challenge in Nepal, where trained health professionals are in very short supply. Meanwhile, counselling for donors who discover they are HIV-positive has to be considered.

The Nepal Red Cross Society runs 56 blood transfusion centres in 41 of Nepal's 75 districts, but they aim to open two new centres a year. Demand has risen due to both maternal haemorrhage and an increase in civil unrest. The society also runs mobile blood donation camps on fixed dates throughout the year in 21 of its district branches. "In order to motivate people to give blood, Red Cross volunteers visit schools, youth clubs, even other aid organizations," says Manita Rajkarnikar, director of the Nepal Red Cross Society's central blood transfusion service.

Raising the profile of voluntary blood donation is a vital task, but not the only challenge. "Nepal is doing well with 100 per cent voluntary blood donation, but other areas of an integrated strategy for blood safety remain somewhat neglected," says Peter Carolan, Senior Officer, Health and Care (Blood), at the International Federation in Geneva. He adds: "There is now a real opportunity to implement changes here and elsewhere. The World Health Assembly recently recognized World Blood Donor Day, on 14 June, as an annual occasion to remind all its member states of the role of voluntary blood donors in healthcare and the responsibilities of governments and their auxiliaries to build the infrastructure needed to implement an integrated strategy for blood safety." Carolan also points out that three of the UN's Millennium Development Goals (to reduce child mortality, improve maternal health and combat HIV/AIDS) are dependent on a safe blood supply. ■

Shortage of skilled health workers compounds risks

Although neither party to the conflict has directly targeted health workers, the climate of danger and violence across much of the country has seriously affected the number of qualified medical staff willing to work in rural areas. "Nepal always had a shortage of skilled manpower and the conflict has made it worse – the rate of absenteeism has increased," says Pitamber Aryal, health director for the Nepal Red Cross Society. "Doctors are not willing to go to conflict zones, so most health facilities lack trained professionals," he adds.

The situation at village level is more complex. A large number of health workers are local and stay put, according to Susan Clapham, health adviser for DFID in Kathmandu. "In some areas, health workers are performing better now as the Maoists supervise their work and hold them accountable," she adds. The Maoists tax them too: "They pay an amount equal to 14 days of their salaries as levy every year," says Daya Shanker Lal Karna from the health centre in Sankhuwasabha, a Maoist-dominated district in far eastern Nepal. Meanwhile, health workers in remote villages have often been interrogated by security forces to reveal rebel locations. And since moving from government-controlled district centres to rural Maoist areas has often proved difficult, district health authorities have been unable to support or monitor village health posts.

Many of Nepal's maternal deaths could be prevented with the help of more SBAs. They could be doctors, nurses or midwives – but they must be competent in internationally-recognized midwifery and obstetric skills. As part of the Millennium Development Goal (MDG) to reduce maternal mortality by three-quarters from 1990 levels, WHO has set a target for 90 per cent of births to be attended by SBAs by 2015. For countries with a very high maternal mortality rate, the target is 60 per cent.

In Nepal, however, 91 per cent of deliveries take place at home, according to the government's Demographic and Health Survey (DHS) of 2001, the great majority without any skilled help. At the outset of the conflict in 1996, the DHS found that 10.1 per cent of all births – at home and in facilities – were attended by a trained health worker. By 2004–2005, this figure had doubled to 20.2 per cent, according to another survey by the government's health management information system (HMIS).

However, says Basnett, "this is a misleading indicator", as trained health workers include anyone from a doctor to a village health assistant with no specific midwifery training. Basnett suggests that a more realistic estimate of birth attendance by SBAs in Nepal today would be around 10 per cent. A key priority is to establish accurate baseline data on how many deliveries are conducted by SBAs. The government aims to introduce this indicator in 2007. Even so, it's clear Nepal is a long way off WHO's 60 per cent target.

Unsafe motherhood threatens newborns

The government has made progress cutting the under-five child mortality rate, particularly through nationwide immunizations which have helped save thousands of young lives every year. "Our real challenge now is to address neonatal mortality," says DFID's Susan Clapham.

Dangerous motherhood practices significantly contribute to Nepal's high infant mortality rate (IMR) of 64 per 1,000 live births. According to the government's 2001 survey, around 50,000 children die each year before their first birthday. Of these, two-thirds die within 28 days, which equates to over 30,000 neonatal deaths annually – one every 20 minutes.

According to the United Nations Population Fund (UNFPA), an infant often dies following the death of its mother during delivery. Motherless newborns are three to ten times more likely to die than those with live mothers. Most neonatal deaths occur as a result of inadequate care during pregnancy, delivery or the first critical hours after birth. Over 16,000 babies born each year in Nepal do not survive for more than 24 hours.

Only half of Nepal's pregnant women receive any antenatal care from a trained health worker, according to the government. Three-quarters of mothers are anaemic, which greatly increases the risks of premature delivery, haemorrhage and underweight babies. Just one in four women reports receiving iron supplements, necessary to combat anaemia. Meanwhile, half of all pregnant women fail to receive a tetanus inoculation.

A WFP survey of 1,359 women across Nepal in 2005 found that 63 per cent of those in the *terai* and 45 per cent of those in the hills and mountains weighed less than the 45kg threshold. Poorly nourished mothers are not only more prone to bleeding and infection, their babies are born smaller and are more vulnerable to potentially deadly diarrhoea and pneumonia. A quarter of Nepal's newborns are underweight, at less than 2.5kg.

Nepal's safe motherhood programmes are focused more on antenatal and delivery care than on postnatal care. According to Save the Children US, the majority of neonatal deaths occur at home. "Many mothers and newborns in Nepal do not make initial contact with the formal health system until the newborn is brought to a health provider at six weeks for the newborn's first immunizations," says a report by the organization.

These factors severely hamper the life chances of Nepal's newest arrivals. "The main reasons [for infant mortality] in Nepal are tetanus, infections and low weight. As the infants are at high risk of infection due to low energy, they often die if proper care is missing," says Save the Children's Nina Khadka.

Some experts argue that neonatal and maternal health should be more closely integrated. According to Clapham, two-thirds of neonatal deaths will be averted by interventions that reduce maternal deaths. However, donors tend to be interested in babies or mothers – not both, says Clapham, adding "although this is changing, we are yet to really integrate the services on a significant scale."

But is this a neglected disaster?

"Of course it is a disaster," says the Nepal Red Cross Society's Pitamber Aryal. The United Nations would appear to agree. In launching its first ever emergency consolidated appeal for Nepal in September 2005, the UN included a budget line of US$ 1.29 million for 'emergency reproductive health services for conflict-affected populations' (see Box 4.3).

Meanwhile, Indira Basnett recalls her experience as a district health officer in the remote hill district of Doti. "When a buffalo suffers birth complications, the community runs to find a skilled attendant, because a buffalo has a high economic value – it carries luggage, it produces milk," she says. "If a buffalo dies, they have to pay a high cost to replace it, but if a woman dies, they can find another without cost. The attitude in rural areas is 'deliver or die.' Women are not perceived to have economic value – for that reason, this is a neglected disaster."

Not all experts agree. "The poor state of maternal health in Nepal can't be defined as disaster, since a disaster is a major deviation from normal," says DFID's Susan Clapham, "yet we have been living with unacceptably high levels of maternal mortality for hundreds of years." To call it a disaster, she adds, implies that something should be done about it immediately. "But we can't do anything in a relatively short time – the evidence shows that progress is only achieved through long-term action." Clapham suggests that 'silent tragedy' would be a more accurate description.

Putting definitions aside, maternal and neonatal mortality are undoubtedly neglected by the media. Since the Maoist insurgency began in 1996, around 13,000 people have been killed as a direct result of the conflict. Over the same decade, by extrapolating current mortality data, an estimated 350,000 mothers and month-old babies have died of largely preventable causes. Yet international reporting of Nepal is dominated by conflict and politics, while maternal and neonatal mortality barely get a mention. A search of the BBC News web site in May 2006 found 1,764 articles on Nepal since November 1997, of which just one focused on maternal mortality.

The same is largely true of the domestic media. Anecdotal evidence suggests a lack of sensitivity to the issue. While a group of journalists from Kathmandu were observing an immunization programme in Dang district hospital during late 2005, two young women were rushed into the emergency ward. They were in fits of pain due to childbirth complications. "This happens all the time in the villages," remarked one reporter. He added: "My editor won't be interested in the story."

For its part, the government of Nepal has been slow to address maternal mortality, although its policy at least has improved in recent years. The global initiative to promote safe motherhood began in the 1980s, but it wasn't until 1993 that Nepal's

Box 4.3 Taking emergency measures

In response to the conflict, aid organizations, including the UN and NGOs, have developed a framework of good practice known as the Basic Operating Guidelines (BOGs) which emphasize that they have the right to suspend aid programmes in the absence of a safe working environment. Nevertheless, both parties to the conflict have, at times, made it difficult for aid operations to continue.

"The conflict has impacted on traditional ways of addressing maternal and child health problems," says Paul Handley, humanitarian officer with the UN's Office for the Coordination of Humanitarian Affairs (OCHA) in Kathmandu. "The basic health services of the state have been clearly affected, as have many other more developmental approaches to delivering services by the international community and local NGOs," he adds.

Susan Clapham, health adviser for the UK's Department for International Development (DFID) in Kathmandu, thinks this overstates the situation. "The conflict does not change the causes of deaths and therefore what we need to do to reduce deaths," she says. "We adapt *how* we work – not what we do."

Last year, the UN launched its first-ever humanitarian appeal for Nepal, asking for nearly US$ 65 million to cover the period from October 2005 to December 2006. The appeal made waves among Kathmandu's resident development agencies, who feared it would divert money from their work. Nick Russell, representative for the International Federation in Nepal, says the appeal process helped bring people together to address humanitarian and development issues in the context of the conflict and the pockets of vulnerability it creates. "The security situation is fluid, it keeps changing." Russell points out: "The aid agencies have to learn to work in a different way."

So, in a climate of violence and political uncertainty, are there any emergency measures that could reduce the terrible toll of nearly 100 mothers and babies dying from mainly preventable causes each day in Nepal? The Nepal Red Cross Society operates a fleet of 90 ambulances in 56 of the country's 75 districts – ready to rush women and children to health facilities when necessary. "Safe motherhood should be integrated into the emergency response of the country," argues Safieh Andersen, deputy representative of the UN Population Fund (UNFPA) in Nepal. She adds that an absence of emergency relief can further escalate the maternal health problem.

The UN appeal included over a million dollars for 'emergency reproductive health services'. UNFPA started by organizing mobile reproductive health surgery camps in eight remote districts. Women with uterus prolapses flocked in to get free surgery, costing about US$ 30 per patient. Clapham, however, remains unconvinced: "Reducing maternal deaths is a long-term development challenge and cannot be fixed by an emergency approach." ■

government launched the national safe motherhood programme. In 2001, a global assessment of 49 developing countries conducted by 750 reproductive health experts concluded that Nepal ranked 47th in all areas of maternal and neonatal health services. Published as part of the *Maternal and Neonatal Program Effort Index (MNPI)* by the United States Agency for International Development (USAID), the survey noted vast disparities between urban and rural access to safe motherhood services.

Meanwhile, accurate data on maternal deaths and safer motherhood indicators are hard to find (see Box 4.4). Basnett argues that "regular surveillance of each maternal death at district level is essential in order to design specific interventions for each district."

Solutions for mother and child survival

With such a range of complex root causes, the hidden crisis of Nepal's lost mothers and newborns demands equally complex solutions. According to DFID's Susan Clapham, maternal mortality is the hardest health problem to crack. The death rate is roughly the same as that of children dying of measles each year. Yet while a recent nationwide measles elimination campaign, costing approximately one dollar a child, is having an immediate and dramatic impact on reducing measles deaths, says Clapham, "we have nothing like that in maternal health".

The government's policy, along with that of the Nepal Red Cross Society, is to address maternal mortality within a broader strategy of reproductive and child health. This encompasses sex education, family planning, safety from sexually transmitted infections, safe motherhood and child survival. Reducing maternal mortality "is not

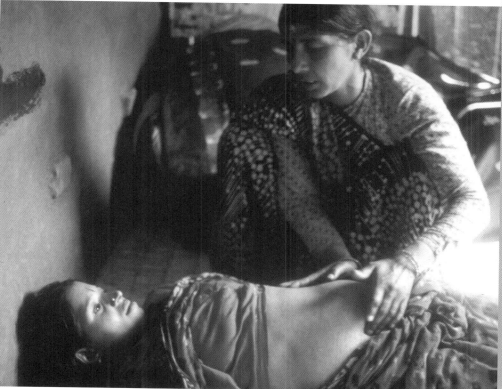

Giving birth in Nepal can be a deadly experience. Between 5,000 and 6,000 Nepali women die each year during childbirth – a silent tragedy that goes largely unreported. Over 90 per cent of deliveries take place at home, usually without the skilled care that's vitally necessary to ensure safe motherhood.

Liliane de Toledo/
International Federation

Box 4.4 Shaky data obscure plight of women and progress of response

Nepal's routine health information systems lack the capacity to determine which districts have the worst infant and maternal mortality rates. Registration of births and deaths is weak and not all hospitals keep accurate records. This contrasts with, for example, Sri Lanka, whose health system reports all maternal deaths down to village level, making it easy to calculate the maternal mortality rate.

One government medical recorder of a major hospital in west Nepal admitted to the *World Disasters Report* that his staff do not even keep records of maternal deaths. He explained, on condition of anonymity, that he did not get enough pressure from the government, civil society or the media to do so. He added that the death of one child from encephalitis or HIV/AIDS received national media coverage, while women dying in childbirth received almost no media attention. A medical recorder is a significant position in the government's health sector – responsible for disseminating information on various public health issues.

The alternative to nationwide registration of all maternal and child deaths is to conduct periodic surveys. However, methodologies vary so surveys cannot easily be compared. The government's figure of 539 maternal deaths per 100,000 live births dates from their 1996 Demographic and Health Survey (DHS), which measures maternal mortality once a decade. The DHS of 2006 will provide the latest figures by the end of this year. However, the confidence interval for the DHS methodology is plus or minus 100 – so the 1996 figure could be anywhere between 439 and 639.

The UN Development Programme (UNDP) highlighted in its *Nepal Millennium Development Goals (MDGs) Progress Report 2005*

that the data on maternal mortality in Nepal are highly problematic, under-reported and misclassified, due to "such issues as variability of the sample, the small number of events, and differences in methodology". In 2004, UNICEF reported a higher maternal mortality rate of 740 per 100,000 live births. The government defends its lower figure by arguing that many deaths that occur in villages or on the way to hospitals cannot be recorded.

The lack of reliable data makes it difficult to determine Nepal's progress towards its 2015 MDG of reducing maternal mortality by three-quarters from 1990 levels. Agencies are not even clear what the mortality rate was in 1990, leading DFID's Susan Clapham to say: "We don't know if we're on course or off course." For its part, the Nepalese government is committed to an MDG target of 134 deaths per 100,000 live births, based on a 75 per cent reduction from its 1996 figure of 539.

There are proxy indicators to measure annual progress towards safer motherhood. One is the percentage of births attended by a skilled birth attendant (SBA) – but up to mid-2006, data are available only on attendance by trained health workers who may or may not be SBAs. This should change with the introduction of SBA registration in July 2006. Another indicator is to measure the number of women with birth complications who receive emergency obstetric care (EmOC). Data on EmOC utilization have been gathered in 13 of Nepal's 75 districts since a baseline year of 1999–2000. But according to SSMP's Indira Basnett, "when the data was compared from baseline to now, it was found that the pace is very slow and there is a need of significant increase in EmOC service." ∎

just about how to have babies, it's about how *not* to have babies", says Manish Pant, senior health manager for the International Federation of Red Cross and Red Crescent Societies in South Asia.

After three or four births, women are more prone to anaemia, while their uterus becomes less efficient at contracting, increasing the risks of post-partum haemorrhage. Teenagers are more vulnerable during childbirth as their bodies are less resilient and they may be less aware of safe motherhood issues. In Nepal, says Pant, 13 per cent of women give birth before they reach 20 years of age. Many pregnancies in Nepal may be unwanted, leading to unsafe abortions by untrained villagers often armed with nothing more sophisticated than a sharp bamboo stick. Complications arising from unsafe abortions in Nepal are estimated to account for 20 per cent of maternal deaths in health facilities alone, not counting the women who never make it to hospital (see Box 4.5).

Red Cross volunteers are counselling adolescent girls in six districts of eastern Nepal in family planning and ways to avoid unwanted pregnancies. Meanwhile, at a national level, the Nepal Red Cross Society has coordinated the annual Condom Day since 1995 to promote birth spacing and disease prevention.

Examining the full range of reproductive and child health responses is beyond the scope of this chapter. However, one approach to safer motherhood is to examine ways of reducing the 3Ds mentioned earlier: delay in deciding to seek care, delay in reaching a healthcare facility and delay in accessing adequate treatment at the facility. The chapter will look briefly at these areas, reviewing what's been achieved and good practices on which to build, before exploring options for home-based care and community participation in making motherhood safer.

Boosting awareness through mass communication

Speeding up the decision to seek care involves building greater awareness among women and men of the benefits of expert help, especially if complications arise. It also means tackling barriers of culture and gender discrimination. Options include raising the profile of safe motherhood through more critical media coverage and mass communication among people at risk.

"If I only knew", says Phulmati's mother as she watches her daughter lying half-conscious in the hospital bed in Dang. She doesn't have the courage to tell Phulmati that she's just given birth to a dead child. Like many Nepalese women, she bitterly regrets not knowing what danger signs to watch out for.

Health awareness programmes are the best way to help people understand the significance of safe delivery, birth complications and health services. Sensitizing the

Complications from unsafe abortions are a major contributor to Nepal's high maternal mortality and morbidity. Because of the sensitive nature of the subject, little hard data is available, but studies by the Ministry of Health have estimated that induced abortion complications are responsible for 53.7 per cent of gynaecological and obstetric hospital admissions and 20 per cent of maternal deaths in health facilities. This does not account for the many women who have died at home, either because they lived too far from a hospital, or could not afford the expense, or were afraid to risk going to a public institution because of the illegal status of abortion, or feared the associated stigma.

In 2002, the Nepalese government legalized abortion and, following implementation of the new law in December 2003, there has been an intensive national programme to train safe abortion service providers and establish simple, safe and women-friendly abortion facilities in public hospitals and private or NGO clinics.

In the two years since the programme began, 226 public and private doctors have received training, 117 safe abortion sites have been established (71 public and 46 private/NGO) and a total of 43,460 women have received services, with minimal complications. Although there is still far to go in building awareness about the legal availability of services and changing attitudes towards abortion, this represents a significant step towards addressing a major cause of maternal death and suffering. ■

whole family is vital to prevent delays in seeking care. "Empowering only women won't be effective," says Deepa Pokhrel, equity and access adviser for SSMP.

In recent years, several organizations have launched 'non-formal education' on safer motherhood, forming community committees to raise awareness and funds. But the conflict has taken its toll on such projects. Agencies have reported difficulty gathering large groups of villagers together in Maoist areas. The migration of educated people from rural communities has undermined information-sharing. And the sustainability of stand-alone projects is limited by short-term funding.

One way of conveying health messages is through existing mothers groups, now numbering over 10,000 nationwide. Members, who include women from all backgrounds, often discuss sensitive issues such as reproductive health. "These groups can help pregnant women not to be shy about discussing their problems," explains Pokhrel.

Radio programmes could reach conflict-affected, remote or illiterate communities. In 2002, NSMP launched a 15-minute weekly radio programme called *Ama* (literally: 'mother'), broadcast in three districts. Listeners' clubs formed and some literate villagers volunteered to explain the issues to less educated families. The programme invited doctors to respond to villagers' queries.

An independent evaluation of *Ama* in Surkhet district found the project helped change attitudes, particularly among husbands and mothers-in-law, and increased local demand for better health services. When NSMP was phased out in 2004 and replaced by SSMP, *Ama* stopped production. Two years later, plans are afoot to resurrect it.

However, for national reach, the best option would be to harness the power of mainstream journalism. "Journalists can play an important role in writing heart-rending case studies, investigating the shortcomings of the government and international development agencies, and informing rural communities about benefits," says Pokhrel. But currently, journalists focus overwhelmingly on political coverage. When they do report on humanitarian issues, it's mainly about infectious diseases.

However, there is experience on which to build. In the mid-1990s, the Nepal Press Institute (NPI), a non-governmental organization (NGO) run by senior journalists, helped promote regular, national newspaper coverage of leprosy. NPI tied up with leprosy-focused NGOs, which sponsored field trips for journalists. Government health officials explained leprosy-related stigma to reporters. The initiative helped change attitudes towards people with leprosy. The same model could be applied to safe motherhood.

Making it cheaper and quicker to reach help

Reducing the delay in reaching a health facility is an issue of access, which in turn depends on ensuring freedom of movement with parties to the conflict, as well as overcoming topographical and financial barriers.

The sheer cost of travel and treatment puts off many of Nepal's poorest families. In 2005, over half of all households borrowed money to pay for hospital deliveries, while one-third sold land and livestock to cover the bills, according to the Ministry of Health.

However, with funding from DFID, the government recently started a cost-sharing scheme in 27 districts. All women delivering a baby at a district hospital or primary healthcare centre receive cash to cover transport and other costs. Those travelling from mountain districts receive US$ 20, while those from hill and *terai* districts get US$ 15 and US$ 7 respectively.

In addition, women from districts with a low human development index (HDI, as defined by the UN) receive free maternity and delivery services at public health institutions. For poorer women from districts with a better HDI, there is an additional travel allowance. Meanwhile, health workers such as SBAs receive US$ 5 per delivery they attend.

Despite this innovative approach, the allowances won't cover everything. On average, it costs over US$ 70 for a normal hospital delivery and US$ 150 for surgery. Add in transport and accommodation and the costs could soar. So poorer families not living in districts with a low HDI may still be forced to sell assets or take out high-interest loans to cover treatment. Added to which, women can only claim the money on leaving the health facility, so the poorest will still need an advance from somewhere.

"When we talk of birth preparedness, we need community-based emergency funds available in the middle of the night," says Suomi Sakai, UNICEF's representative in Nepal. One solution could be to approach mothers groups to advance emergency funds or low-cost loans to pregnant women in need. With hundreds of monthly fees coming in from members, many mothers groups serve as micro-banks.

In Jumla district, the local government is helping fund healthcare by taxing cigarettes, alcohol and air travel, levying an extra US$ 1.30 per passenger. Jumla plans to raise US$ 3,500 a year, which could go towards mothers' travel expenses or even a resident SBA. In Dang district, UNICEF is working with the government to promote safe motherhood groups and easier access to facilities (see Box 4.6).

Engaging private practice is another option. In Lamjung district, the government is piloting a safe motherhood project in which the private sector and local community are free to decide the allowances of service providers, who receive a government incentive of US$ 5 per delivery. This scheme has helped increase coverage of maternity services among rural women.

Improving service delivery at health facilities

Raising awareness of the need to deliver babies in health facilities and improving access to those facilities will be of limited use if Nepal's hospitals and health centres lack the equipment and staff necessary to ensure a safe delivery. Creating an effective nationwide health service (which Nepal has arguably never had) is a vital part of reducing unnecessary maternal and neonatal deaths. While a full analysis of this is beyond the scope of this chapter, there are some key issues to consider, including increasing the numbers of SBAs and considering options for better home-based care.

At the current rate, Nepal will miss WHO's 2015 target of 60 per cent of births attended by SBAs – and by a wide margin. Training more skilled birth attendants and, crucially, retaining them is a vital priority. At present there are 1,259 doctors and 6,216 nurses working in the governmental health system, mostly in city and district hospitals. Not all of them are trained to the standards required of SBAs by the International Confederation of Midwives. There are no accurate data on the numbers of SBAs in Nepal – although nationwide registration was due to begin in July 2006.

International Federation
of Red Cross and Red Crescent Societies

Box 4.6 Model hospital reaches out to community

The district hospital of Dang, 400 kilometres west of Kathmandu on the *terai* plains bordering India, has become a model for safer motherhood. The government, with support from UNICEF, now runs 24-hour maternity services at the hospital. They have helped to strengthen village health posts throughout the district and their delivery services reach every level of society. Safe motherhood groups, comprising women from each community, keep watch on all expectant mothers and ensure they go for regular antenatal check-ups. The groups help organize emergency funds so that any of their members with pregnancy-related complications can use the money to travel to hospital. Last year alone, healthcare centres across the district treated 344 life-threatening complications.

Most women still deliver babies at home in Dang district, but local attitudes towards maternal and newborn health are changing for the better. The hospital is helping to promote the idea of deliveries in hospital or at the hands of skilled birth attendants (SBAs). These SBAs (often nurses) train locally at the district hospital, where they learn to handle normal births and complicated cases. The hospital has a fully functional and well-equipped 15-bed maternity unit and a 24-hour blood transfusion service. ∎

The Ministry of Health plans to strengthen existing health centres sufficiently to provide adequate birthing facilities and to train existing doctors and nurses in SBA skills. Far more SBAs are needed to cover remote areas. SSMP is proposing that in order to hit the WHO target, one SBA is needed per 50 births in the mountains, one per 100 births in the hills, and one per 150 births in the *terai*. This means over 4,000 SBAs are needed across the country.

While skilled birth attendants can manage minor complications, doctors are needed to operate EmOC facilities and manage major complications. According to Geeta Rana, head of the safe motherhood programme for UNICEF in Nepal, "there is a need to increase the numbers of general practitioners [medical doctors] so that there is at least one in every district hospital and eventually two." However, at present there are only 45 Nepalese general practitioners, of which just 15 work for the government.

Most rural communities currently make do with traditional birth attendants (TBAs), who number approximately 15,000. Confusingly, however, TBAs – like maternal and child health workers (MCHWs) – are not special birth attendants and cannot handle birth complications. As many of them are poorly educated and trained, the best they can do is refer patients on to SBAs. Since the late 1980s, the Nepalese government has invested in expanding the numbers of MCHWs and TBAs. However, evaluations suggest that they have had little impact on improving safe motherhood practices, so government policy is now focused on increasing the number of SBAs.

Role for community-based care?

One key issue is whether to invest more resources in improving health facilities or to send more SBAs into the homes of vulnerable women – especially given the enormous barriers which poorer women in remote locations face in reaching an adequate health facility.

In the late 1990s, donors like DFID concentrated on health facilities, but this is changing. "There's a lot more that can be done to prevent complications in the home," says DFID's Susan Clapham. Reducing post-partum haemorrhage is critical. This can be done by managing labour correctly, including the use of essential drugs. But it requires skilled health workers such as SBAs, plus a drug supply system. So the key priority is to ensure there are enough SBAs to provide care in the home as well as in community-based facilities in vulnerable, high-risk areas. Considering that 46 per cent of maternal deaths in Nepal are caused by bleeding, which could largely be managed at home or in local facilities, Clapham believes such care by SBAs could achieve "not far off a 50 per cent cut in maternal mortality".

However, the barriers preventing women from accessing health facilities also apply to SBAs accessing communities. Persuading skilled health workers to operate in remote, dangerous locations will take sustained financial incentives and more support from the health system. This is primarily the state's responsibility. "If the government is really committed to the MDGs, it needs to invest more money in training and retaining SBAs," says Indira Basnett.

In the meantime, should the roles of community health volunteers – including TBAs – be re-examined? They could be trained to register pregnancies and forward the information to the nearest SBAs, to facilitate antenatal visits. They could learn to recognize birth complications in time to refer women to expert care. They could distribute iron supplements to combat anaemia. And they could promote simple health messages before and after birth – such as the need for mothers to improve their nutrition and take sufficient rest.

Proper postnatal care is vital, but often neglected by SBAs. One pilot project, conducted by Save the Children US with the government, has shown that TBAs can conduct effective home-based postnatal care. The project targeted 24 villages in Kailali, one of the least developed districts in the far western *terai*, and trained community-based health workers and TBAs in how to conduct basic examinations of newborns in the home, recognize danger signs and refer to appropriate health centres. They had to make at least three visits to the home of each newborn, physically examining babies and counselling mothers.

As a result, half the mothers and 44 per cent of newborns in the project area received postnatal care. Unfortunately, the project staff had to pull out in 2004 for security

International Federation
of Red Cross and Red Crescent Societies

CHAPTER 4

reasons, but the intervention showed that TBAs can be a valuable resource in the fight against neonatal mortality.

Conclusion: political champions, new partners

Solving the hidden crisis of maternal and neonatal mortality is a complicated, long-term process. Put simply, the solution involves two broad approaches which need concurrent action:

- **Supply side:** improving the healthcare system by equipping more health centres with basic EmOC facilities, training and retaining more SBAs, improving safe abortion services, and enabling better access for the most vulnerable.
- **Demand side:** building greater demand for reproductive health services by tackling socio-cultural barriers to a greater awareness of maternal and neonatal health among vulnerable communities.

To achieve this in the current political and security climate will require the cooperation not only of communities and government, but also the private sector, the media and power-brokers across the country. Binding these disparate players together will take a high level of advocacy and coordination among humanitarian and development organizations.

Find political champions: "Unsafe motherhood is not a quick fix. We need more political champions to address this issue strongly," says DFID's Susan Clapham. For example, abortion was legalized after a high-profile campaign led by lawyers, civil society, politicians and the prime minister's wife. Journalists were mobilized through regular seminars and coverage of the court trials of women imprisoned for abortion.

Engage mainstream media: A similar campaign to that for abortion could be effective for safer motherhood. Aid organizations could collaborate on concrete communication strategies and build stronger ties with mainstream media – a major untapped resource with nationwide reach. Identifying a National Safe Motherhood Day, as in India, would be a good start.

Partner with the private sector: Building effective partnerships with the private sector could help supplement overstretched public health services. But district government officials need more autonomy for such schemes to succeed.

Advocate with rebels and security forces: Aid organizations and human rights groups could advocate more strongly with Maoists and security forces to ensure absolute security, unhindered access and respect for health workers conducting life-saving missions across the country.

Principal contributors to this chapter and Boxes 4.1 – 4.4 and 4.6 were Naresh Newar, a reporter with the Nepali Times *who also works as a freelancer for IRIN and Bishnu Sharma, who is a reporter for* Rajdhani National Daily *newspaper. Cherry Bird, consultant with the Technical Committee for the Implementation of Comprehensive Abortion Care (TCIC) advising the Nepalese government, contributed Box 4.5. We would also like to acknowledge the invaluable assistance and advice of Dr Indira Basnett, consultant with Nepal's Support for Safe Motherhood Programme (SSMP) and Dr Susan Clapham, health adviser in Nepal for the UK's Department for International Development (DFID).*

Sources and further information

Adhikary, K. *Qualitative Investigation of NSMP's Radio Programme Launched in Surkhet District.* Kathmandu: NSMP, 2004.

Aitken, J-M. and Thomas, D. *Synthesis of Final Evaluation Findings From the Nepal Safer Motherhood Project.* Kathmandu: Family Health Division, Department of Health Services, Ministry of Health, HMG Nepal, Options, DFID, 2004.

Beun, M. and Neupane, B.D. *Impact of Conflict on Accessibility of EmOC Health Services.* Kathmandu: Family Health Division, Department of Health Services, Ministry of Health, HMG Nepal, Options, DFID, 2003.

Chhetry, S., Clapham, S. and Basnett, I. *Community Based Maternal and Child Health Care in Nepal: Self-Reported Performance of Maternal and Child Health Workers.* Journal of Nepal Medical Association, 2005.

The Center for Reproductive Rights. *Women of the World: Laws and Policies Affecting Their Reproductive Lives – South Asia.* New York: The Center for Reproductive Rights, 2005.

Consolidated Appeals Process. *Nepal 2005.* New York: United Nations, 2005.

Freedman, L.P., Waldman, R. J., de Pinho, H., Wirth, M.E., Mushtaque, A., Chowdhury, R. and Rosenfield, A. *Who's got the power? Transforming health systems for women and children.* London: Earthscan, 2005.

International Federation. *Maternal and child health care.* Geneva: International Federation, 2005.

Ministry of Health, *National Maternal Mortality and Morbidity Study 1998.* Nepal: Ministry of Health and Population, HMG Nepal, 1998.

Ministry of Health. *National Neonatal Health Strategy.* Nepal: Family Health Division, Department of Health Services, Ministry of Health, HMG Nepal, 2004.

Save the Children. *State of the World's Mothers 2006 – Saving the Lives of Mothers and Newborns.* London: Save the Children, 2006.

Taylor, M.E. *Analysis Of Systems: The Jumla Community Health Program.* Maryland, USA: Unpublished doctoral thesis, January 2000.

Thomas, D., Messerschmidt, L. and Devkota, B. *Increasing Access to Essential Obstetric Care: A review of progress and process.* Kathmandu: Family Health Division, Department of Health Services, Ministry of Health, HMG Nepal, Options, DFID, 2004.

UN Children's Fund. *Needs assessment on the availability of emergency obstetric care services.* Kathmandu: UNICEF, 2000.

UN Population Fund. *State of World Population 2005.* New York: UNFPA, 2005.

World Food Programme. *Household Food Security in Nepal.* Nepal: WFP/VAM, December 2005.

World Health Organization. *Beyond The Numbers: Reviewing Maternal Deaths And Complications To Make Pregnancy Safer.* Geneva: WHO, 2004.

World Health Organization. *Improving Maternal, Newborn and Child Health in the South-East Asia Region,* p. 70. New Delhi: WHO, 2000.

World Health Organization. *Regional Health Forum WHO South-East Asia Region (Volume 6, Number 2).* New Delhi: WHO, 2002.

World Health Organization, United Nations Children's Fund, United Nations Population Fund. *Maternal Mortality in 2000.* Geneva: WHO, UNICEF, UNFPA, 2004.

World Health Organization. *Skilled Attendant at birth 2005 Estimates.* Available at http://www.who.int/reproductive-health/global_monitoring/ skilled_attendant_at_birth2005_estimates.pdf

Web sites

UK's Department for International Development (information on Nepal)
http://www.dfid.gov.uk/countries/asia/nepal.asp

Maternal and Neonatal Program Effort Index
http://www.policyproject.com/pubs/MNPI/Nepal_MNPI.pdf

Nepal Red Cross Society **http://www.nrcs.org**

Nepal Safer Motherhood Project **http://www.nsmp.org**

Save the Children US **http://www.savethechildren.org**

UN Population Fund Nepal **http://www.unfpanepal.org**

UN Children's Fund (information on Nepal)
http://www.unicef.org/infobycountry/nepal_nepal_latest.html

UN Integrated Regional Information Networks News **http://www.irinnews.org**

UN Millennium Project **http://www.unmillenniumproject.org**

World Health Organization Regional Office for South-East Asia
http://www.whosea.org

CHAPTER 4

CHAPTER 5

Death at sea: boat migrants desperate to reach Europe

One night in November 2004, Canary Islands photojournalist Juan Medina was on the deck of a Spanish police boat off Fuerteventura as it drew alongside a patera *carrying, by the police count, 40 migrants from West Africa. As the coastguards got within reach, the Africans rushed to the same side of the already overloaded vessel. In an instant the* patera *– not much more than a large rowing boat with an outboard motor – flipped over, trapping almost all the passengers under its hull. The police watched in horror as the would-be migrants fought their way to the side of the cutter. At least 11 people drowned in this single incident. Medina could do nothing but photograph the dreadful scene. His pictures won a Spanish press award and are still the only ones actually showing a mishap on the high seas involving boat migrants trying to get into 'Fortress Europe' from the coast of north-west Africa.*

No one knows how many migrants have died in the last ten years attempting to cross in small boats from Western Sahara, Mauritania and, most recently, Senegal to the Canary Islands; from Morocco to Spain; from Libya and Tunisia to several Italian islands and Malta; from Turkey and Egypt to the Greek Islands; and – some with the eventual aim of reaching Europe – from Somalia to Yemen.

No single international agency is tracking the whole disaster, although it is transnational by definition. The collection of hard data has been left to academics, journalists, smaller non-governmental organizations (NGOs) like the Spanish Asociación Pro Derechos Humanos de Andalucía (APDHA) and local Red Cross or Red Crescent branches.

The most authoritative research on boat migration worldwide is probably still that carried out in 2004 by Michael Pugh, now a professor of peace studies at Bradford University in the UK. It suggested that up to 2,000 people were drowning every year in and around the Mediterranean trying to reach European Union (EU) territory. He derived this figure from interviews with migrants, records of bodies recovered, numbers of wrecked vessels and government statistics.

This chapter focuses on the plight of 'irregular' migrants attempting to reach Europe by sea. It explores options for reducing the death toll and analyses the legal and humanitarian implications of assisting 'mixed flows' of economic migrants and refugees, including a brief discussion of the recent history of migration into the EU.

Photo opposite page: Would-be migrants sit on a police boat after being intercepted off the coast of Fuerteventura, one of Spain's Canary Islands, 1 May 2005. Around 70 people were intercepted aboard two makeshift boats on their way to reach European soil from Africa.

© REUTERS/Juan Medina, courtesy www.alertnet.org

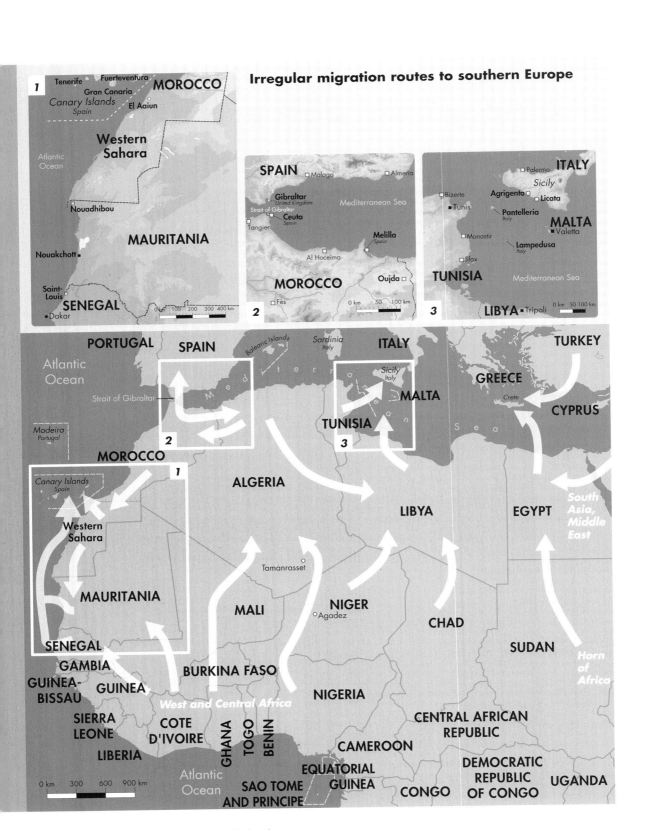

Irregular migration routes to southern Europe

1
Tenerife Fuerteventura
Gran Canaria
Canary Islands El Aaiun
Spain

MOROCCO

Western Sahara

Atlantic Ocean

□ Nouadhibou

MAURITANIA

Nouakchott □

Saint-Louis
■ Dakar

SENEGAL

0 km 100 200 300 400 km

2

SPAIN
□ Malaga   □ Almeria
Gibraltar *United Kingdom*   Mediterranean Sea
Strait of Gibraltar □ Ceuta *Spain*
□ Tangier   Melilla *Spain*

□ Al Hoceima   Oujda □

MOROCCO
□ Fès

0 km 50 100 km

3

□ Palermo   ITALY
Sicily
□ Bizerte   Agrigento □ Licata
■ Tunis   Pantelleria *Italy*
MALTA
■ Valetta
□ Monastir   Lampedusa *Italy*
□ Sfax

TUNISIA   Mediterranean Sea

LIBYA ■ Tripoli

0 km 50 100 km

PORTUGAL   SPAIN   *Balearic Islands*   *Sardinia Italy*   ITALY   TURKEY

Atlantic Ocean   *Med*   *Sicily Italy*   GREECE   *Crete*   CYPRUS

Strait of Gibraltar   MALTA

2   TUNISIA   **3**

Madeira Portugal

MOROCCO   **1**   ALGERIA   LIBYA   EGYPT   *South Asia, Middle East*

Canary Islands Spain

Western Sahara

Tamanrasset ○

MAURITANIA   MALI   NIGER   CHAD   SUDAN   *Horn of Africa*
○ Agadez

SENEGAL
GAMBIA   BURKINA FASO
GUINEA-   GUINEA   NIGERIA   CENTRAL AFRICAN
BISSAU   REPUBLIC
SIERRA   COTE   GHANA TOGO BENIN   CAMEROON
LEONE   D'IVOIRE
LIBERIA   EQUATORIAL   DEMOCRATIC
Atlantic Ocean   GUINEA   REPUBLIC   UGANDA
SAO TOME   CONGO   OF CONGO
AND PRINCIPE

West and Central Africa

0 km 300 600 900 km

"Major humanitarian crisis"

In February 2006, the Italian intelligence agency reported to parliament in Rome that the number of people arriving illegally on Sicily and other Italian islands had surged to nearly 23,000 in 2005, from just over 13,500 the year before. NGO statistics indicated this upward trend was continuing in the first half of 2006 (see Table 5.1).

There is no recent estimate of the death toll in the Sicilian Channel. However, in 2004, a European Commission technical mission to Libya concluded that of an estimated 15,000 people who tried to reach Italy from the Libyan coast, about 2,000 (or 13 per cent) had died.

During winter 2005–2006, Moroccan police drove people smugglers down the coast of Western Sahara and into Mauritania; in early March came confirmation from the Canary Islands that a new influx from Mauritania was under way. The islands' governor, José Segura, said more than 3,500 sub-Saharan Africans had arrived since the beginning of the year, dramatically reversing a downward trend for 2005 reported earlier by the Spanish interior ministry. Segura added that the boat-migrant phenomenon had become "catastrophic" because people were leaving countries like Mali and Senegal where locusts and droughts had wrecked entire harvests.

The story broke in the international media when 45 African migrants – from Gambia, Guinea-Bissau, Côte d'Ivoire, Mali, Mauritania and Nigeria – were confirmed to have

Table 5.1	Irregular boat migration to Mediterranean islands surges					
Confirmed arrivals of migrants	Canary Islands	Spanish mainland	Italian islands	Malta	Greece	TOTALS
2002	9,875	6,795	23,719	1,680	3,945	46,014
2003	9,382	9,794	14,331	568	2,439	36,514
2004	8,426	7,249	13,635	1,400	3,047	33,757
2005	4,715	7,066	22,824	1,800	1,280	37,685
2006 (Jan–June)	10,896[1]	n.a.	7,236[2]	967[3]	n.a.	19,099*

Note: n.a. signifies no data available.

*provisional total

Sources: Data from central government ministries unless otherwise stated; figures for Malta were compiled by www.maltatoday.com.mt from various sources and may have been rounded. If the total of confirmed arrivals for 2005 (37,685) represents 95 per cent of those who embarked, almost certainly an overestimate, nearly 2,000 migrants must have been lost at sea last year.

[1] Spanish Red Cross, figure for 1 January–12 July.

[2] Medici Senza Frontiere figure for Lampedusa and Linosa only; does not include the Sicilian mainland. This is a large increase on corresponding month-by-month data for 2005, when 4,933 migrants arrived from January to June. (Migration flows to Italian islands are more seasonal than the Canaries.)

[3] Statement by Malta's foreign minister Michael Frendo to EU ambassadors, 3 July 2006. (The figure is almost double that for the corresponding period in 2005.)

drowned in two separate accidents off the Mauritanian coast on the same day in March 2006. Ahmedou Ould Haye, coordinator of the Mauritanian Red Crescent, told the Spanish *Cadena Ser* radio station: "They are prepared to commit suicide. It's a game of Russian roulette: either I get there or I die."

The Mauritanian Red Crescent estimated that more than 1,200 migrants had died at sea in the five months from November 2005. News reports in spring 2006 from the Canary Islands said that a third of the boats setting off from Mauritania were being lost.

In the case of West Africans, the sea voyage is often preceded by an equally hazardous trek across the Sahara, and there are not even guesstimates of the number of people who have died in the desert. For this is irregular, illegal migration and, in the Mediterranean region (defined as including the Canary Islands) it is a highly lucrative business which seems to be firmly in the hands of organized criminals.

In March 2006, just as the new seaborne exodus from Mauritania gathered pace, Spain's *El Pais* newspaper carried a detailed report on a three-year-long investigation by the Spanish intelligence service into illegal migration to the Canary Islands. It found that the people-smuggling business was firmly in the hands of nearly 50 Moroccan gangs, including some in Mauritania, who had lost interest in tobacco once they realized how profitable migrants are. They were said to have inveigled struggling Senegalese and Mauritanian fishermen into acting as skippers with the promise of a free passage to Spain.

It's possible that people-smuggling is even serving as a kind of unofficial redundancy scheme for the hard-pressed fishermen of Mauritania, whose bountiful waters – usually teeming with tuna, mackerel, snapper and sardinella – are in danger of being fished out by, ironically, the EU fleet.

From one side of the African continent to the other, smugglers have used ruthless methods. Once land is sighted, they sometimes force migrants overboard at gunpoint to avoid being arrested themselves. As many as 200 Somalis on a boat bound for Yemen drowned in a single such incident in September 2005.

There is some reason to believe that in 2005–2006, as people-smuggling became better organized in the eastern Mediterranean, losses at sea in the region might have fallen. But in the west, as boat migrants have been forced to attempt the longer route to the Canaries from Mauritania and Senegal, they have almost certainly risen.

As defined by international conventions, people-smuggling, unlike human trafficking, is in theory not based on a deception of the person smuggled (across an international border). But first-hand contact with smuggled – and often bewildered – people in Spain and Italy reveals that a significant degree of deception is involved. Some migrants arriving on the tiny Italian island of Lampedusa, for example, believing they were being taken to the mainland, ask where they can catch a train (see Box 5.1).

In November 2005, the Office of the United Nations High Commissioner for Refugees (UNHCR) described the situation in the Mediterranean region as a "major humanitarian crisis". UNHCR also called on states to reaffirm their commitment to protection and not engage in the summary repatriation of boat groups which might include refugees.

The Red Cross Societies of the EU member states, together with Croatia, Serbia and Montenegro, Norway and Switzerland, issued a joint statement in January 2006 expressing "grave concern" about the precarious humanitarian situation facing migrants at the EU's borders.

Most of these new migrants, especially young men from the Maghreb countries of North Africa who are usually deported if identified, have destroyed their documents and attempt to conceal their national origins. The police in countries like Spain and Italy use linguists and consular officials to try to identify them.

In the first decade of the new century, Europe seems to be facing the consequences of failed development in the global South, above all in sub-Saharan Africa. Drawn by the prospect of earning their fortunes and driven by desperation born of grinding poverty, unemployment, insecurity and hopelessness, many migrants view Europe as a promised land that they're prepared to risk their lives to reach.

Get there or die

Fuerteventura is closer to Africa than any of the other Canary Islands, lying just 100 kilometres or a day's sail from Western Sahara and well known to northern Europeans as a winter holiday destination. It was the first island in the chain where African boat migrants started landing, in the mid-1990s, using a route pioneered by Saharawi fishermen.

When the migrant flow to Fuerteventura spiked in 2004, both the authorities and the local branch of the Spanish Red Cross were nearly overwhelmed. According to a meticulous record kept by the Red Cross branch president, Gerardo Mesa Noda, a retired banker, nearly 1,000 boat people arrived on the island in October alone, the busiest month. That year, the Red Cross on Fuerteventura assisted the *Guardia Civil* (police) with 65 bodies.

Mesa Noda's data records the work of the branch's emergency corps of 75 volunteers. His figures show a fall in arrivals from Western Sahara from the beginning of 2005 onwards, probably due to tighter Moroccan and Algerian land-border controls. They

Box 5.1 Lampedusa: an island in the spotlight

If *Lampedusani* have any objections to the island's ramshackle detention centre for boat migrants, there's no sign of them in its only town. No anti-immigrant graffiti; no hint in the election posters that cover all the empty wall space that immigration is even an issue at all; and Veronica Besengo, the Kenyan wife of the local Medici Senza Frontiere (MSF) doctor and one of the few black Africans actually resident on Lampedusa, says she has never had any problems.

Mayor Bruno Siragusa is proud of the presidential medal awarded to Lampedusa – *la roccia* (the rock) – for humanitarian ser-vices to migrants. Though some local traders dispute it, he says tourism actually increased by 10 per cent in 2005 – the year after the tiny island became the epicentre of an international crisis over irregular migration that caused bitter divisions within the Italian body politic and threatened to tarnish Italy's human rights record. But Siragusa adds: "Everyone agrees the time has come to replace the old detention centre with a better building."

For a facility that has caused so much international uproar, Lampedusa's *Centro di accoglienza temporanea* (temporary reception centre) next to its airport, from which Italy was accused of carrying out several indiscriminate deportations of boat migrants in 2004 and 2005, is quite unimposing. A little cluster of former aviation buildings and shipping containers turned into sleeping-quarters, it's sandwiched between the runway and the immaculate rows of olives, figs, grapes and *fico d'india* (cactus) of an allotment field. The tatty perimeter fence would not thwart a determined escapee, but on Lampedusa – three kilometres wide and eleven long – there's truly nowhere to go.

Tourists arriving at the airport, which ironically can only handle domestic flights because there's no customs base, would not know it was even there unless they looked carefully.

The small size of the detention centre, intended to accommodate a maximum of 190, however, is part of the problem. Only two or three migrant boats need arrive and it's forced to take several times more people than it really should.

This year arrivals are up; way up.

Among the best data on irregular boat migration anywhere in the Mediterranean are statistics for Lampedusa compiled by Dr Stefano Valentini, Veronica's husband, as a by-product of his work as MSF's emergency physician based at the *Guardia Costiera* (coastguard) jetty. Valentini and his wife provide water, food, first aid – and do a head count. They're called every time a migrant boat or a coastguard cutter carrying rescued migrants comes in.

In January 2006, a bad month to embark, a scarcely credible 767 migrants arrived by boat compared with a third that number in January 2005. In February – again a bad time to sail – 181 arrived compared with 13 the previous February. In March, 1,626 migrants arrived compared with just over 1,100 in March 2005. In April, a month of high winds, 84 migrants arrived compared with none at all in April last year.

In May, as the *World Disasters Report* was going to print, a rusty fishing trawler with about 500 people crammed aboard limped into Lampedusa's tiny clover-shaped harbour – believed to be the largest number of migrants ever to arrive on a single vessel. The total figure for May, the first month of the real migration season, was 2,412 arrivals compared with 1,662 in May 2005.

The consensus on Lampedusa is that the overwhelming majority of migrants set off from Libya and that the people smugglers are much better organized than they were.

Luciana Mirto leads Sicily's Italian Red Cross (CRI) voluntary nurses, who do solo two-week stints at the Lampedusa detention centre. She says arriving migrants have very little idea what to expect or even exactly where they are. "Some ask where they can catch the train," she says. "Some say they're minors, so the police use X-rays of hands to try to age them." Under Italian law, minors cannot be deported.

The nadir of the Lampedusa centre's human rights image probably came in October last year, when a journalist from *L'espresso* magazine, Fabrizio Gatti, went undercover as a migrant and wrote of a catalogue of abuse by *carabinieri*. The article led to demands on Lampedusa itself for the centre to be closed. But the chairman of the Italian parliament's immigration committee, Alberto di Luca, a member of the then-governing Forza Italia party, described the *L'espresso* article allegations as "unfounded and defamatory".

As of March 2006, the United Nations High Commissioner for Refugees (UNHCR), the International Organization for Migration (IOM) and the CRI have been sharing a small permanent office at the Lampedusa centre and finally have access to the detainees, if not the central wired-in zone which is the preserve of local staff of the Misericordia NGO. It hardly matters: once inside the main gates there's nothing but flimsy chicken-netting between you and the detainees. Migrants speak freely to visitors.

It's difficult to imagine abuses of the kind alleged by *L'espresso* – or, for that matter, rushed and indiscriminate deportations of mixed groups that might contain refugees – going unnoticed now. Not from Lampedusa, at any rate. Newly arrived migrants spend only a few days there now before going on to other centres in Italy, such as Crotone, for processing. ∎

Boats used by migrants wait to be broken up for scrap in Lampedusa.

© Alex Wynter, 2006

also show that boat migrants reaching the Canaries are overwhelmingly sub-Saharan African men: 6,584 out of a total for Fuerteventura in 2004 of 7,543. Fewer than 200 women and children of any nationality made the crossing that year.

"Government statistics available to us do not provide a breakdown of the percentage of people in need of international protection," says William Spindler, Senior Public Information Officer at UNHCR. Of those involved in irregular movements to Europe by land or by sea, "the majority are people looking for better economic prospects", Spindler says, "but there is a significant minority of people fleeing persecution, conflict or generalized violence."

Fodé, a 41-year-old father of three from Guinea-Bissau staying in one of the two Spanish Red Cross hostels on Fuerteventura, remembers his own voyage as uneventful: "We set off from the Moroccan coast at five in the morning and at seven that evening we were in Spain." He has mastered Spanish in his four years in the Canaries, but he's suspended in a legal limbo, barred from seeking work, yet, under Spanish law, he cannot be returned to Guinea-Bissau as there is no bilateral repatriation agreement. Fodé fled poverty and the diffuse, brutal conflict that across Africa is often quite random in its impact. But he is not seeking refugee status or even temporary humanitarian protection.

Whether they are actually refugees or not, many irregular boat migrants transiting the Mediterranean at least behave as if they were fleeing for their lives, accepting the hazards often inherent in desperate flight. Juan Medina's professional archive is a photo gallery of death at sea: African bodies floating in the tranquil waters of what are ironically also known as the Fortunate Islands; or literally washed up at the feet of tourists; or frozen where they huddled together in the bilges of their open boats.

This desperation originates in the tradition in some parts of Africa of "sending young men off to seek their fortunes abroad, sometimes with the financial backing of whole villages," according to Josephine Shields-Recass of the International Federation's regional office for North Africa in Tunis. "That's how they can afford to pay the smugglers. And it is a big disgrace for them to go home empty-handed."

The head of the Africa unit of the Spanish Red Cross, Jaime Bará Viñas, who was in Mauritania in early 2006, agrees: "For them, there is no turning back. Many migrants prefer to risk death rather than return to their communities with nothing." He says: "It's a question of pride mixed with poverty and misery."

A Senegalese fisherman, Mamadou Ba, sitting in a Canary Islands police station in March waiting to be deported but vowing to try again, told a Reuters correspondent: "Die or succeed is the motto."

International Federation
of Red Cross and Red Crescent Societies

Mesa Noda, a humane and thoughtful man, is dismayed at the idea of his young volunteers counting bodies on the shores of a beautiful island better known as a tourist playground. For him, the human tragedy he observes week-in-week-out is, above all, a measure of crisis in Africa. "The world must know what's happening here," he insists. "People do not leave their homes and their countries for nothing."

Morocco: EU border guard

It was actually a sequence of events on dry land last year that transformed 'Fortress Europe' from metaphor to blunt fact and helped change the dynamics of the boat-migrant crisis throughout the north-west Africa region.

In late September 2005, hundreds of sub-Saharan African migrants stormed the razor-wire fences around the Spanish North African enclave of Ceuta in what was described in news reports as a coordinated assault. Five died, two of them on the Spanish side of the wire. Another incident in October at Melilla, the other Spanish enclave, left six migrants dead. Ceuta and Melilla are the EU's only land border with Africa.

Exactly what happened is still not clear. Journalists and reported eyewitness accounts said Spanish *Guardia Civil* officers protecting the border fired rubber bullets at the migrants on the Moroccan side, through and above the fence, while Moroccan police used live ammunition. Morocco admitted its police shot four of the migrants who died at Melilla; Spain has insisted the *Guardia Civil* did not fire the bullets that killed the two migrants who fell dead on Spanish soil at Ceuta, or use any live ammunition at all.

A day after the Melilla incident, Médicos Sin Fronteras, the Spanish branch of Médecins Sans Frontières (MSF), disclosed it had found a group of more than 500 sub-Saharan African immigrants "left to their fate" in a remote desert area in the south of Morocco. MSF said the migrants told how they had been transported into the desert by Moroccan police after being expelled by the *Guardia Civil* from Ceuta and Melilla.

Morocco initially denied it had dumped people in the desert, but responded to international pressure by retrieving more than 1,000 Africans and taking them to the town of Oujda on the border with Algeria for repatriation.

Observers who have been tracking the Mediterranean migrant story agree that Morocco, in particular, has been successfully coaxed into policing Europe's borders. "The EU has persuaded Morocco to get tough," says Mehdi Lahlou, a professor of economics at the National Institute of Statistics and Applied Economics in Rabat. "Officially, Morocco does not want to be Europe's border guard, but on the ground that's what's happening."

And it is no secret. The police in Oujda themselves, for example, were quoted by Agence France-Presse (AFP) in late February as saying they'd deported to Algeria more than 750 people "trying to make their way to Europe". They included "sub-Saharan Africans, Algerians, Indians, Pakistanis and Syrians", arrested in various cities. Most of the migrants that were camped out around the Spanish enclaves also left or were moved on last winter.

In the immediate aftermath of the violence at Ceuta and Melilla, the NGO Amnesty International said its delegates had found "numerous irregularities in the treatment of migrants, including possible asylum seekers, during a ten-day mission to Spain and Morocco, including the towns of Ceuta, Melilla, Oujda, Nador and Tangier". Amnesty interviewed people, mostly from Central and West Africa, "fleeing poverty and repression" who were trying to get into the Spanish enclaves.

Whatever a fair assessment of its human rights record might be, Morocco's clamp-down on irregular 'transit migrants' seems, at the time of writing, to have succeeded mainly in shifting the migrant issue elsewhere.

To Mauritania, for example. The Spanish NGO Médicos del Mundo, after watching would-be migrants arriving in the country's northernmost port, Nouadhibou, in late 2005, reported at one stage that up to 15,000 sub-Saharans were camped on the coast waiting to sail in mafia *cayucos* – slightly larger and sturdier boats than the *pateras* that are typical of the Saharawi route (see Box 5.2).

And to Libya, from where most migrants hope to reach Italy.

Smugglers "established" in Libya

Official Italian statistics for seaborne *clandestini*, as the media often call them, show annual arrivals falling from a peak of nearly 24,000 in 2002 to around 14,000 during both 2003 and 2004. For 2005, the numbers leapt back to nearly 23,000 and more boat migrants than usual reached Sicily itself.

This is borne out by data for arrivals in the Sicilian port of Licata, collected by the Italian Red Cross (CRI) Agrigento branch, on the island's southern coast. In 2004, a single boat carrying 130 migrants arrived; but in 2005, between May and October, there were 12 boats, carrying no fewer than 1,433 people.

In 2005–2006, boat migrants arrived all along Sicily's southern shores. Local newspapers reported that there were hundreds of thousands of people waiting in Libya to "try their luck". The true number in spring 2006 was more like 20,000, according to sources in North Africa familiar with the situation in Libya.

Generally, boat migrants arrive in Italy in good condition, "clean-shaven and in nice new clothes", according to one Italian aid worker with first-hand experience of

International Federation
of Red Cross and Red Crescent Societies

arrivals. Dehydration and the crippling stiffness typical of extended small-boat voyages are rare. This has led to suspicions that people smugglers are using larger ocean-going vessels to cover the bulk of the distance from North Africa and transferring migrants to small boats for the final leg.

Members of the European Parliament (MEPs) visiting Libya in September 2005 were told of "an increased emphasis on cooperation" between Libya and the EU over migration, according to an official report from the parliament's human rights unit. But much of the rest of what the MEPs heard – with its implication of large-scale human vulnerability – will have disturbed them.

The report detailed a briefing from the British ambassador in Tripoli: uncontrolled immigration into Libya, a revolutionary country with a long tradition of welcoming African citizens, was "putting a serious strain on society". It was clear that "traffickers have established themselves". Currently, around 7,000 people are repatriated from Libya every month, most of them of sub-Saharan origin, the ambassador told MEPs.

For their part, Libyan government officials said they were interested in "humanitarian aid assistance, helicopters in order to rescue people in the desert, or even in the constructions of roads in the south… to facilitate the control of entry into the country".

In Tunisia, stepped-up law enforcement is said to have driven people smugglers across the border into Libyan territory, while some sub-Saharan transit migrants, driven out of Morocco and into Algeria, are bypassing Tunisia altogether and travelling deep into the Sahara to get to Libya.

Seaborne influx strains refugee convention

The concept of asylum is "a central tenet of democracy", UN High Commissioner for Refugees António Guterres said in a speech last year. Yet as seaborne mixed flows in Europe have grown, so have suspicions that exasperated governments are sometimes less than thorough in identifying genuine refugees within them.

Refugee specialists have argued that seaborne irregular migration has, to a greater extent than perhaps any other migrant flow of the post-war era, led Western states with otherwise strong humanitarian traditions to bend the spirit – some say the letter – of the 1951 refugee convention.

In 2004 and 2005, Italy was explicitly accused of breaking the convention by deporting boat migrants from Lampedusa, one of three small Italian islands between Sicily and Tunisia, without properly ascertaining whether any of them were refugees.

Box 5.2 From Africa to Spain: "strong men in flimsy boats"

"They arrive soaked to the skin, vomiting and shitty," Rubén Fernández of the Spanish Red Cross (CRE) told Spanish newspaper *El Pais* one weekend in May 2006, when more than 100 paramedics had helped nearly 400 sub-Saharan African boat migrants who'd just come ashore in the Spanish Canary Island of Tenerife.

"The first thing is to give them a change of clothes and a blanket." Next, injuries. "They have abrasions because of the saltiness of the water. They're seasick, dehydrated and sometimes weak from hunger. But in just 15 minutes, they're fine again. Of this 400, we only had to send four or five to hospital with severe dehydration."

"The sub-Saharan migrants are very strong," added CRE coordinator Juan Antonio Corujo. But the *cayucos* they sail in from Mauritania and Senegal – a kind of flat-hulled African fishing canoe, bigger than the *pateras* used on the Western Sahara run – "are really very flimsy".

"And they come in complete silence," Corujo said. "They're very reluctant to speak initially, but we gradually win their trust and they tell us how tough the sea crossing was, how they have tried before from Morocco, how they left home two years ago.

"Each *cayuco* has its own story. And not all the migrants come from coastal African states. Many of them started their journey in Central Africa years ago."

On 18 May 2006, the arrival in Tenerife of nine open boats carrying between them almost 650 people beat the previous single-day record for the Canaries by nearly 200.

In March, *The Washington Post* told the story of Magat Jope, 34, "an electrician and a polite father of two" from Senegal, who borrowed US$ 1,100 from his mother and travelled to Mauritania to get on a migrant boat to the Canary Islands.

After four days of seasickness and "constant bailing", the leaky *cayuco* was intercepted by the Moroccan coastguard and towed back to Nouadhibou, Mauritania's northernmost port about 800 kilometres from the Canary Islands. Some of his fellow passengers swam ashore and fled, to avoid being repatriated.

Jope later heard other friends had drowned when their boat carrying nearly 30 people sank at night. "Death on the water", as *Washington Post* correspondent Kevin Sullivan put it, kept the gravediggers of Nouadhibou busy early this year.

Throughout 2005, unreported and almost unnoticed by anyone but locally based agencies, sub-Saharan African migrants (later followed by the international media) streamed into the port, by tradition an open and cosmopolitan town, boosting its population from around 90,000 to 100,000. Exactly why the flow of migrants transiting Mauritania increased is not clear, but the tightening of borders by Morocco and Algeria must have played a part.

Stories of tragedy on the high seas soon began to abound.

Mauritania's only search and rescue patrol boat found a *cayuco* which had apparently set sail from Saint-Louis, Senegal, some 600 kilometres even further to the south. It had been at sea for two weeks. Of the more than 40 people on board, half were dead.

Father Jerome Otitoyomi Dukiya remembers it was early last year when an excited young man rushed into his office with the news that a group had made it "all the way to Las Palmas" in a *cayuco*. The Nigerian missionary, who has worked in Nouadhibou for four years, is well placed to evaluate the scale of the humanitari-

International Federation
of Red Cross and Red Crescent Societies

an crisis surrounding irregular migration. He says no one can give precise figures, "but there is always information", he said.

"The first thing they do is try to contact someone to say they've arrived," he says. "And then it becomes the talk of the town. [Likewise when they *don't* arrive.] It's very dangerous, very risky. Do you realize how many people we've lost?"

The Mauritanian Red Crescent's Ahmedou Ould Haye, using information from a variety of sources, including Spanish ones, estimated that more than 1,200 migrants had died at sea in the six months from November 2005.

But there's no way of knowing exactly how many African boat migrants to the Canaries have been lost at sea. The condition of those who arrive, and the stories they tell, must lend credence to reports that one boat in three doesn't make it. Father Jerome, frustrated that by its very nature this disaster cannot be measured properly, says the true numbers could be much worse. "I think it could be 30 per cent who do make it," he says.

On land, the Spanish Red Cross and the Nouadhibou branch of the Mauritanian Red Crescent established a humanitarian assistance programme for migrants detained by the local authorities in a newly built centre. "Many of them have survived mishaps at sea," said Jaime Bará Viñas, head of the Africa unit of the Spanish Red Cross who was in Mauritania early this year.

Three Spanish delegates and 15 Red Crescent volunteers provided water and hot food, medical care, blankets, hygiene kits, clothes and free telephone calls. When asked if they risked creating a 'pull factor', Bará Viñas replies: "These people are not *delincuentes*. Many of them are just young people, between 15 and 45, looking for a better future. Some are selected by their own community to make the dangerous voyage."

"The origin of this migration is complex," Bará argues, "but its origins must be addressed through a developmental approach, creating job opportunities, providing training, education, basic services to people."

The Spanish government announced in May that it had agreed *Plan África* – a diplomatic effort in at least six West African states, headquartered in Senegal, the latest jumping-off point for the Canaries, aimed at stemming the flow of irregular migrants through security measures, repatriation agreements and aid.

It will be too late for many. ■

According to Christopher Hein, Director of the Italian Refugee Council (IRC): "The Italians were engaging in mass expulsions from Lampedusa, sending people back to Libya irrespective of whether they are refugees or not." A European Parliament resolution on 14 April 2005 took the view that "collective expulsions" of migrants by Italy to Libya constituted a "violation of the [1951] principle of non-refoulement" and that the Italian authorities had "failed to meet their international obligations" under the refugee convention. There were also serious concerns about the conditions in which migrants detained on Lampedusa were being held.

Italy denied these accusations, and exactly what happened on Lampedusa – in many ways the legal, political and diplomatic epicentre of the Mediterranean boat-migrant crisis – was not independently verified. The Italian authorities consistently asserted that their actions did meet international obligations. Their defence appeared to be that some nationalities (such as Eritreans, Ethiopians, Somalis, Palestinians and Iraqis) were allowed to claim asylum if they wanted to; others, mainly Egyptians, weren't.

Since then, according to Amnesty International, Italy has been building three detention centres in Libya which, it's believed, will be used to conduct procedures to determine the status of migrants in Libya and identify refugees. Such 'offshore processing' has raised concerns among refugee and human rights organizations, while it is often pointed out that Libya is not a signatory to the 1951 refugee convention. Christopher Hein says the IRC might support the offshore asylum-processing of people in third countries but is "completely opposed to the deportation to such centres of people who have already arrived in a safe destination country."

While UNHCR does not oppose governments' rights to set migration policies, says the organization's William Spindler, "what must always be ensured is that persons in need of international protection have an effective opportunity to seek asylum and access to fair and efficient asylum procedures". Spindler adds that offshore processing "raises many question marks, from a legal, practical and logistical point of view". Any measures put in place should "not be aimed at preventing asylum seekers from reaching Europe and offshore processing should not be used as a reason for refusing to process applications in Europe."

What the Lampedusa episode seems to illustrate best is that it is unlikely that refugee organizations, human rights campaigners and EU governments facing a seaborne influx of mixed groups of migrants and refugees will ever interpret 1951 in the same way. Perhaps the least controversial thing that can be said is that the widely publicized repatriations of people who transited Lampedusa did nothing to stem the flow of boat migrants towards Italian territory. MSF's figures for the first half of 2006 for Lampedusa show, pro rata, the number of arrivals this year rising far above even 2005.

In peril on the sea

The boat-migrant crisis brings two distinct humanitarian codes into play: sanctuary on land and the maritime tradition of rescue at sea.

International maritime law, not to mention the time-honoured practice of mariners everywhere, compels ships to go to the aid of anyone in distress on the high seas. But the law offers no guidance on a key issue, in the context of seaborne mixed or refugee flows, of where people rescued at sea should be disembarked.

According to a senior official at the London-based International Maritime Organization (IMO), the mariner's code is largely being observed in the Mediterranean region, despite some well publicized (and, for shippers and insurers, expensive) wrangles over where to disembark rescued migrants. But there have also been allegations of people in distress being ignored by ships for fear of incurring delay and cost in rescuing them.

In July 2006, various amendments to both the Safety of Life at Sea (SOLAS) and Search and Rescue (SAR) conventions were coming into force. They're intended to ensure that boat migrants are assisted regardless of nationality, legal status or the circumstances in which they're found, and that ships are able to disembark survivors in a safe place. Above all, according to the IMO official, "for the first time, it will be primarily states, not just ships' masters, who have to find a safe disembarkation point for boat migrants found in their SAR areas."

But some migration specialists like Martin Baldwin-Edwards, co-founder of the Mediterranean Migration Observatory at Panteion University, Athens, believe European governments are moving towards the model of interception at sea used by the United States and Australia – an entirely different maritime concept from rescue. "In particular, Spain, with its *Sistema Integrado de Vigilancia Exterior* [a coastal network of surface radar, sensors and cameras]," says Baldwin-Edwards, "but also Italian coastal patrols and collaboration with Libya and Egypt."

There are no explicit allegations, however, that either the Spanish or Italian coastguards are plucking people off migrant boats at sea and returning them directly to countries of embarkation without transiting EU soil. This is a key humanitarian and political threshold which it appears has not yet been crossed by EU states.

Seaborne interception (or interdiction) of migrants, in the sense of swiftly returning boat people to the country from which they sailed, has been practised by the US coastguard since 1980, mainly in the Caribbean. Australia, especially since 2001 and the *Tampa* incident, has been a "trailblazer in policies on interception at sea, particularly in terms of… regional processing agreements and deterrence policies," according to a January 2006 report by the Migration Policy Institute (MPI), a Washington DC-based independent think tank.

The inevitably cursory asylum procedures available on coastguard vessels make interception, especially in international waters, a highly controversial issue. According to MPI, all migrants intercepted by the US coastguard in the Caribbean (except Cubans and Chinese, who are subject to special rules), including the largest group, Haitians, are only given an on-board 'credible-fear interview' if they spontaneously show they are afraid to return once the ship changes course. This has been dubbed the 'shout test'.

According to MPI, it is still too early to tell if interception at sea is leading to a "rejection of the concept of territorial asylum on which the international refugee system is currently based [but] profound concerns about refoulement, deterrence and discrimination need close examination."

In the short term, however, maritime options – such as increased coastal patrolling (whether of sending or receiving countries) – are not the solution to the problem of boat migrants dying at sea. While the possibility of interception might deter some migrants and assist states to control borders, it would be unlikely to reduce the death toll significantly, particularly in the Canary Islands region. The Spanish organization APDHA has produced figures for losses at sea in 2004 which show that some of the most dangerous moments in irregular voyages come shortly after casting off in shallow inshore waters and during interception on the high seas by coastguard cutters too large for the task.

EU migration policy to blame?

APDHA blames the human tragedy of irregular boat migration on what it calls the EU's *política de cierre de fronteras* (closed-border policy).

"We have to send a clear signal that there are other ways to reach Europe," says the Italian Refugee Council's Christopher Hein. "There also has to be the possibility of remaining in a third country under humane conditions while you wait for the chance to come to the EU as a migrant worker."

An African would-be immigrant holds on to a makeshift boat he was in which capsized during a rescue operation at sea off the coast of Fuerteventura, 12 November 2004.

© REUTERS/Juan Medina, courtesy www.alertnet.org

International Federation of Red Cross and Red Crescent Societies

In a speech in 2004, UN Secretary-General Kofi Annan said Europe's populations are getting smaller and older and argued that without immigration "your economies would shrink and your societies could stagnate... I would therefore encourage European states to open up greater avenues for legal migration – for skilled and unskilled workers, for family reunification and economic improvement, for temporary and permanent immigrants."

But Europe's dilemma is that for immigration to offset the EU's growing demographic crisis (in countries like Germany, for example), it would have to rise beyond what seems to be politically acceptable.

Even as things stand, during the period that the Mediterranean boat-migrant crisis reached its initial peak, from the late 1990s until 2004, the "net inflow of [legal] international migrants" to the EU rose from just under 0.5 million to nearly 2 million a year, according to preliminary statistics for 2005 issued by Eurostat in January 2006. Spain, Italy, the UK and Germany – respectively the two countries most irregular boat migrants arrive in and the two many say they want to go on to – were most receptive to legal migrants (not necessarily sub-Saharan Africans), between them accounting for 76 per cent of all inward migration into the EU in 2005.

In Spain, the estimated number of international migrants leapt from just over a million in 1995 to nearly 4.8 million in 2005, or 11.1 per cent of the population, according to UN figures. Italy hosted nearly 1.5 million international migrants in 1995 and more than 2.5 million in 2005. Just over 7 per cent of the Irish population were international migrants in 1995, rising to 14 per cent a decade later.

So while opening up legal channels for economic migration still further would self-evidently benefit successful applicants, it does not seem likely this would lure migrants away from smugglers. It is arguable that it's precisely the recent huge expansion in primary immigration into, above all, Spain and Italy, that has increased the flow of irregular migrants.

Joanne van Selm, a migration specialist affiliated with the University of Amsterdam and a co-author of the 2006 MPI report, argues that those migrants not qualifying even for wider categories of legal entry would still continue to find their own way into Europe illegally. She adds that: "It's most unlikely that either governments or employers will admit to needing unskilled workers who come from situations of abject poverty and often widespread violence, famine and disease, and who are unlikely to return home without some sort of miracle in Africa.

"This is one of the most pertinent humanitarian issues in the story of irregular migration to Europe. If people cannot survive in Africa but also cannot make it in Europe as workers, they are truly stuck."

Helene Lackenbauer, the International Federation's specialist on migration issues, argues that sub-Saharan Africans have not really benefited from increased migration into the EU. "Rich countries still hand-pick migrants," says Lackenbauer, "consciously only taking, say, IT professionals from India, medical personnel from Africa, tradesmen from EU accession states, rather than the unskilled irregular migrants who actually prop up entire sectors like agriculture, building and catering in some countries – and for lower wages than they would get if their status was regularized."

She would like to see more labour programmes targeting underemployed workers from the countries providing most of the Mediterranean's boat migrants. "Then they could apply for a work permit, rather than risk their lives crossing the Mediterranean in unseaworthy boats. This would also guarantee that their basic rights in immigration countries would be honoured."

Action against smugglers

Boat migration is dauntingly complex in its political and legal dimensions. Many experts argue that Africa is already losing far more skilled and professional people to the North than it can afford to, and that emigration is actually damaging the continent's chances of successful development; that is, it more than cancels out the case for 'development by remittance'.

But the issue's humanitarian core is simple: if people set sail in vessels that are not seaworthy, a proportion of them will die. Can anything be done within existing humanitarian norms to mitigate this neglected crisis?

One short-term answer to people-smuggling might be the same as the response to human trafficking, its more vicious criminal sibling: action against smugglers. This does not mean increased coastal security in receiving countries (the so-called militarization of the EU's outer borders) or interception (turning vessels back on the high seas). Patrol boats are not the answer. Still less should it rely on the indiscriminate mass deportation of migrants from or to transit countries like Morocco, Mauritania and Libya. This could jeopardize the vital principle of non-refoulement, which states say they still want to honour.

Action against smugglers means exactly that: targeting smugglers not migrants. This means better land-based policing of beaches and ports in sending countries and a purge of corrupt officials. News reports in March said control of Mauritania's beaches had to be transferred from the police to the country's gendarmerie after the former were found charging migrants nearly US$ 600 a head to turn a blind eye to small-boat departures.

Measures against the logistics of smuggling could be introduced or toughened: more rigorous checks on wholesale importers of outboard motors, for instance. Journalists have noticed that confiscated outboards in the Canary Islands sometimes bear consecutive serial numbers, suggesting bulk imports that would be difficult without the connivance of corrupt officials. The *Guardia Civil* car park in the Fuerteventura capital, Puerto del Rosario, has been turned into a graveyard for confiscated outboards – hundreds of them, in row upon identical row, together representing a multimillion-dollar turnover for the smugglers.

However, some legal experts have sounded a note of caution. They point out that it would be a breach of the 1951 convention to prevent would-be refugees from seeking sanctuary across an international border – even, provided certain conditions are met, with the aid of smugglers. While the great majority of migrants waiting to board boats to Europe are not seeking asylum, it would be important to ensure that measures to tackle smuggling do not prevent people from fleeing a well-founded fear of persecution.

António Guterres, in a speech late last year, described the balance that needs to be struck by states, which should "act forcefully to eliminate the smuggling and trafficking of human beings and severely punish the profiteers. But guarding borders must not prevent physical access to asylum procedures or fair refugee status determination for those entitled to it by international law. A tough and uncompromising crackdown on abhorrent criminals must go hand-in-hand with a humanistic concern to protect their needy victims."

Local heroes: sharing information, meeting needs

When Jean-Philippe Chauzy of the International Organization for Migration (IOM) travelled to Oujda, Morocco, late last year to visit stranded Malians, he found they had been unaware of the risks they would be taking. "In the desert, we were abandoned by smugglers and robbed of all our belongings," 38-year-old Bourama from Bamako told Chauzy. "We only survived thanks to the generosity of local shepherds who provided us with food and water."

According to Barbara Harrell-Bond, professor of forced migration and refugee studies at the American University in Cairo and founder of the Refugee Studies Centre in Oxford: "One thing that does not happen now is any serious effort to communicate through the media in Africa about the loss of life at sea, in particular, including lists of nationalities or even names of the dead.

"In the African media, the only messages impoverished, desperate people get about the West is through advertisements or false information sent back by migrants and refugees who have made it there."

One vital task is to gather information about the Mediterranean boat crisis and produce a reasonably accurate regional death toll. Much of the work is already being done on local initiative – it just needs to be collated at international level, disseminated and publicized. Credible public information campaigns about the risks of illegal boat migration could then be undertaken in sub-Saharan source countries. This would most likely be a role for governments. Organized gangs of people smugglers will not take kindly to having vulnerable and possibly gullible clients seduced out of their clutches by well-meaning aid workers.

So what options are available for humanitarian organizations keen to reduce the suffering of irregular migrants? Mario Musa, deputy head of the International Committee of the Red Cross's regional delegation in Tunis, has this advice: "Given the involvement of organized crime in smuggling, the best time for National Societies to address the needs of vulnerable migrants seems to be once their journey has failed and they are retained by the authorities in the process of being repatriated."

Or once they're dead. Musa points out that National Red Cross and Red Crescent Societies could also help confirm the fate of the thousands of migrants who never arrive.

Further afield, trained volunteers from the Canadian Red Cross Society regularly monitor the situation of foreigners, especially Chinese boat people, detained under Canadian immigration laws. "This is part of our humanitarian mandate and has been recognized as such by the Canadian government," said the society's Johanna Hökeberg in an interview in early 2006, adding: "We consider these detainees a particularly vulnerable group in need of protection."

The Australian Red Cross visits government detention centres to help detained migrants communicate with their families through Red Cross messages, as well as to organize recreational activities and provide clothing, phonecards and foreign newspapers.

In December 2005, the IOM launched a new programme to help stranded migrants return home voluntarily, speaking of "a dramatic increase in demand for such help across the world, particularly during the last decade."

Conclusion: migration out of choice, not necessity

The broad picture that emerges from a study of the recent history of boat migration in the north-west Mediterranean region shows that, although it might not be their declared policy, countries like Spain and Italy – in terms of refugee rights and protection – regard the whole of the Maghreb as safe (including, most controversially,

Libya), as well as most West African source countries. But the region's mixed flows include people fleeing from more dangerous situations in the Horn of Africa, the Middle East and South Asia.

While tougher action against criminal people smugglers would appear to be one realistic short-term option to reduce the numbers of unnecessary deaths at sea, any attempt to prevent the departure of irregular migrants on dangerous sea voyages from transit states immediately raises the issue of what should happen to the refugees who might be among them.

There is a possible conflict here between the physical safety of migrants and the rights of asylum seekers. It is a dilemma for humanitarians; one to which there isn't even a difficult answer, let alone an easy one. Nevertheless, there remains an urgent need for humanitarian organizations to ensure that migrants are treated legally and humanely wherever they find themselves detained by authorities.

The long-term answer to this grievous humanitarian problem, which surely has as much to do with globalization and the expectations it raises as anything else, is "here", according to the secretary general of the Tunisian Red Crescent, Tahar Cheniti. "It's not enough just to see this as a security issue for EU states," he argues. "We have to find a global approach."

Unlike its sub-Saharan neighbours, Tunisia enjoys a surplus of highly educated people and the country would undoubtedly benefit from expanded EU managed-migration programmes. But that wouldn't help the poorly educated and often unemployed young men of which Tunisia also has a surplus and who often find themselves behind barbed wire "on the other side", as Cheniti puts it. "We must do much more for them," he insists, "and give them a reason to stay."

In the words of the first "principle for action" of the 2005 Global Commission on International Migration: "Women, men and children should be able to realize their potential, meet their needs, exercise their human rights and fulfil their aspirations in their country of origin, and hence migrate out of choice, rather than necessity."

Principal contributor to this chapter and Boxes is Alex Wynter, a UK-based journalist, who edits The Bridge, *the International Federation's magazine for Europe. We would like to acknowledge the assistance and advice of Joanne van Selm, a migration specialist affiliated with the University of Amsterdam and the Migration Policy Institute, a Washington DC-based independent think tank, and Professor James C. Hathaway of the University of Michigan Law School, Ann Arbor, USA.*

CHAPTER 5

Sources and further information

Amnesty International. *Italy: Temporary Stay – Permanent Rights.* London: June 2005. Available at http://web.amnesty.org/library/index/engeur300042005

Amnesty International. *Spain: the Southern Border.* London: June 2005. Available at http://web.amnesty.org/library/index/engeur410082005

Asociación Pro Derechos Humanos de Andalucía. *Informe sobre la inmigración clandestina durante el año 2005.* Seville: APDHA, January 2006.

Asociación Pro Derechos Humanos de Andalucía. *Informe violaciones de los derechos humanos en Marruecos.* Seville: APDHA, October 2005.

Baldwin-Edwards, M. *Between a Rock and a Hard Place: North Africa as a region of emigration, immigration and transit migration.* Athens: 2006.

Bowcott, O. '4,000 refugees believed drowned at sea every year', *The Guardian*, 9 October 2004. Available at http://www.guardian.co.uk/international/story/0,,1323294,00.html

Cooper, B. and van Selm, J. *The New "Boat People", Ensuring Safety and Determining Status.* Washington DC: Migration Policy Institute, January 2006.

Corsini, V. and Lanzieri, G. *First demographic estimates for 2005.* Luxembourg: Eurostat, January 2006.

Delicato, V. *National Legislation and Good Practices in the Fight Against Illegal Immigration, the Italian Model.* Rome: Interior Ministry, October 2004.

European Commission. *Technical Mission to Libya on Illegal Immigration 27 November–6 December 2004.* Brussels: EC, 2004.

European Commission. *Visit to Ceuta and Melilla – Mission Report. Technical mission to Morocco on illegal immigration 7 October–11 October 2005.* Brussels: EC, October 2005.

European Parliament, Directorate General – External Policies Human Rights Unit. *Report on the visit of an ad hoc delegation to Tripoli, Libya on 4 to 6 December 2005.*

Global Commission on International Migration. *Migration in an Interconnected World.* Geneva: GCIM, October 2005. Available at http://www.gcim.org/attachements/gcim-complete-report-2005.pdf

International Maritime Organization. *Unsafe Practices Associated with the Trafficking or Transport of Migrants by Sea (First biannual report).* London: IMO, 31 January 2006.

International Organization for Migration. *World Migration 2005.* Geneva: IOM, 2005.

Lutterbeck, D. *Policing Migration in the Mediterranean.* Mediterranean Politics, Vol. 11, No. 1, pp. 59–82. Oxford: Routledge, March 2006.

Manuel Pardellas, J. '45 organizaciones mafiosas controlan el tráfico illegal de personas desde 15 asentamientos', *El Pais*, 8 March 2006.

Médicos Sin Fronteras (MSF). *Violencia e inmigración, Informe sobre la inmigración de origen subsahariano (ISS) en situación irregular en Marruecos.* Barcelona: MSF, September 2005.

Organisation for Economic Co-operation and Development (OECD). *Migration, Remittances and Development.* Paris: OECD, 2005.

Pugh, M. 'Drowning not Waving: Boat People and Humanitarianism at Sea' in *Journal of Refugee Studies*, Vol. 17, No. 1. Oxford University Press, 2004.

Pugh, M. *Europe's boat people: maritime cooperation in the Mediterranean.* Brussels: Institute for Security Studies of the Western European Union, July 2000.

Rennie, D. 'Death stalks boat people of the Canaries', *The Daily Telegraph*, 18 March 2006. Available at http://www.telegraph.co.uk/news/main.jhtml?xml=/news/2006/03/18/wcanaries18.xml

Tattersall, N. *European trawlers threaten Mauritania's fishermen*, The Associated Press, 10 April 2006. Available at http://www.localnewsleader.com/elytimes/stories/index.php?action= fullnews&id=173348

Web sites

Amnesty International **http://www.amnesty.org**
Asociación Pro Derechos Humanos de Andalucía **http://www.apdha.org**
BBC News **http://news.bbc.co.uk**
European Commission **http://europa.eu.int/comm/index_en.htm**
Eurostat **http://epp.eurostat.cec.eu.int**
Forced Migration Review **http://www.fmreview.org**
International Maritime Organization **http://www.imo.org/home.asp**
International Organization for Migration **http://www.iom.int**
Médicos Sin Fronteras **http://www.msf.es**
Migration Policy Institute **http://www.migrationpolicy.org**
Spanish Red Cross **http://www.cruzroja.es**
UN High Commissioner for Refugees **http://www.unhcr.org**

International Federation
of Red Cross and Red Crescent Societies

"Please don't raise gender now – we're in an emergency!"

Faced with a major disaster, some argue that attending to gender concerns is a luxury that must wait until more important matters have been addressed. Yet evidence shows that the failure to address gender-based inequalities immediately after disaster and throughout the response can condemn women and girls to less aid, fewer life opportunities, ill health, violence and even death. This chapter challenges the 'tyranny of the urgent', which leads to the neglect of gender before, during and after disaster – drawing on fieldwork from three continents.

Analysis of the impact of recent disasters reveals that women suffer disproportionately. However, this chapter also explores gender issues relating to men and boys in disasters, as well as the often neglected resilience of women in the face of crisis. Moving beyond a beneficiary model of disaster response, the chapter argues that, in order to reduce future risks, aid organizations must adopt a rights-based approach to address the causes of social vulnerability which are rooted in gender inequality.

Multiple identities of women

All women and men have multiple identities and a simple categorization along one axis of perceived vulnerability or capacity (e.g., gender) can be misleading. Nevertheless, there is sufficient evidence to say that in disasters, as in everyday life, women and girls across the world experience greater discrimination than men and boys, and are more likely to have their needs and contributions ignored or undervalued.

Gender inequality can be subtle or explicit. It can mean more women die in disasters than men. Last year's *World Disasters Report* related how 3,972 women died when the Indian Ocean tsunami hit Ampara, Sri Lanka, compared with 2,124 men. In the Bangladesh cyclone of 1991, 71 women per 1,000 died compared with 15 men per 1,000 (aged 20–44). This has been blamed on male-to-male warning systems, women not getting men's permission to evacuate and cyclone shelters not designed for women's needs.

Women who survive disasters are often worse affected than men. According to American writer Kathleen Bergin, Hurricane Katrina was "a highly racialised and gendered event" which hit African American women hardest. "More than half of the women in the city of New Orleans were single mothers, independently responsible for ensuring they and their children survived the storm," says Bergin. "These women lived in greater poverty than

Photo opposite page: Following October 2005's earthquake in Pakistan, many women from remote mountain areas were forbidden by their families from coming down to relief camps in the valleys, in case their honour was compromised. Most women could only access relief supplies through male relatives.

Arne Hodalic/
Slovenian Red Cross

men, owned fewer assets than men, had less formal education than men, and worked in less lucrative jobs than men. Women in New Orleans also comprised a majority of the elderly population, most of whom were destitute."

Consequently, African American women formed the majority of those trapped in the city or confined to mass evacuation centres as flood waters rose – exposing them to "unprecedented risk of rape and sexual assault". However, it would be wrong to characterize women as victims of Katrina – there are many examples of women acting with great ingenuity and courage (see Box 6.1).

Box 6.1 Women's networking during Katrina saves lives

On 29 August 2005, Hurricane Katrina made landfall as a category 4 hurricane in Plaquemines Parish, Louisiana, south of New Orleans on the Bird's Foot Delta that extends into the Gulf of Mexico. A month later, Hurricane Rita – a category 3 storm – lashed the same coastline.

Between them, the two storms turned around 76,000 acres of Louisiana's wetlands into open water – almost half of which was in Plaquemines Parish. Katrina resulted in around 1,300 deaths and major disruption to people's lives and livelihoods. It also had political ramifications as the poor management of the disaster challenged those in government responsible for emergency response.

Lower Plaquemines Parish, with a population of African American, Cajun French, Vietnamese, Atakapa Indian and Euro-American citizens, was swamped by a 28-foot storm surge of sea water during Hurricane Katrina and again during Rita. Communities inside and outside the levee system of dykes were destroyed. Flood waters formed a lake inside the levees for months following the storms. Although the parish was more vulnerable and exposed to the storms than more protected areas to the north, such as New Orleans, it had fewer deaths. Women's local knowledge and networking ability played a key part.

Six women in the sheriff's office – all dispatchers (telephone operators who convey information between the public and emergency workers) with no official authority – were instructed to stay at their positions during Katrina. Their supervisors (emergency operations officials) evacuated, leaving the six women on their own and unaware of any emergency plans. Concerned not to lose their jobs, these women stayed and quickly devised a spontaneous rescue plan, which they communicated to a response network of friends and family before the storm knocked out phone lines and electricity.

The women contacted communities in the more vulnerable areas and made lists of who would still be in the area during the hurricane, their strategy for survival and what resources they had to offer – such as boats, fuel, able-bodied companions and property on higher ground.

They then mapped where those staying behind would be located, along with their needs and resources. They linked possible boat drivers with available boats, keys and fuel and directed them to the neediest of the stranded people. They also instructed all boats to use radios to contact the coastguard, helping rescue crews from outside the region to locate them via their radio coordinates.

The women's local knowledge of the area, its networks and resources, along with their quick thinking and ingenuity, saved several hundred lives. ■

Gaps in measuring gender impacts

Disaster impacts on women are not consistently quantified. For example, EM-DAT (the international disasters database compiled by the Centre for Research on the Epidemiology of Disasters (CRED)) does not disaggregate by gender, as such data are rarely available, especially for the more numerous small- to medium-sized disasters.

According to Debarati Guha-Sapir, CRED's director: "Gender has not been seen as an issue in disaster prevention and preparedness, except as a blanket policy statement. Therefore, ground-level evidence on what the gender-related risks are remains unknown and so cannot be translated into concrete action. For example, the CRED/ISDR [the United Nations International Strategy for Disaster Reduction] epidemiological study in Tamil Nadu on the victims of the tsunami show age and gender patterns that could have useful insights for disaster preparedness, but studies like these are few and far between. So right now, we all agree that gender is a significant issue in disaster, but we can say practically nothing quantitatively about its patterns or magnitude."

In order to protect people's lives, livelihoods and dignity in emergencies, it is important to recognize their particular identities and cultural contexts. Gender-based inequalities, combined with ethnicity, age and class, lead to great differences in women's experiences in disasters. While humanitarian workers seem increasingly aware of gender issues, research suggests many of them do not know concretely what this means.

The 2003 annual review of the Active Learning Network for Accountability and Performance in Humanitarian Action (ALNAP) reports that, overall, the promotion of gender equality by humanitarian organizations is variable or poor. Analysing 127 evaluations of humanitarian action (2000–2003), ALNAP says the evaluation of gender equality was unsatisfactory in 73 per cent of cases. The review points to major gaps in training and gender mainstreaming that need to be addressed.

However, there have been some advances by international agencies (including United Nations Development Programme (UNDP), World Food Programme (WFP), Food and Agriculture Organization (FAO), Inter-Agency Standing Committee (IASC) and the International Red Cross and Red Crescent Movement), which have recently developed policies and tools for gender mainstreaming.

Women's multiple roles

Typically, women are seen as being located mainly in the home. But researchers have identified at least three types of women's activity:

■ **Reproductive role:** household, domestic, childbearing, family health.

- **Productive role:** earning benefits in cash or in kind.
- **Community role:** contributing to community well-being – in this context, focusing on women's roles in disaster response.

Disasters and their aftermath impact on all three. This simple conceptualization gives structure to the material which follows. However, referring to roles can make women's and men's lives seem static, when in reality they are dynamic and influenced by complex gender power relations.

Women's reproductive role

During disasters, women predominantly carry out their normal, socially assigned roles. They hold their families together in the basic conditions offered by temporary shelters, often managing with little support.

Women are at the biological and social centre of family life and, in many cultures, they embody the family honour. Some are chaperoned when going outside and protected from outsiders even when inside the home. Inevitably, this can restrict their access to disaster relief, so specific procedures must be in place to offset gaps in delivering aid.

In Pakistan, women from remote mountain areas were trapped in wrecked houses because they feared (or were forbidden from) coming down to relief camps in the valleys. *Dawn* newspaper reported the views of two (male) survivors from Shangla district, in November 2005: "We are Pukhtun people," said Abdul Hameed, who left his mother, wife and sister in the mountains. "For us, the woman's honour matters more than life."

Because they are often confined to the home, women and girls are particularly at risk from death and injury when buildings collapse. In the 1993 earthquake in Maharashtra, India, more women were crushed in their homes than men, who worked or slept outside. This is one reason why women and their particular needs must be included in the planning and reconstruction of damaged homes.

Despite being closely associated with the home, women often lack rights to land, tenancies and other property. When husbands died in the Pakistan earthquake, their land went to the eldest son – even though the late owner's wife had occupied and worked it. Meanwhile, in drought-stricken Kenya, Maasai women have to negotiate their right to cultivate family land, putting household food security at risk (see Box 6.2).

While looking after children is seen as a primary concern of women, the tsunami and Katrina left many children separated from their families (2,430 children after

Box 6.2 Maasai women's role in reducing vulnerability to drought neglected

Loitokitok is a sub-district in southern Kenya which lies near the foot of Mount Kilimanjaro. Populated by traditionally semi-nomadic Maasai people, the more arid parts of Loitokitok have, since the 1950s, experienced increasing temperatures, droughts and rainfall variability. The Maasai's pastoralist livelihoods – based mainly around cattle – have also become increasingly constricted by the demarcation of grazing lands for cultivation and wildlife conservation.

In response, the Maasai are reducing their reliance on keeping livestock and embracing crop farming and new herding strategies. Such livelihood diversification has important implications for gender roles and relations.

Historically, crop farming among the Maasai has been used to recover from drought, but following the severe drought of 1984 it became a more permanent form of land use in Loitokitok. Crop farming is predominantly for cash and is becoming dominated by men. As a result, women are now more involved in livestock production, which was once the preserve of men.

The new divisions of labour have an impact on the role women play in managing household food security in this semi-arid zone. Women grow food which is intercropped with men's cash crops on irrigated fields near their homesteads. But although women's crops provide a critical (if small) source of nourishment for the family during droughts, their share of irrigated land is extremely low. This is because priority goes to men's cash crops and women only gain cultivation rights on family land through their husbands. The important role that women's food crops play in drought conditions is not widely recognized.

Meanwhile, Maasai women still have to maintain the health of their families' livestock and ensure a sufficient milk supply for their children. During droughts and extended dry periods, women have to work much harder to care for the livestock. They must gather high-quality fodder from acacia trees for their sheep and goats, as well as a variety of plants from the swamps and forests for their cattle. On the lower slopes of Mount Kilimanjaro and in Loitokitok's swampy areas, many families feed high milk-yielding cattle in stalls. This means more work for the women, who must gather and deliver fodder and water to the cattle stalls.

Across this area, women are working significantly harder than men in livestock production – but this hasn't been recognized by practitioners in government and development organizations who perpetuate the stereotype that Maasai pastoralism is a predominantly male activity. Recognizing and reinforcing the role played by pastoral women is critical to understanding how the Maasai strengthen the resilience of their livelihoods in the face of greater climate variability and drought.

As livelihoods diversify, the dynamics of vulnerability also change. So organizations intervening in arid and semi-arid areas must ensure that their activities are participatory, instead of being based on outdated assumptions. Recognizing women's roles will only prove productive if this is combined with an active incorporation of women's voices in intervention policies.

In the context of Loitokitok, this would require seeking out women in their own spaces and meeting with them at times convenient for them. However, meetings are mostly held at times of day when only men can attend. Donors, non-governmental organizations (NGOs) and policymakers should pay more attention to the important role that women's crop and livestock production activities play in reducing vulnerability to drought in pastoral communities. ■

Katrina). This has untold psychological effects on family members, while raising serious protection issues.

Women can be at risk throughout their life: from sexual abuse, trafficking or loss of education (when young); from forced marriages, nutritional deficits and birth complications (when childbearing); and from poverty, neglect or abandonment (when elderly). At any time, they may be vulnerable to violence, honour killings or punishment.

Mother/child health neglected during disasters

In November 2005, just a month after the earthquake, the United Nations Population Fund (UNFPA) estimated 17,000 disaster-affected women in Pakistan would give birth in the next few months. Around 1,200 would face major complications and 400 would require surgery. Yet there was a critical lack of female doctors and health workers. Women from conservative areas sought professional care as a last resort, mainly because modesty and family honour prevented them from consulting male doctors.

From March 2006, temporary camps began to close, leaving many pregnant Pakistani women with long, difficult journeys home. Basic reproductive health services are not available in most of the areas to which they have been returning. Lady health workers (LHWs) traditionally provide primary healthcare in remote mountain communities. They normally operate from their homes, but the earthquake destroyed their houses and threatened this vital service. Some agencies have provided support: the Pakistan Red Crescent Society (PRCS) supplied LHWs with tents and supplies for 200 new health posts in affected areas. In some cases, this means people are getting better healthcare than before the quake.

After giving birth, breastfeeding women provide a vital, safe food supply for their young children. Transferring to formula feeding during disaster greatly increases the risk of child morbidity and mortality, as the water which must be added to make up the formula may be contaminated. Signatories to the 1990 Innocenti Declaration on the Protection, Promotion and Support of Breastfeeding (including UN agencies and governments) have estimated that during emergencies, child illness and death rates can increase 20 times due to increased exposure to infections and inadequate feeding and care.

Promoting breastfeeding before and after disaster, especially floods and earthquakes, is a fundamental part of disaster management, yet how often is it included in emergency plans? It is important to train aid workers to assist mothers in breastfeeding, as their infants are at the greatest risk. This may also be the case in crises where transmission of HIV/AIDS is a risk. Current UN infant feeding guidelines say: "When replacement feeding is acceptable, feasible, affordable, sustainable and safe, avoidance of all breastfeeding by HIV-positive mothers is recommended; otherwise, exclusive breastfeeding is recommended during the first months of life."

Men's psychological health neglected

The stereotypical expectation of men to 'be strong' means that their specific health needs during disasters have not been widely recognised. Men's psychosocial needs go untreated because of cultural norms, which inhibit men from expressing pain, fear or their own perceived inadequacy to fulfil their traditional role as family provider. Feminized care-giving systems disadvantage men, as they often don't speak to women about their problems.

After the 1990 Towyn floods in Wales, UK, men seemed to cope initially and then, sometimes years later, sought help from doctors for stress-related symptoms associated with the flooding. Humanitarian workers can overestimate men's emotional strength; men and boys may need gender-sensitive support to deal with trauma, loss and the challenges of recovery.

In the absence of culturally acceptable support, men can resort to destructive forms of 'coping', which are well documented by researchers, such as substance abuse and physical aggression, and which put themselves and the women around them at risk of harm.

The tsunami aftermath amply demonstrated this. According to a report on the situation in Sri Lanka, published in 2006 by Amnesty International: "Many men displaced by the conflict and tsunami are unemployed and traumatized, which is resulting in higher levels of alcohol abuse and violence." This problem may have inadvertently been fuelled by the generous aid response, whether in cash or in kind. "NGOs told Amnesty International that growing incidences of domestic violence among tsunami IDPs are partly due to the fact that the financial support is given to the male household heads and can easily be spent on alcohol, as well as the fact that many relief items can be easily sold and the money spent on alcohol." However, a UN Office for the Coordination of Humanitarian Affairs (OCHA) situation report from early 2006 noted an increase in alcohol abuse among women and children in Sri Lanka – not just men.

Many men who have lost wives during disaster lack the domestic skills to cope and have struggled to rebuild family life, says Sri Lankan gender and disaster specialist Madhavi Malalgoda Ariyabandu. In traditional societies, it is unusual – even socially unacceptable – for men to do household work or live in close proximity to their daughters. Some men widowed by the earthquake in Pakistan said they wanted to remarry soon to ensure they had a chaperone for their young children. They suggested that an organization could help them remarry women who had lost their husbands and children in the earthquake.

Gender-based violence

Humanitarian crises can be a trigger or cover for violence towards women and children. In conflicts, women and girls are increasingly being trafficked, forced into prostitution or sexual slavery, and used as weapons against the enemy.

Violence in the home can be attributed to the increased stress of disaster pushing people beyond what they can cope with – although disasters may simply reveal underlying power relations that existed before. Gender-based violence during disaster is under-researched, although the body of evidence is growing. Reports of domestic violence have increased after major storms in the United States, Canada, Latin America, Australia and New Zealand – as well as after the tsunami.

Meanwhile, disturbing evidence of sexual abuse in UN peacekeeping missions emerged after Sarah Martin, an expert on the subject at Refugees International, conducted investigations in Haiti and Liberia in 2005. "Since the bulk of personnel in peacekeeping missions are men, a hyper-masculine culture that encourages sexual exploitation and abuse and a tradition of silence have evolved within them," she said. Who will protect people from the protectors?

In Pakistan after the earthquake, honour killings remain a threat. Farida Shaheed, coordinator of Pakistan's Shirkat Gah women's collective, reported the case of one woman who was forced to provide sexual favours in return for aid; but nobody would discuss it openly because to do so could result in the woman's death.

Women's productive role

Damaged homes can mean damaged workspaces. For many women whose income is based in the home, destroyed housing means a loss of workspace, as well a loss of tools, equipment, stock and markets. While working at home provides significant household benefits, it is often not recorded in the same way as formal employment. So women may not be fully compensated after disasters.

Opportunities for employment outside the home vary around the world, but are often fewer for women than men. And competing demands in the wake of disaster may lead women to lose such jobs. In San Alfonso, a Salvadorean community hit by Hurricane Stan in October 2005, one mother said: "Here we had women who lost their jobs washing and ironing for others because they had to stay at home and tend their children. The employers didn't understand. Three days of not showing up for work is cause for termination. Women said: 'I don't care about the job, I don't want to lose my children'."

The specific impacts of disasters on women and girls are not routinely assessed, which can lead to their needs and priorities being neglected. Nor are women always victims of disaster – their roles in networking and organizing for disaster response are often overlooked.

Marko Kokic/
International Federation

In Pakistan, none of the women interviewed in a rapid assessment by the International Federation of Red Cross and Red Crescent Societies claimed to have undertaken paid work before the earthquake. Nor had they been encouraged to take part in cash for work promoted by some international non-governmental organizations (INGOs). Many said they'd be happy to help remove rubble, with or without men, if paid in cash. As plastering mud houses is traditionally women's work, they were willing to help with reconstruction.

Some Pakistani women did find work. In tent villages in Balakot, the International Labour Organization (ILO) employed women to be responsible for cleanliness. This was a rare opportunity, regarded as acceptable because it replicated the type of work they would normally do in the home. ILO also initiated a quilt-making enterprise, encouraging women to cut up piles of unsuitable donated clothes (which were being burned to keep warm) and sew the pieces into quilts. This was so successful, the women started to receive orders.

In Muzaffarabad, Pakistan, after her daughter was killed and her house destroyed by the earthquake, Shazia Noreen defied convention and built a small corrugated iron shop next to the tent where her family lived. "It is our family tradition to keep women in the house, but I'm going to change that tradition," she told Reuters news agency in January 2006. However, she did so with her husband's permission. As one Islamic scholar in Muzaffarabad said, a woman was free to work – as long as her husband, brothers or father had no objections and she covered her face and body.

Just a few weeks after the 2001 earthquake in Gujarat, India, women began returning to work inside makeshift shelters, stitching together canvas bags and embroidering linen. "If they don't start again then what are they going to eat in future?" asked one woman textile worker. But while Gujarati women worked, most men lost their livelihoods. "After the earthquake, the men of the family stopped working," said one woman. "The men are all in trauma."

There are similar reports from Sri Lanka. Madhavi Malalgoda Ariyabandu, visiting a camp in Hambantota a year after the tsunami, found numerous women who had started tailoring, trading vegetables or making food packets for sale, while still living in temporary shelters. But the men sat passively in the camp common room, making comments such as: "So many agencies and teams of people come and go promising to give various things, that we are waiting for their return," or: "For labour work one has to go very far, and we cannot do that."

Disasters can destroy access to markets. A group of 25 women traders from inland villages were caught in the tsunami while attending the Sunday market in Hambantota, which borders the coast. Subsequently, they were too traumatized to return to the market. When the market moved to a new location, these women lost their places and nearby markets refused to accommodate them. Securing a place in a regular market is extremely competitive and often depends on who you know and what you can pay.

Since these women lived inland, they couldn't access the massive amounts of relief available to coast dwellers. They received government rations, but more than a year after the disaster, they were still struggling to recover their lost livelihoods.

Women's community role

Following all disasters, formal teams are set up in camps, villages and at higher administrative levels to manage disaster response. But these often lack gender equity because:

- Socially constructed restrictions on mobility – especially regarding female safety – may prevent women from participating.
- Approval is needed from a father/husband/brother for women to engage in activities outside the immediate family.
- Responsibility for multiple roles (e.g., domestic, childcare) leaves women little time for activities outside the home or workplace.

- Officials may lack gender awareness and see no need to engage women.
- Women themselves often lack confidence to play a public role – especially in male-dominated disaster management.

These barriers hinder women's participation in formal recovery – so specific measures are necessary to include women.

Gender-aware NGOs and civil society groups have improved women's engagement in relief and recovery, but these efforts remain largely isolated and insufficient. Fieldwork in Pakistan suggested gender awareness was much more likely within NGOs, the Red Cross and Red Crescent, and UN agencies as opposed to Pakistani government organizations.

Women in Pakistan faced socially constructed barriers to receiving adequate relief supplies following the October 2005 earthquake. Farida Shaheed argues that disasters cannot be separated from the everyday. Women's pre-existing physical, environmental and social vulnerabilities – measured in terms of less education, less access to economic resources, fewer social assets and skills with no market value – underpinned how they fared during and after the earthquake.

Women were heavily dependent on men for access to relief after the Pakistan disaster, although there were exceptions (see Box 6.3). Few women received tents or rations directly; most received them through male family members. The majority of volunteers were male, particularly in the early stages of relief, although many agencies worked hard to recruit more females after this problem was recognized. However, it was a challenge to find qualified women to work as volunteers. Women typically work in pairs if part of a male team and this meant there were often not enough women available to meet rapid assessment timetables. This problem needs to be overcome in future disasters.

A local government woman told the International Federation that when she went to the Pakistani army's distribution camp to request their support for a tented village nearby, she was told: "Bring a man, we don't talk to women." According to female respondents to the International Federation's needs assessment, some army camp managers required all widows and female-headed families to enter under the name of a male relative as head of their family.

However, this practice was not typical of all of Pakistan's governmental responses. The IRIN news service reported in December 2005 on a camp in Hattian, Punjab province, which housed nearly 300 women and children who'd lost their male family members. The shelter was set up within a week of the disaster by the Khubab Foundation, a local NGO, and the Pakistani government's Ministry of Social Welfare.

CHAPTER 6

Box 6.3 Training overcomes tradition in Pakistan quake

© Jonathan Walter, 2006

The winding mountain road from Balakot to Old Sanghar village is still scarred by landslides, six months after the earthquake that devastated northern Pakistan in October 2005. Boulders the size of buses hover above the road, halfway down their headlong plummet, waiting for the next aftershock to shake them loose. Looking up at the snow-dusted ridgelines three or four thousand metres high, it's hard to imagine the raw power of a tremor capable of moving mountains.

"I was planting garlic in the field with my children when the earth shook," says Saeeda Bibi. "I looked back and saw my house had collapsed. My husband was inside. I thought: 'Everything is finished'."

Saeeda has lived in Old Sanghar village all her life. Now aged 25, she is married with two children. In September 2005, three weeks before the earthquake, she was one of seven women and 18 men who attended a Pakistan

Red Crescent Society (PRCS) training session in community-based disaster preparedness.

For four days, Saeeda and her fellow participants learned about different types of disaster, how to prepare before the event, how to react afterwards and where to go for help.

"There was an earthquake here in Balakot in 2004," says Mufti Mansoor, the disaster management officer for the North West Frontier Province (NWFP) branch of the PRCS. "A thousand houses were damaged then. Floods and landslides are even more common. So it was clear to us that this is a disaster-prone district." By early 2005, Mufti had already laid plans to establish a disaster management cell and warehouse nearby, as well as to conduct preparedness training in eight districts at risk across the province.

Mufti encountered considerable opposition in recruiting women as well as men to his training. The mountain regions of the North West Frontier are deeply conservative. The male village elders control what goes on, discussing matters of importance by squatting in a circular jirga (council) from which women are excluded.

Once in the mountain villages, we saw almost no women outside their homes. When they do work in the fields, they are forbidden from speaking to men from neighbouring villages. Female literacy in some districts of NWFP is less than five per cent, according to the UN's IRIN news service.

"Before my training, people of the area criticized me for going to the town, alone as a woman, for training," says Saeeda. The men in Chitrali caps clustered around Saeeda nod in agreement. "They called my husband and told him to stop me," she continues, "but he said I could go."

International Federation
of Red Cross and Red Crescent Societies

Saeeda takes up her earthquake story again. Once she had found somewhere safe for her children, she saw her husband emerge unscathed from the ruins of their home. Dazed survivors began gathering on a nearby terraced field. The mountainside to which Old Sanghar clings is so sheer that the terraces are no more than two or three metres wide. "I heard that my uncle, his wife Naseema Bibi and eight-month-old child were trapped under the ruins of their collapsed home. We used farming tools and our bare hands to dig them out. Aftershocks kept shaking the ground. After five hours, we rescued them – they all survived."

Not everyone in the village shared Naseema's luck. On top of the hill lies the ruined rubble of the village school. Pages of discarded exercise books still flap in the wind. A wooden class chair is buried to the arms by severed chunks of reinforced concrete.

Of the 11 people who died in Old Sanghar when the earthquake struck, 10 were schoolchildren, aged between 5 and 15 years.

How did Saeeda react in the face of disaster? Did her training help? "After the earthquake in 2004, we didn't know what to do," she says. "But with the training I realized I had to rescue people, mobilize people. I left my home and organized other people to help."

She provided water for survivors and cleaned mud from the bodies of victims. She told villagers to get blankets and assist the injured. She helped rescue some schoolchildren and pulled out dead bodies.

Together, Saeeda and those with her saved 40–50 people from their collapsed homes. "We also learned the need for psychological support from our training," she adds, "so I asked people not to cry. I told them the disaster came from God, that it was not our fault."

For a week or ten days, no aid arrived in Old Sanghar village. With temperatures below freezing, the villagers were sleeping rough in the fields – too scared to venture back inside their homes as dozens of aftershocks shook the region. Eventually, Saeeda decided to go in search of aid herself. "I knew I had to communicate to other people what had happened," she says.

She set off on foot to raise the alarm. Once more, the whole village objected to her going to a strange town on her own. Undeterred, she trekked for five hours across landslides and past ruined houses, until she reached the Red Crescent office in Balakot. They responded by sending tarpaulin sheets, tents, blankets, kitchen sets and stoves back to her village.

We ask Saeeda how the disaster preparedness training could be improved – in the light of her experience. She requests that the women of the village be taught first aid. In many parts of the world, this is included in Red Cross/Red Crescent community disaster training. But before the earthquake struck, the PRCS simply lacked the resources: the annual community disaster preparedness budget for the whole province was just 30,000 rupees (US$ 500). Following the earthquake, that is set to change, with a month of intensive disaster management training planned for PRCS volunteers in this district alone.

Saeeda's top priority, however, is for villagers to be taught how to rebuild their homes in an earthquake-safe way, using local materials. Most of the villagers continue to live in tents, six months afterwards. "We still live in fear of another earthquake," she says, to more nods. Like the experts, Saeeda knows that it is bad buildings, not earthquakes, that kill people. And she knows that the only way she and countless thousands of other survivors across the region will sleep without fear at night is if they can rebuild safer than before. ■

In this camp, unlike many others, a school, hospital, playgrounds, community dining hall, general store and mosque were built. Some of the rooms had attached bathrooms. Security was enforced by uniformed guards who allowed no unauthorized men inside. "Unlike other camp settlements, where families tend to huddle together in scared clusters, young girls and children run freely through the area, vying for a turn on one of the swings, and women sit outside in the sunshine mending clothes or knitting," reported IRIN.

Other humanitarian organizations also made provisions for women. The international NGO ActionAid found that Pakistani women had faced harassment in camps due to a lack of private and public spaces for women. The agency constructed 20 women-friendly spaces, incorporating health services, psychosocial support, first aid and the inclusion of women in disaster preparedness. The Pakistan Red Crescent Society implemented a psychosocial support programme for women, men and children in four tent villages. Of the 31-person team, 16 were women. "We work with women because men can't," said Tapassum Naz, one of the female team members. "Women want to be involved in recovery, but they complain that men are dominant in making decisions," she said.

Absence of women in camp management

After the tsunami, Sri Lankan women were largely absent from the management teams running the camps where nearly 250,000 survivors lived.

The women inhabitants among the 100 families housed in Dharma Kabeer mosque in Hambantota lamented the lack of opportunities to express their concerns or contribute to daily management. When interviewed in May 2005, the women said they hadn't had a single opportunity to discuss their concerns, nor had any women's support groups visited them. The husband of one woman remarked: "It's alright for women to engage in recovery planning activities, to go out and take part in the meetings, because it is a crisis situation. But in normal times, it's a man's job and it will remain so."

This limited participation is mirrored at national level: the Sri Lankan Parliament Select Committee on Natural Disasters, mandated to examine disaster preparedness and mitigation, has just two women on its 22-member committee.

One major area of concern cutting across many recent disasters is the poor management of women's and girl's personal hygiene needs. A female government official from Kalutara, Sri Lanka, who was part of the district team responsible for disaster relief, admitted that – even as a woman – it took her several days to ensure sanitary supplies were included in emergency distributions. In the male-dominated world of disaster management, it takes experience and gender training to consider such issues from the start.

Meeting menstruation needs can be community, culture and class specific. Pakistani women didn't know how to use Western sanitary items. Poorer women often use washable rags rather than sanitary towels. In most cultures, menstruation is an extremely private female issue. This posed difficulties for women queuing up publicly to obtain sanitary items from mainly male relief teams. Organizations such as UNFPA, UN Children's Fund (UNICEF) and the International Federation took measures to provide appropriate female hygiene packs. But Pakistani women survivors told Tapassum Naz that, even six months after the earthquake, their most personal needs hadn't been met because of a lack of female doctors or nurses.

Meanwhile, power relations exert a strong influence over food distribution. Awareness of such family dynamics is vital if relief camps are to be managed effectively and justly. If food rations are distributed through a male householder, when traditionally women buy, grow or forage for food, it can change the power dynamics of the household, disempowering women. On the other hand, females accessing food in camps can be perceived as a threat to men's authority. If men are no longer providing what they used to provide for their family, they may fear losing the respect of others as well as their own self-respect.

The security of displaced women and children in many relief camps remains a concern. In Sri Lanka, women complained that their toilets were inadequately lit and located too close to men's toilets – they would never normally visit the toilet in the presence of unknown men.

In Pakistan, fieldwork in early 2006 by Khadim Hussain, from Islamabad's Rural Development Policy Institute, identified many tent villages with no proper security arrangements. In Muzaffarabad, the manager of the Chattar Class camp was beaten up by locals after one of the girls in his camp was abused. Although this case was never publicized, camp residents knew of similar examples which fuelled their fears for the security of women and girls.

Ismail, a tsunami survivor from Ampara, Sri Lanka, lost his wife and elder daughter in the disaster. He lived in a camp for six months with his unmarried younger daughter – but was anxious about her safety and emotional well-being when he was away queuing for relief or attending meetings. He used money provided by the government for family funerals to buy two mobile phones, so that he and his daughter could stay in contact and reassure each other.

Windows of opportunity

In Pakistan, argues Fareeha Ummar, from the Aga Khan Rural Support Project: "The earthquake was the worst kind of catastrophe, but it brought out women and girls. There are opportunities, especially in the North West Frontier Province. In these areas, women and girls had not been allowed to come out of their homes unaccompanied, even to see the sky. Since they have now lost their homes, they must come out."

Disasters, although destructive in so many ways, can open windows of opportunity for empowering women and enabling them to take an active role in building disaster-resilient communities (see Box 6.4).

During the response to Hurricane Stan, which hit El Salvador in October 2005, women gained new strength and self-esteem by being active members of the many community-based emergency preparedness committees set up by the NGO Plan El Salvador. Marisol Carmen Arevalo of La Laguna municipal civil protection committee said: "Maybe we women are not used to share our experiences but I am going to dare to share. I have a problem: my husband is not keen on me attending committee meetings and I have problems going out to assess damages, but I delivered food aid in Hurricane Stan. I was doing home visits to my neighbours despite mud going up to my knees but I realized we had to save them. Sometimes women don't know about our strength. It was us women who dared to go in the canyons, going after the victims. It was us women who took the elderly out of their houses."

Importantly, even older women – a group often seen as most vulnerable and given the least opportunities to be active – play a significant role in these committees. Christina del Carmen from El Portillo said: "As soon as I joined this project I began learning. I am an old woman but still able to learn!" During emergency and first-aid training drills, these women discovered new strengths in themselves: "I had to carry a man! I didn't know I could do it," said another female participant.

Plan adopted a rights-based approach, with a strong focus on gender and age equality, integrating risk reduction across disasters, health and environment. Over 1,200 women, men, girls and boys joined community or school emergency committees and received training from the Salvadorean Red Cross Society in disaster mitigation and preparedness. Training in gender equity and child rights produced much mutual respect between committee members and encouraged them to challenge age- and gender-based norms of behaviour.

Following the tsunami in Sri Lanka, researchers have found that many NGOs are very interested in acquiring knowledge and skills to address gender issues in recovery. To achieve this, large-scale, systematic skills development is needed by all agencies engaged in disaster response and recovery.

More gender analysis needed

In disasters, as in everyday life, men's lives tend to be understood as normal while women are seen as a 'special population'. However, women's and men's disaster experiences and needs may simply differ. For example, in research conducted by Shrader and Delaney for the World Bank in 2000, a Nicaraguan community was asked: What was the worst thing about Hurricane Mitch? Women said: fear. Men said: decreased coffee production. How can both be better understood and addressed?

A considerable body of evidence has now been amassed on the 'gendered terrain of disaster', although it is still small compared with what is known about other, more mainstream aspects of disasters.

While humanitarian organizations are increasingly practising a gender-disaggregated approach in needs assessments and other aspects of their work, there remain many instances where such a breakdown is not available. An analysis of the likely effect on gender equality of different kinds of distribution (e.g., preference for cash) is an area ALNAP regards as "ripe for investigation with primary stakeholders".

Although a number of humanitarian organizations have initiated gender-related data collection, it remains largely ad hoc and has not been incorporated into the regular programmes of national statistics offices. This is a barrier to gender-sensitive disaster project planning and evaluation.

If we are ever to know how disasters affect women and men differently, even at the most fundamental level of fatalities, then analysts must be trained to use a gender-sensitive lens. Until the quantification of gendered disaster impacts becomes a commonplace part of disaster datasets, aid organizations cannot fulfil their mandates of saving lives, reducing avoidable suffering and increasing the resilience of communities to disaster.

When gender is neglected in disaster response and risk reduction, impacts, needs and priorities are also overlooked; poverty and inequity are exacerbated; vulnerability is intensified and new categories of 'victims' are created.

The issue is fundamentally a question of rights. A UN resolution from 2002 urges governments and aid organizations to "ensure the full enjoyment by women and girls of all human rights – civil, cultural, economic, political and social, including the right to development – including in disaster reduction, response and recovery; in this context, special attention should be given to the prevention and prosecution of gender-based violence."

It is time to end the neglect of gender in disasters and ensure the rights of women to be equal partners throughout all aspects of disaster risk reduction and response.

Box 6.4 Women organize for disaster response and risk reduction

El Salvador. The women of San Alfonso know the value of community organization, after being hit by Hurricane Mitch in 1998, two earthquakes in 2001 and Hurricane Stan in October 2005. Following Stan, Teresa Rivera, a member of the community committee (formed with the help of the NGO Plan El Salvador) said: "When we faced Hurricane Mitch, it destroyed our houses. So this is the second time we've gone through this. That's why some people are struggling here. The river took their houses. They live in tin shacks near the river. In Mitch we weren't organized. We were like crazy bees after the beehive is shaken. We were improvising. After Mitch we learned to get organized. Now in Storm Stan we had that experience and all houses were evacuated in time."

While leading a discussion under a mango tree, Marta García, their leader said: "The river is a risk here. Right now it looks harmless, but the river is a traitor. The latrines collapsed, houses were damaged, we don't have drinking water and have chronic diseases." Since Stan, they have constructed a risk map which combines health and environmental data. "After the storm, we worked on our map so now we know the risk areas. We are really motivated. We are monitoring the river and we know how to evacuate safely," said García, adding: "In spite of what we've gone through, we are better organized. We work together in different sectors and we've also worked on organizing the youth. When we have an emergency we know we can count on each other. We have various committees – support, sanitation, emergency – here in San Alfonso. We know what our goal is and our purpose."

Tamil Nadu, India. Sasikala, Mari and Janaki are three women's leaders who formed self-help groups after surviving the tsunami of December 2004. A year later, when heavy rains and floods afflicted Tamil Nadu state, they found themselves wading for 15 kilometres through water a metre deep, holding hands to avoid falling into potholes, evading water snakes and creepers to provide emergency relief to the people of Poovalai, one of the worst affected villages.

They went against the advice of men who warned that nearby villages were marooned and reaching them by foot would be dangerous. But these tsunami survivors knew how to take control of their lives in the wake of disaster. "When the tsunami struck, people from outside helped us rebuild our lives. We decided it was time to act quickly and help our neighbours in whatever way we could," they said. "If we found it so difficult even to visit the villages, imagine the plight of the villagers who live there!"

The women raised money to buy food and prepared 650 food packets. The youth team and local men helped them distribute the food by boat. It became a well-coordinated relief effort which lasted several days.

Gujarat, India. Following the earthquake that shattered Kutch district, Gujarat, in 2001, Naviben Subhbhai Rajput studied low-cost earthquake-resistant technology. She rebuilt her house and convinced other villagers to follow her example and become self-reliant.

"I knew the importance of living in a safe house and was determined to know more about various training programmes. Post-earthquake, we have learnt a lot. Many people in my village have done retrofitting and several women have attended mason-training programmes," she said. "Our women's group is now aware of the techniques involved and materials needed in making our houses earthquake-resistant. Just as the post-earthquake reconstruction activities emphasized the need to adopt new and appropriate technology, the women's groups have encouraged us to be economically self-reliant. Today, I run a small grocery shop and plan to take a loan from the group to expand my shop."

Meanwhile, Jamunaben Someswara, an enterprising but uneducated woman from the same district, helped inspire the women of her village to work together for the benefit of the community after the earthquake. Previously, there was no public role for women and they seldom left their homes. But, following the example of women's groups in the aftermath of the earthquake in Maharashtra in 1991, Someswara formed five women's credit groups to encourage local enterprise. "Earlier, we were not organized and were never acknowledged for anything we did," she said, "but we have started giving loans to women members for various needs." Out of 25 members, five of them now have businesses.

Working as a collective gave the women confidence to tackle other major problems that beset the village, such as water shortages. Every day, women had to walk three kilometres to collect drinking water. The women's group approached the water supply office 25 kilometres away, met the concerned officer and obtained written confirmation that the village would receive a daily water tanker. There are now three women on the village council and their next target is to improve the village's healthcare facilities.

Pakistan. In February 2006, the IRIN news service reported that the United Nations High Commissioner for Refugees (UNHCR) had established a female committee in the earthquake-affected town of Muzaffarabad. Attended by up to 80 women from 60 camps across the district, their aim was to include women in camp management and decision-making. The women shared their concerns about issues such as food, debt, water and sanitation.

For most of the women, it was the first time they'd voiced their problems in public. "Little by little these women are waking to a new reality," said Sumeera Mehboob Qureshi, the elected chairwoman. "As one woman said to me: 'God caused the earthquake and it has brought a lot of destruction, but it has shaken the roots of society and has brought change into women's lives and has given us a voice'."

Bangladesh. In response to recurrent windstorms and flooding, the Bangladesh Red Crescent Society (BDRCS) has made efforts to increase the number of its female volunteers. The society has been running a cyclone preparedness programme since the 1970s, but preparedness teams were male-dominated. In the 1990s, BDRCS began recruiting at least two female members per 12-person team. In the 1998 floods, women were active in BDRCS's response – alerting communities to rising flood waters, engaging in needs assessments, providing health education and first aid to flooded communities. Subsequently, BDRCS developed a major disaster preparedness programme in which volunteer teams recruited in disaster-prone areas should include at least eight women out of a total of 25 members.

Sri Lanka. In Batticaloa district, Oxfam and others helped form a Women's Coalition for Disaster Management, which found an innovative way of communicating the need to respect women's security and privacy. The coalition painted colourful murals on the water tanks inside tsunami camps, with slogans such as: "My father is always shouting at my mother. Why? Violence destroys the whole family."

Disaster Watch. A new international network of women's grass-roots organizations active in disasters, Disaster Watch brings women together across borders and other barriers. Through field studies and peer training, disaster-affected women share what they have learned about coping with cyclones in India or earthquakes in Turkey and Iran, and rebuilding structures in ways that leave women stronger. ∎

Recommendations

The following recommendations call for an explicit commitment and clearly articulated strategy on gender issues from humanitarian organizations and the civil society groups (from grass-roots to national and international) with whom they (should) work. However, it is important not to conclude that disasters are divorced from the daily, lived experiences of women and girls, men and boys, since the everyday is where the root causes of disaster vulnerability are located and resilience is generated.

In order to address gender inequalities, such organizations must take action in the following areas:

Gender training
- Mandate and promote gender training.
- Ensure staff and volunteer teams are gender-balanced.

Protection
- Prioritize protection issues.
- Ensure identification of all at-risk populations, including women and girls at risk of gender-based violence and trafficking.
- Include strategies for dealing with children.
- Provide for women's physical safety post-disaster, including safe spaces and facilities for women and girls.
- Ensure support for legal redress.

Health
- Address the specific health needs of women and girls in disaster situations.
- Provide sufficient female health workers and doctors, prenatal and maternity care.
- Provide suitable latrines and sanitary supplies.
- Address, in a gender-sensitive manner, the psychosocial needs of women and girls, and men and boys, to cope with the loss of family and the ongoing challenges of disaster.

Livelihoods
- Include strategies for creating long-term, income-generating projects for women, especially those who have lost livelihoods and/or key providers.

Education
- Ensure girls' education is protected post-disaster.
- Rebuild/relocate schools quickly and safely.
- Train more women teachers.

Gender analysis
- Ensure all data collected are, at the minimum, disaggregated by sex.
- Strive to include other axes of vulnerability, including race/ethnicity, age and ability.

International Federation of Red Cross and Red Crescent Societies

This chapter was contributed by Maureen Fordham, Programme Leader for the MSc in Disaster Management and Sustainable Development at Northumbria University, UK; Madhavi Malalgoda Ariyabandu, a Sri Lanka-based development researcher specializing in the political economy of development and disasters; Prema Gopalan, the India-based global facilitator for the Women and Disaster Reduction Campaign of the Huairou Commission, a global grass-roots network; and Kristina J. Peterson, a community activist and doctoral student at the Center for Hazards Assessment, Response and Technology (CHART), University of New Orleans, USA. Box 6.1 was contributed by Kristina J. Peterson. Box 6.2 was contributed by Dr Elizabeth Edna Wangui, Department of Geography and Human Environmental Studies, San Francisco State University, USA. Box 6.3 was contributed by Jonathan Walter, editor of the World Disasters Report. *Box 6.4 includes contributions from Maureen Fordham, Prema Gopalan, Kristina J. Peterson and Elaine Enarson, who teaches disaster sociology at Brandon University, Manitoba, Canada. We would also like to acknowledge the assistance of Elaine Enarson in reviewing this chapter.*

Sources and further information

Active Learning Network for Accountability and Performance in Humanitarian Action (ALNAP). *Annual Review of Humanitarian Action: Improving Monitoring to Enhance Accountability and Learning.* London: ALNAP, 2003.

Ahmad Aftab, S. *Earth Quake Response Relief Programmes Mansehra, Battagram and Abbottabad Districts.* Pakistan: Sarhad Rural Support Programme, December 2005.

Amnesty International. *Sri Lanka: Waiting to go home – the plight of the internally displaced.* London: Amnesty International, 2006.

Ariyabandu, Madhavi Malalgoda and Wickramasinghe, Maithree. *Gender Dimensions in Disaster Management.* New Delhi: Zubaan Books, 2005.

Asian Development Bank, World Bank. *Pakistan 2005 Earthquake: Preliminary Damage and Needs Assessment.* Islamabad, Pakistan: 12 December 2005.

Chew, Lin and Ramdas, Kavita N. *Caught in the Storm: The Impact of Natural Disasters on Women.* San Francisco: The Global Fund for Women, 2005.

Enarson, E. P. and Morrow, B. H. (eds.). *The Gendered Terrain of Disaster.* New York: Praeger, 1998.

Fordham, Maureen. 'Gender, disaster and development: the necessity for integration' in Mark Pelling (ed.), *Natural disasters and development in a globalizing world.* London: Routledge, 2003.

Human Rights Commission, Sri Lanka. *Report of the Women's Division: Disaster Relief Monitoring Unit.* Sri Lanka: Human Rights Commission, August 2005.

International Federation. *NWFP Early Recovery Needs Assessment – Gender and Community Participation Analysis Report.* Unpublished draft, 2006.

International Federation. *Training Pack on Gender Issues*. Geneva: International Federation, 2003.

International Federation. 'Sharing information for tsunami recovery in South Asia' in *World Disasters Report 2005*. Geneva: International Federation, 2005.

International Labour Organization (ILO). *A Survey of the Demand for Temporary Employment in Cash for Work Projects, April–May 2005*. Technical Paper 3, 24 June 2005, Sri Lanka.

International Strategy for Disaster Reduction (ISDR) and Centre for Research on the Epidemiology of Disasters (CRED). *Understanding risks of death and injury: Evidence from the tsunami in Tamil Nadu*. Press release, Bonn, 28 March 2006.

Martin, S. *Must Boys Be Boys? Ending Sexual Exploitation and Abuse in UN Peacekeeping Missions*. Washington DC: Refugees International, 2005.

Moser, C. *Gender Planning and Development: Theory, Practice and Training*. London: Routledge, 1993.

Oxfam International. *The tsunami's impact on women*. Oxfam briefing note. Oxfam International, March 2005.

Shrader, E. and Delaney, P. *Gender and Post-Disaster Reconstruction: The Case of Hurricane Mitch in Honduras and Nicaragua*. World Bank, 2000.

Tercier Holst-Roness, F. *Violence against girls in Africa during armed conflicts and crises*. International Committee of the Red Cross, Second International Policy Conference on the African Child: Violence Against Girls in Africa. Addis Ababa, 11–12 May 2006.

United Nations. *The World's Women 2005: Progress in Statistics*. New York: United Nations, Department of Economic and Social Affairs, Statistics Division, 2006.

United Nations. *Women 2000 and Beyond: Making Risky Environments Safer*. New York: United Nations Division for the Advancement of Women, Department of Economic and Social Affairs, 2004.

United Nations. *Agreed Conclusions on Environmental Management and the Mitigation of Natural Disasters*, proposed by the United Nations Commission on the Status of Women, forty-sixth session, 4–15 and 25 March 2002, and adopted as ECOSOC resolution 2002/5.

UN Office for the Coordination of Humanitarian Affairs (OCHA) Situation Report, Sri Lanka, 27 January–2 February 2006.

World Health Organization (WHO). *Gender and Health in Disasters*. Geneva: WHO, 2002.

World Health Organization. *International Code of Marketing of Breast-milk Substitutes*. Geneva: WHO, 1981.

Yonder, A., Akcar, S. and Gopalan, P. *Women's Participation in Disaster Relief and Recovery*. New York: SEEDS, The Population Council, 2005.

Web sites

Active Learning Network for Accountability and Performance **http://www.alnap.org**

Bangladesh Red Crescent Society **http://www.bdrcs.org**

Centre for Research on the Epidemiology of Disasters, the international disasters database **http://www.em-dat.net**

Disaster Watch **http://www.disasterwatch.net**

Gender and Disaster Network **http://www.gdnonline.org**

15th Anniversary of the Innocenti Declaration on the Protection, Promotion and Support of Breastfeeding **http://www.innocenti15.net**

Oxfam GB **http://www.oxfam.org.uk**

Population Council **http://www.popcouncil.org**

Refugees International **http://www.refugeesinternational.org**

Reuters AlertNet **http://www.alertnet.org**

UN Division for the Advancement of Women **http://www.un.org/womenwatch/daw**

UN Integrated Regional Information Networks **http://www.irinnews.org**

UN Population Fund **http://www.unfpa.org**

Note: The title of this chapter is based on the reply of a (male) official to a (female) gender specialist's request for gender issues to be considered during the response to the Pakistan earthquake in October 2005. This chapter refers to the South Asia earthquake of October 2005 as the 'Pakistan earthquake', since research on the earthquake for this chapter was conducted only in Pakistan.

International Federation
of Red Cross and Red Crescent Societies

Adequate? Equitable? Timely? Humanitarian aid trends in 2005

How do we know which disasters or crises are neglected? Analysing flows of humanitarian aid against emergency appeals is one measure. This helps track which countries, types of disaster and sectors are underfunded – at least, within the scope of crises for which humanitarian appeals are made.

This chapter tracks flows of humanitarian aid during 2005 and over the past five to ten years, analysing them by sector and amount per beneficiary – including public and private donations – and comes up with some striking key findings (see Map).

With the advent of the Good Humanitarian Donorship (GHD) initiative – launched by a group of key donors in 2003 to promote humanitarian aid according to need – interest has never been higher in how donors are responding to disasters and humanitarian crises. Have wealthier countries met their commitments to distribute humanitarian aid coherently and equitably across the world? What are the trends among other donors? What priority areas need to be addressed?

The chapter begins with an overview of the context of global humanitarian aid, exploring the key factors which have shaped trends in 2005 and their implications for adequate, equitable and timely response. Part 2 compares aid for natural disasters and complex political emergencies. Part 3 analyses different ways of measuring equitable and adequate humanitarian response. Part 4 looks at the latest attempts to improve the equity of response and draws out some recommendations.

Part 1: Overview of trends

Humanitarian aid from wealthy Western donor governments in 2005 is estimated at over US$ 12 billion, according to preliminary figures released in April 2006 by the Development Assistance Committee (DAC) of the Organisation for Economic Co-operation and Development (OECD)[1]. This is an increase of over US$ 3 billion in real terms (37 per cent) from 2004, and is particularly striking as the preliminary figures don't include all multilateral contributions to United Nations (UN) agencies.

Photo opposite page: Amounts of humanitarian aid committed to crises vary enormously from one place to another. Here in Chad, the UN appealed for US$ 32 per beneficiary in 2005, but received just US$ 18 per head. In neighbouring Sudan, it appealed for US$ 588 and received US$ 310 per head. Does global inequity in emergency aid start with the widely divergent amounts of money for which agencies appeal?

Rosemarie North/ International Federation

2005: the year of inequitable humanitarian aid?

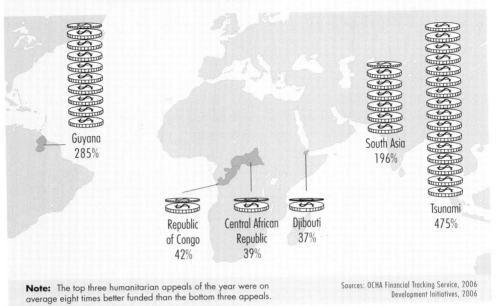

 Total per cent coverage of priority needs, in 2005 (inside and outside UN appeals).

Guyana
285%

South Asia
196%

Republic of Congo
42%

Central African Republic
39%

Djibouti
37%

Tsunami
475%

Note: The top three humanitarian appeals of the year were on average eight times better funded than the bottom three appeals.

Sources: OCHA Financial Tracking Service, 2006
Development Initiatives, 2006

Figure 7.1

Total humanitarian aid from DAC government donors, 1970–2004 in real terms (2003 prices)

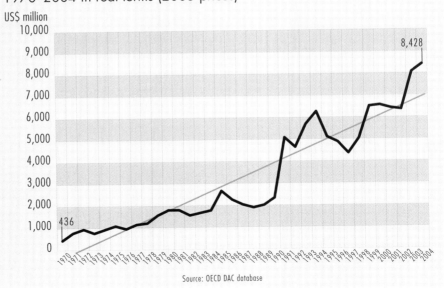

US$ million

8,428

436

Source: OECD DAC database

International Federation
of Red Cross and Red Crescent Societies

Looked at in real terms (2003 prices), humanitarian aid from OECD donors was less than US$ 1 billion in 1974. During the 1980s, it averaged around US$ 2 billion per year. The 1990s saw humanitarian aid more than double in real terms, averaging over US$ 5 billion a year. In 2004, it stood at US$ 8.4 billion (2003 prices) (see Figure 7.1).

As well as increasing in real terms, humanitarian aid has been rising as a percentage of global aid, or official development assistance (ODA). The steepest rise took place during the first half of the 1990s – when ODA was falling, while post-cold war instability in Europe and complex emergencies in Africa were receiving global attention. A key question, now that ODA has started to rise (with substantial growth predicted to 2010), is whether humanitarian aid will maintain its current share. For more information on levels of ODA, see Annex.

Tsunami generates unprecedented attention and funds

Even before December 2004's Indian Ocean tsunami focused global attention on humanitarian needs with such tragic force, 2005 was expected to put both development and humanitarian issues in the spotlight as never before.

Several factors ensured widespread public and political awareness last year: the Millennium Review Summit (assessing progress towards the UN Millennium Development Goals), the Make Poverty History campaign, the Global Call to Action Against Poverty, LIVE 8 and the 20th anniversary of famine in Ethiopia and Somalia, the poverty and development orientation of the G8 Summit at Gleneagles, Scotland, plus the association of humanitarian needs with the global security agenda.

Public interest in humanitarian issues during early 2005 was strongly focused on the aftermath of the tsunami, which prompted unprecedented donations. The factors spurring the generous response were clear soon after the disaster: its timing while many Westerners were enjoying seasonal holidays; the vast death toll involving so many nationalities; the vivid, immediate and extensive media coverage (including amateur video footage of the moment of disaster); the perception that the tsunami was an act of nature and therefore nobody's fault; and a strong identification with the victims, through personal connections with affected countries.

International funds raised and pledged for the tsunami totalled over US$ 14 billion – substantially more than is pledged most years to all emergencies in developing countries. This total included money from governments, aid organizations and private donors, some of it to be spent up till 2010 (see Figure 7.2).

Pledges from governments and international financial institutions (IFIs), including the World Bank, totalled US$ 8.5 billion – a very large amount in relation to 'normal'

Figure 7.2
International funding for the Indian Ocean tsunami
(US$ million and percentage)

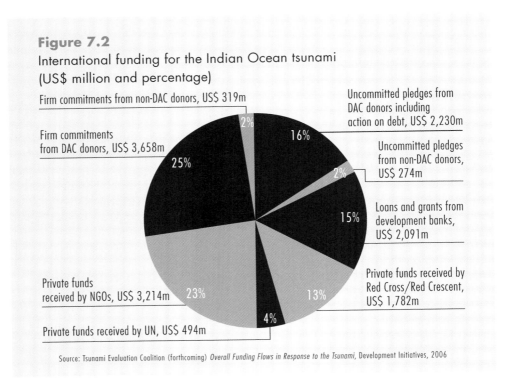

Firm commitments from non-DAC donors, US$ 319m

Firm commitments from DAC donors, US$ 3,658m

Uncommitted pledges from DAC donors including action on debt, US$ 2,230m

Uncommitted pledges from non-DAC donors, US$ 274m

Loans and grants from development banks, US$ 2,091m

Private funds received by Red Cross/Red Crescent, US$ 1,782m

Private funds received by NGOs, US$ 3,214m

Private funds received by UN, US$ 494m

2% 16% 2% 15% 13% 4% 23% 25%

Source: Tsunami Evaluation Coalition (forthcoming) *Overall Funding Flows in Response to the Tsunami*, Development Initiatives, 2006

humanitarian aid, though not quite as large as official pledges in response to 1998's Hurricane Mitch, which amounted to approximately US$ 9 billion.

The most striking aspect of the response was the very high level of individual giving. At least US$ 5.5 billion was donated by the public, an amount greater than non-governmental organizations (NGOs) had ever before collected in a year from all sources of humanitarian aid. Private funds given through NGOs accounted for 23 per cent of all tsunami donations, while 76 National Red Cross and Red Crescent Societies together contributed nearly US$ 1.8 billion – 13 per cent of total tsunami funding.

The enormous interest generated by the tsunami, plus the fact that some agencies received more money than they had requested (or could spend, in some cases), threw the issue of neglected disasters into sharp relief. Did the focus on a few high-profile emergencies during 2004–2005 come at the expense of other, unreported disasters or chronic humanitarian crises? Part 3 explores this question in more detail.

The emergence of non-DAC donors

Over the last 15 years, OECD-DAC donor countries have provided 95 per cent of official development assistance. But during the 1970s and 1980s, non-DAC donors (including China, the former Soviet Union, several Middle Eastern and OPEC countries, and countries such as Poland and the Czech Republic which are now members of the European Union) provided significant amounts of aid. OPEC countries contributed 30 per cent of global aid in 1978.

In response to the tsunami, non-DAC governments pledged US$ 593 million, 9 per cent of overall funding pledged by governments. Over the period 2000–2005, non-DAC donors provided 6 per cent of total humanitarian aid from governments, although in 2001 it was 13 per cent and since 2003 the share of the total from non-DAC donors has been growing each year (see Figure 7.3).

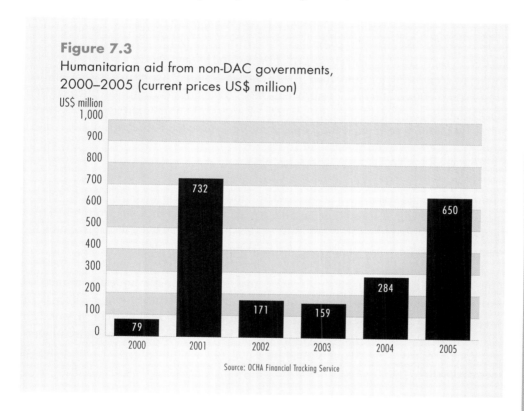

Figure 7.3
Humanitarian aid from non-DAC governments, 2000–2005 (current prices US$ million)

Source: OCHA Financial Tracking Service

From 2000 to 2004, around 20 non-DAC donors a year provided humanitarian aid on average, but in 2005 the tsunami response boosted this to 64 countries. There are several reasons for assuming that, in future years, non-DAC donors will become increasingly significant. Firstly, for countries without long-established patterns of giving, humanitarian crises provide obvious opportunities to channel resources. Secondly, several non-DAC countries, including South Korea, Turkey, Hungary and the Slovak Republic, are committed to increasing their aid significantly. Lastly, emerging donors will want to spend money in a way that reinforces domestic support for a growing aid programme – and domestic constituencies are normally strongly supportive of responding to clear humanitarian needs.

What will this increase in the number and range of donors do for neglected emergencies? Historical trends suggest that while the effect may be modest overall, it will be highly significant for some crisis-affected countries. The strength of the oil market increases the potential for countries such as Saudi Arabia to provide substantial aid and, if the past is a guide to future action, OPEC and Middle Eastern donors are likely to concentrate on their neighbours in the Muslim world.

For example, between 2000 and 2005, Saudi Arabia provided over US$ 1 billion in humanitarian aid to 47 countries – principally the Occupied Palestinian Territory (OPT) (US$ 671 million), Pakistan (US$ 144 million), Iraq (US$ 44 million), Afghanistan (US$ 23 million) and Niger (US$ 19 million).

In 2001, the OPT received US$ 645 million and North Korea (DPRK) US$ 68 million – accounting for more than 97 per cent of all non-DAC humanitarian aid that year. From 2000 to 2004, just four beneficiaries (Afghanistan, Iraq, North Korea and the OPT), received more than 80 per cent of non-DAC humanitarian aid. Of these, non-DAC donors accounted for 35 per cent of all humanitarian contributions to the DPRK and 20 per cent of such aid to the OPT, from 2002 to 2004 – according to UN OCHA's Financial Tracking Service (FTS).

Humanitarian aid reported from non-DAC donors appears quite volatile – but the extent to which this is a result of variable reporting is not clear. Data from non-DAC governments available on FTS are only reported voluntarily, which may account for the very big year-on-year changes in the total figures.

One source of aid invisible in almost every analysis (because it is not easily monetized and accounted for) is local response – both from governments and affected or neighbouring communities. This is often the earliest and most important response in terms of saving lives. No institution appears to be measuring what host governments are spending on disaster response in their own countries and reporting it internationally.

Part 2: Which types of disaster get most attention?

Humanitarian aid tends to be categorized and accounted for, at least by the UN, in two parts – natural disasters, for which 'flash appeals' are issued, and complex emergencies, for which 'consolidated appeals' are made. Somewhat confusingly, both types of appeal form part of the UN's Consolidated Appeals Process (CAP).

Since 1997, a total of US$ 29.4 billion has been requested under the CAP. Of this, by far the larger amount (almost US$ 27 billion) has been for complex emergencies. Just US$ 2.6 billion has been requested for natural disasters under flash appeals – most of this during 2005 (see Figure 7.4).

International Federation
of Red Cross and Red Crescent Societies

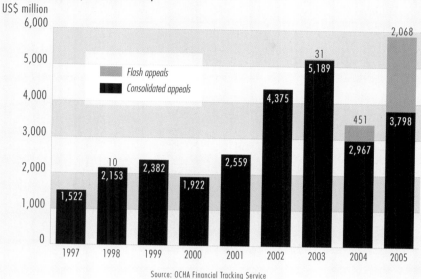

Figure 7.4

Total requirements for UN consolidated and flash appeals, 1997–2005 (US$ million)

US$ million

Source: OCHA Financial Tracking Service

Over the last decade, there has been a fairly steady rise in the number of consolidated and flash appeals, from 16 a decade ago to a peak of 31 in 2004, dropping slightly to 25 last year. Much of this increase is due to a recent rise in flash appeals for natural disasters. Between 1996 and 2002, there were only three flash appeals, but since 2003 there have been 21 (see Figure 7.5).

To some extent, this may be attributed to an upsurge in the impact of natural disasters. According to the latest data from the Centre for Research on the Epidemiology of Disasters (CRED), the average number of natural disasters reported each year increased by over 60 per cent during 2003–2005, compared with 1996–1998. The numbers reported killed and the estimated costs of damage increased by a similar margin.

It also appears that the increase in flash appeals has come about because the CAP is now seen by donors as an increasingly important trigger for response and the flash appeal mechanism provides them with a reliable vehicle through which to contribute. Certainly, in 2005, the response to the two most prominent natural disasters – the tsunami and the South Asia earthquake – was well above historic response rates.

As there have been few flash appeals since 1997, it is difficult to give a more reliable explanation of trends. But the gathering momentum around the

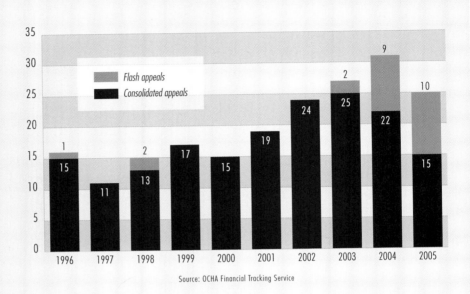

Figure 7.5
Total numbers of UN consolidated and flash appeals, 1996–2005

Flash appeals
Consolidated appeals

Source: OCHA Financial Tracking Service

coordination of flash appeals under OCHA suggests that the increase of such appeals in response to natural disasters will continue. Even without the tsunami, total requirements under flash appeals increased from US$ 451 million in 2004 to US$ 762 million in 2005. With the tsunami appeal, requirements totalled more than US$ 2 billion.

It is easier to assess trends in consolidated appeals because there have been 176 appeals over the decade. While there has been a decline in the number of consolidated appeals from 25 in 2003 to 15 in 2005, this is still in line with the average number of appeals from 1996 to 2001.

The recent reduction is as likely to be due to a consolidation in the way appeals are developed as to a reduction in need related to fewer complex emergencies. In fact, the average amount requested per consolidated appeal in 2005 was US$ 253 million – well above the average since 1997 of US$ 164 million.

In volume terms over the decade, total requirements were at their highest in 2003 (over US$ 5 billion), due to a US$ 2.2 billion request for Iraq. Between 1997 and 2005, only three appeals had requirements over US$ 1 billion – Afghanistan in 2002, Iraq in 2003 and Sudan in 2005.

International Federation
of Red Cross and Red Crescent Societies

Part 3: How adequate and equitable is humanitarian response?

Concern about equitable response to emergencies has been on the international agenda for years, notably since 1994's *Code of Conduct for the International Red Cross and Red Crescent Movement and NGOs in Disaster Relief*, which now has over 300 signatories and whose second principle states:

> Within the entirety of our programmes, we will reflect considerations of proportionality. Human suffering must be alleviated whenever it is found; life is as precious in one part of a country as another. Thus, our provision of aid will reflect the degree of suffering it seeks to alleviate... The implementation of such a universal, impartial and independent policy can only be effective if we and our partners have access to the necessary resources to provide for such equitable relief, and have equal access to all disaster victims.

The enormous response to the tsunami heightened awareness of the need to address equitable responses *between* emergencies and coherent responses (which ensure that priority needs are met first) *within* emergencies. There are several ways of measuring equitable, coherent and adequate responses:

- Tracking per cent coverage of appeals (measuring commitments against requirements).
- Comparing funding by targeted beneficiary (both requirements and commitments per head).
- Analysing the regional distribution of global humanitarian aid.
- Measuring coverage by individual sectors to reveal whether responses are coherent within crises.
- Measuring the timeliness with which aid is committed – as the adequacy of humanitarian response depends on speed as well as quantity.

The chapter will now examine each of these measures in turn, using data from both the CAP and the DAC. It should, however, be noted that large numbers of people in need of humanitarian aid are out of reach of aid agencies and so may not figure in a consolidated or flash appeal. In addition, an analysis of CAP data cannot capture the full nature of humanitarian aid flows, which include funding given directly to governments and resources channelled through NGOs or the International Red Cross and Red Crescent Movement, which are not recorded as 'inside the CAP'.

Tracking appeal coverage

The UN's Consolidated Appeals Process has been operational since 1992. It is the international community's primary method for ensuring that everyone affected by a humanitarian crisis receives an adequate response. But over the last decade, there has been no real improvement in the extent to which appeals are funded. At the same time, the volume of requirements has increased substantially and, as a result, the volume of funding through the CAP has also increased.

In the case of the tsunami, the flash appeal requested US$ 1.28 billion, but FTS recorded over US$ 6 billion in humanitarian response alone during 2005 – most but not all of which will have been available for spending in 2005. This means that the tsunami appeal was funded to the tune of 475 per cent. By contrast, most appeals are underfunded by about one-third (see Figure 7.6).

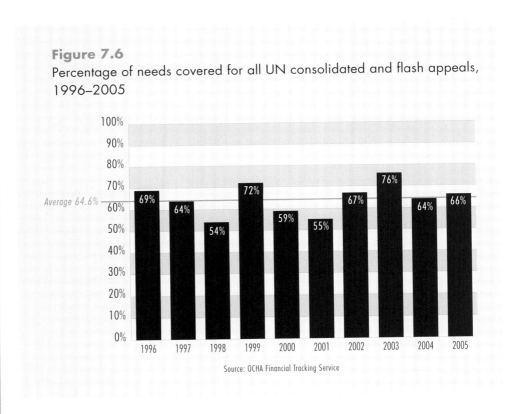

Figure 7.6
Percentage of needs covered for all UN consolidated and flash appeals, 1996–2005

Source: OCHA Financial Tracking Service

Disaggregating the picture, it is clear that there is a huge range in the extent to which appeals are funded. On average since 2000, the five best-funded appeals in each year have had well over four-fifths of their needs met. However, the five most poorly funded have received around a quarter to a third of their requirements. The widest gap came in 2003, when 96 per cent of needs were covered for the top five emergencies while only 27 per cent were met for the bottom five. The gap narrowed somewhat in 2005, with the top five appeals 77 per cent covered and the bottom five 36 per cent covered (see Figure 7.7).

International Federation
of Red Cross and Red Crescent Societies

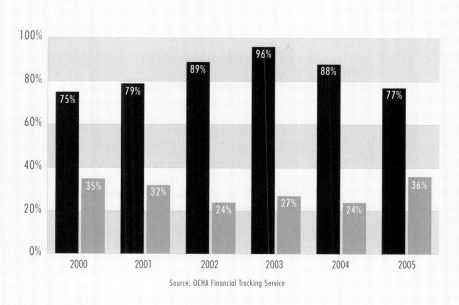

Source: OCHA Financial Tracking Service

Looking at the impact of these variations on particular countries in 2005, the flash appeal for Guyana had the lowest coverage, at 30 per cent. When torrential rain deluged this small South American country in January 2005, two-fifths of the entire population were affected in the country's largest disaster for a century. Close on Guyana's heels were the Djibouti flash appeal (34 per cent covered), Central African Republic (35 per cent), Republic of Congo (38 per cent) and the West Africa cholera flash appeal (45 per cent).

The appeals with the highest percentages of needs covered in 2005 were the Angola flash appeal (72 per cent), Malawi flash appeal (76 per cent), Uganda (76 per cent), the Great Lakes (77 per cent) and, of course, the tsunami flash appeal (see Figure 7.8). However, according to FTS data, Malawi's appeal was revised downwards after a disappointing donor response – just over half of the original appeal requirements were met.

What are the reasons for these disparities? It is not to do with the volume of funding needed. Ironically, the most poorly funded appeals have had only modest requirements. Guyana's appeal was for less than US$ 3 million, while the complex emergencies in the Central African Republic and the Republic of Congo needed around US$ 25 million each, but only received US$ 9 million.

CHAPTER V

Figure 7.8
Per cent coverage of consolidated and flash appeals,
(inside the UN appeal) 2005

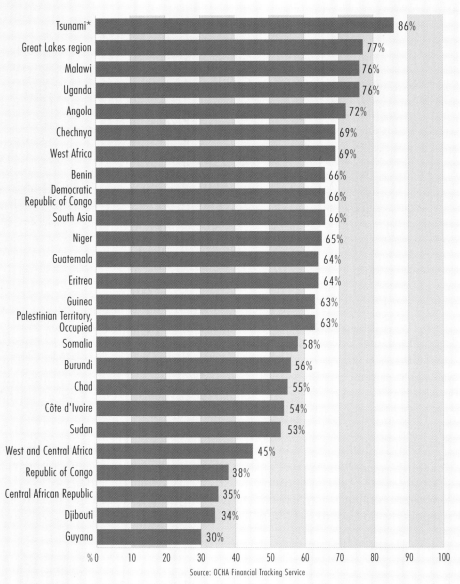

Tsunami*	86%
Great Lakes region	77%
Malawi	76%
Uganda	76%
Angola	72%
Chechnya	69%
West Africa	69%
Benin	66%
Democratic Republic of Congo	66%
South Asia	66%
Niger	65%
Guatemala	64%
Eritrea	64%
Guinea	63%
Palestinian Territory, Occupied	63%
Somalia	58%
Burundi	56%
Chad	55%
Côte d'Ivoire	54%
Sudan	53%
West and Central Africa	45%
Republic of Congo	38%
Central African Republic	35%
Djibouti	34%
Guyana	30%

Source: OCHA Financial Tracking Service

*Note on tsunami: for technical reasons, the tsunami was only 86% funded within the UN appeal, but 475% funded when all humanitarian response for 2005 is considered.

International Federation
of Red Cross and Red Crescent Societies

The data suggest that the reasons for neglect are rooted in the policy priorities given to different countries – possibly linked to the capacity to deliver. A country may be very needy, but access may be difficult and other obstacles may prevent an effective response. However, this should be reflected in the appeal requirements, which are not a statement of needs alone, but a prioritized, costed set of programmes designed to meet needs as far as possible.

The same countries appear continually at the top and bottom of the table for the share of needs met. In the past ten years, the Great Lakes region of Africa has had an appeal every year. For eight of those years it was in the top five, in terms of per cent coverage. Angola appeared five times in the top five, while Sierra Leone, Tajikistan and the DPRK each appeared four times.

However, the Republic of Congo has had an appeal for five of the past ten years and each of those has been in the bottom five and below 40 per cent coverage. Zimbabwe has appeared three times in the bottom five. Yet, while the Republic of Congo has received very little media attention – which may help to explain its position as a neglected emergency – the same cannot be said of Zimbabwe. The difficult political context in Zimbabwe may inhibit the work of donors, but the country's plight is certainly not overlooked.

Analysing DAC data reveals a similar concentration of humanitarian aid in a few countries – far more so than for development assistance. In 2004, the latest year for which DAC data are available, the top five recipients shared 31 per cent of total humanitarian aid from DAC donors, while 137 other countries shared the remaining aid. These figures include all contributions to UN consolidated and flash appeals, but also humanitarian aid to countries which are not the subject of an appeal.

Some of the 137 countries will have had very small, local crises and a small volume of funding cannot be interpreted as an inadequate response. However, the CAP is supposed to include all countries where the crisis is on a sufficient scale to require a consolidated UN response. So the unevenness to which UN appeals are funded makes it clear that there is a big variation in international response, even between globally prioritized emergencies.

Comparing funding per beneficiary

The other way of measuring neglect is by comparing responses between emergencies, looking at the data per targeted beneficiary.

The following analysis uses UN figures, where available, to work out humanitarian aid per beneficiary. OCHA's 2005 Humanitarian Appeal provides numbers of beneficiaries targeted by all consolidated appeals for complex emergencies. Since this information is less easily available for flash appeals, the analysis uses the best data available from the appeal documents.

However, this does not always provide a like-for-like comparison. Some appeals, such as the 2005 flash appeal to combat cholera in six countries across West and Central Africa, are principally for information-sharing rather than for meeting the needs of affected people.

In the case of the tsunami, estimates of the number of people affected ranged from 1 million to 5 million, so estimates of per capita spending will vary widely depending on which estimate is taken. The UN tsunami appeal states that it aims to meet the needs of 5 million people and this is the figure used for the analysis in this chapter. However, it is worth noting that the Tsunami Evaluation Coalition and the World Bank put the number of people affected at 2 million.

A further complicating factor is the lack of humanitarian benchmarks which would set standards across all emergency situations for minimum adequate outcomes. Without these, the amounts requested (let alone donated) are determined to some extent by what can be delivered or by subjective criteria, rather than by the consistent application of a common denominator of need. Since appeals combine needs assessment with a call for resource mobilization, there is an ongoing risk that they will request funds based, at least in part, on what the donor market can bear.

Added to which, humanitarian appeals are not in principle intended to fund recovery and reconstruction. But it's not always easy to draw clear lines between these phases and the emergency phase.

Analysing funding within the UN appeal process, it is striking that while contributions per targeted beneficiary were very diverse for different emergencies during 2005, this is at least in part because the funds requested were equally wide-ranging (see Figure 7.9).

Contributions inside the UN humanitarian appeal during 2005 ranged from US$ 3 per targeted beneficiary in Guyana to US$ 310 per head in Sudan. Meanwhile, funds requested per beneficiary for Guyana and Sudan were US$ 9 and US$ 588 respectively.

Taking the bottom five appeals of 2005 (West and Central Africa flash, Guyana flash, Malawi flash, Niger flash and Côte d'Ivoire), the average requested per beneficiary was US$ 16 and the average contributed inside the appeal was US$ 9. At the other end, the top five appeals (Djibouti flash, Chechnya, Benin flash, Republic of Congo and Sudan) averaged US$ 373 requested per beneficiary and US$ 190 contributed.

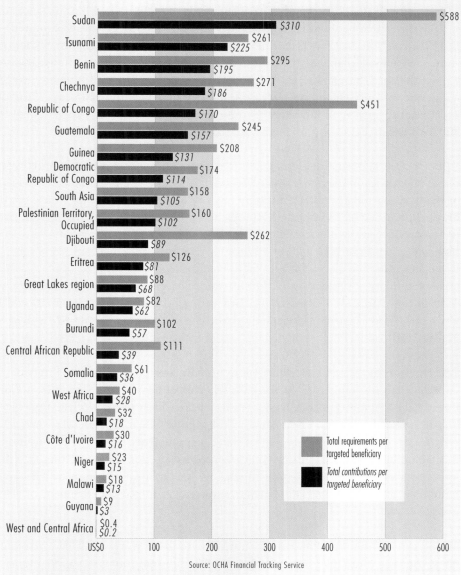

Figure 7.9
Total requirements and contributions per targeted beneficiary (inside UN appeal), 2005 (US$)

Country	Total requirements	Total contributions
Sudan	$588	$310
Tsunami	$261	$225
Benin	$295	$195
Chechnya	$271	$186
Republic of Congo	$451	$170
Guatemala	$245	$157
Guinea	$208	$131
Democratic Republic of Congo	$174	$114
South Asia	$158	$105
Palestinian Territory, Occupied	$160	$102
Djibouti	$262	$89
Eritrea	$126	$81
Great Lakes region	$88	$68
Uganda	$82	$62
Burundi	$102	$57
Central African Republic	$111	$39
Somalia	$61	$36
West Africa	$40	$28
Chad	$32	$18
Côte d'Ivoire	$30	$16
Niger	$23	$15
Malawi	$18	$13
Guyana	$9	$3
West and Central Africa	$0.4	$0.2

Source: OCHA Financial Tracking Service

Legend:
- Total requirements per targeted beneficiary
- Total contributions per targeted beneficiary

Note: the Angola flash appeal is not counted because of uncertainty over numbers of targeted beneficiaries.

The difference between the top and bottom five appeals, in terms of both requests and contributions per head, is greater than a factor of 20. But is it 20 times more expensive to run an aid operation in Sudan, Congo or Benin than it is in Niger, Malawi or Guyana?

One reason for the huge difference in requirements per beneficiary may be due to the context, the nature of the appeal and what needs to be resourced. For instance, there is a big difference between the appeals for Sudan (US$ 588 per head requested) and neighbouring Chad (US$ 32 per head requested). The 2005 appeal for Sudan was a countrywide work plan which aimed to restore peace in the country after years of war. It encompassed humanitarian, protection, recovery and development needs with requirements totalling around US$ 1.4 billion. Meanwhile, the 2005 appeal for Chad was launched principally to meet the needs of refugees entering eastern Chad from Sudan's Darfur region and totalled US$ 182 million.

What is also striking from this analysis is that some well-covered appeals actually didn't raise much money per targeted beneficiary. Malawi's appeal, noted above as one of the best covered at 76 per cent, only raised US$ 13 per person in need – the third lowest figure out of 25 appeals. Conversely, the Republic of Congo's appeal, one of the worst covered at 38 per cent, raised US$ 170 per person in need – the second highest figure of the year.

However, many countries with UN humanitarian appeals also attract contributions outside those appeals – often channelled through NGOs or the International Red Cross and Red Crescent Movement – and these figures are tracked by FTS (see Figure 7.10).

Ten crises are revealed as receiving more humanitarian aid (inside and outside their appeals) than was requested by the UN: Chechnya, Democratic Republic of Congo, Great Lakes region, Guyana flash appeal, Malawi flash appeal, Niger flash appeal, South Asia flash appeal, the tsunami flash appeal, Uganda and West Africa. But 14 appeals still fell short of the CAP's stated requirements, even when counting total humanitarian donations. All funding provided for the Republic of Congo, Djibouti and the Central African Republic, whether given inside or outside the appeal, amounted to less than half of what was requested in the CAP's statement of priority needs.

In the case of the tsunami, private donations outside the appeal were particularly large, totalling more than US$ 3.8 billion – which meant four times more money was donated outside the appeal than inside. This boosted tsunami contributions in 2005 for humanitarian aid alone to US$ 1,241 per targeted beneficiary (using the UN's figure of 5 million beneficiaries) or over US$ 3,000 per head, using the World Bank's figure of 2 million affected people.

International Federation
of Red Cross and Red Crescent Societies

Figure 7.10

Total requirements and contributions per targeted beneficiary (inside and outside UN appeal), 2005 (US$)

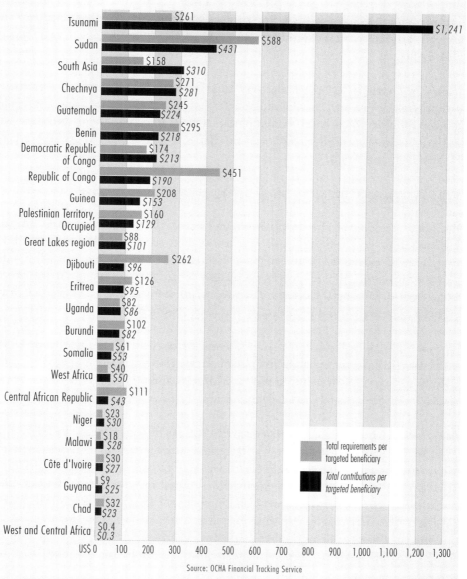

Source: OCHA Financial Tracking Service

Notes: 1) The Angola flash appeal is not counted because of uncertainty over numbers of targeted beneficiaries.
2) The tsunami contributions figure is calculated as follows: total humanitarian assistance of US$ 6.2 billion for 2005, reported by FTS as inside and outside the UN appeal, divided by 5 million beneficiaries as stated by the UN appeal. Using the total tsunami aid of US$ 14 billion (including reconstruction funding, pledges and loans as reported in Figure 7.2) would clearly result in an even higher per capita figure.

Another appeal to attract considerably more aid outside the UN appeal than inside was the South Asia earthquake, boosting the per capita figure to US$ 310 – nearly double what was requested through the UN appeal.

At the other end of the spectrum, however, the same five countries appear near the bottom in terms of per capita aid, whether calculated inside or outside the appeal: Niger, Malawi, Côte d'Ivoire, Guyana and Chad. Taken together these appeals attracted total humanitarian aid of less than US$ 27 per targeted beneficiary.

It may be appropriate to treat the very large funding per person for the tsunami as exceptional, given the overwhelming public response. But, discounting the tsunami, it is clear that when total humanitarian aid is analysed, there are even wider disparities between high-profile, well-funded emergencies and those where people are relatively neglected.

The regional distribution of humanitarian aid

Are some regions of the world more neglected than others when it comes to humanitarian aid? According to the latest data from CRED, over 2.2 billion people in Asia have been killed, made homeless or otherwise affected by natural disasters over the past ten years, compared with 202 million in Africa over the same period. But Asia (including Afghanistan) receives less than 30 per cent of global humanitarian aid recorded by the DAC (see Figure 7.11).

The overall rise in funding for sub-Saharan Africa over the decade from 1995 to 2004 was 182 per cent, while for North Africa the rise was 257 per cent, thanks mainly to increases in bilateral aid to Morocco and Algeria. This compares with rises of 138 per cent to the Middle East and 124 per cent to Asia.

Only two or three Asian countries are the subject of consolidated or flash appeals each year, compared with around 15 African countries, which raises the issue of why Asia is comparatively neglected. Several factors are at play. Perhaps the strongest is the tendency of wealthier donors to give humanitarian aid to countries in their own region or with which they have strong economic, social or political ties. This partly explains high levels of assistance to the Balkans from EU member states throughout the 1990s. Most Japanese aid is focused on Asia; Latin America receives proportionately more aid from the US than from other donors.

Another factor is that complex emergencies are more prevalent in Africa than Asia and have received more sustained political attention than natural disasters in Asia over the decade to 2004 – and consequently more funding.

Figure 7.11

Regional distribution of humanitarian aid, 1995–2004 (US$ million)

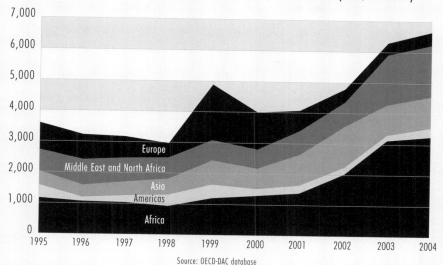

Source: OECD-DAC database

Note: this graph shows bilateral humanitarian aid, according to the DAC definition, together with multilateral contributions to UN agencies. It does not include private contributions. The graph shows only humanitarian aid which can be allocated by region – this leaves just over US$ 1 billion which is not reported by region.

Tracking coverage by sector

Measuring aid coverage by sector is one way of tracking whether aid is coherent – whether it is committed equally across all priority areas. However, by far the largest share of aid to humanitarian appeals is for the food sector, which represents 55 per cent of the US$ 15.5 billion in commitments made by donors through UN appeals from 2000 to 2005 (see Figure 7.12).

The next largest category is multi-sector aid; for example, interventions that cover a number of sectors such as food, health, education, water and sanitation. This is different from the 4 per cent of aid classified as 'sector not specified' – which is funding not allocated to a particular sector at the time of commitment (giving agencies flexibility to allocate those funds to real-time priorities).

The volume of commitments to food (US$ 8.6 billion over the past six years) is greater than that allocated to all other sectors combined. Priorities such as health (US$ 781 million), education (US$ 432 million), shelter and non-food items (US$ 318 million) and water and sanitation (US$ 269 million) receive much less attention, despite being the kinds of priorities favoured by the taxpayers who ultimately fund most humanitarian aid.

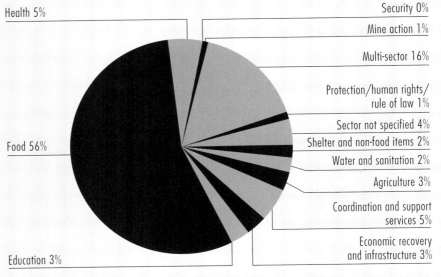

Figure 7.12

Percentage of donor commitments to all sectors, 2000–2005

Health 5%

Security 0%

Mine action 1%

Multi-sector 16%

Protection/human rights/ rule of law 1%

Sector not specified 4%

Shelter and non-food items 2%

Water and sanitation 2%

Agriculture 3%

Coordination and support services 5%

Economic recovery and infrastructure 3%

Food 56%

Education 3%

Source: OCHA Financial Tracking Service

Note: percentages may not add up due to rounding

Food is not only by far the largest sector – it is also the sector which is best covered in relation to requests (79 per cent covered from 2000 to 2005). By contrast, the needs of vital sectors such as economic recovery, shelter, protection, water and sanitation, and health and agriculture were all on average less than 40 per cent covered between 2000 and 2005 (see Figure 7.13).

Food aid to Iraq worth US$ 1.4 billion in 2003 helped boost spending on food that year to almost US$ 2.8 billion – after which the value of food aid has fallen back to under US$ 1.5 billion. Food aid is subject to different driving forces compared with cash aid. For some large donors, food is given in kind – it cannot be converted into cash.

Other much smaller sectors showing an increase from 2000 to 2005 include water and sanitation (up 17 times), economic recovery (up 33 times) and shelter (up 153 times) – but all of these increases are from very low levels. Given the scale of food aid, a small shift from food to other sectors could leave room for greatly increased spending on other priorities. Health, for instance, went up from US$ 37 million in 2000 to US$ 266 million in 2005 – but this still only represented 5 per cent of spending last year.

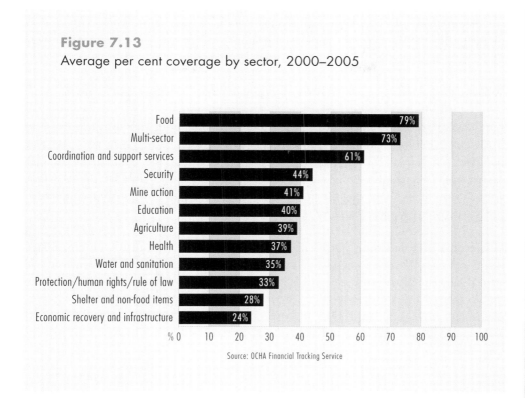

Figure 7.13

Average per cent coverage by sector, 2000–2005

Sector	Coverage
Food	79%
Multi-sector	73%
Coordination and support services	61%
Security	44%
Mine action	41%
Education	40%
Agriculture	39%
Health	37%
Water and sanitation	35%
Protection/human rights/rule of law	33%
Shelter and non-food items	28%
Economic recovery and infrastructure	24%

Source: OCHA Financial Tracking Service

Making the global needs assessment and the UN's Consolidated Appeals Process more inclusive would improve the analysis of sectoral shortfalls. Up to now, NGOs and the International Red Cross and Red Crescent Movement have not been consistently involved in either the needs assessment or the CAP. If they have a particular focus on one sector, for example Oxfam on water and sanitation, their actions in that sector may not be properly reported within the CAP data.

Timeliness: too late, as well as too little

A key issue on the adequacy and efficiency of humanitarian interventions is how quickly donors respond to need. If an emergency is neglected in its early stages the consequences can be serious, not only for the people affected, but for the wider international community. Interventions that are life-saving cannot wait. Even less extreme needs must be met in a timely way – there are often only very small windows of opportunity for an effective response.

As related in last year's *World Disasters Report*, the delays in responding to Niger's locust and food crisis from 2003 to 2005 proved costly in terms of lives, livelihoods and aid. During a multi-donor meeting in Paris on 24 October 2004, there was agreement that only US$ 1 million would have been needed to contain the locust threat in July 2003, whereas the delayed response meant that, in the end, 100 times that figure was needed.

What is the record on timeliness for different kinds of UN appeal last year?

For 2005's flash appeals (for natural disasters), 73 per cent of all contributions were made either before or within the first month of an appeal launch – an improvement on 2004's figure of 37 per cent. It is partly a result of the tsunami factor: the catastrophe's very high profile, the fact that budgets were available for the new year and the media's focus on the need to convert pledges into disbursements all provided incentives for quick, reliable funding.

However, when analysing 2005's consolidated appeals (for complex emergencies), just 7 per cent of contributions were made before or within the first month of the appeal launch. Within three months, just over one-third of contributions had been made, rising to just over two-thirds by the six-month stage (see Figure 7.14). This was an improvement on 2004, when the majority of contributions (54 per cent) were made six months after the appeal start date.

Figure 7.14
Timing of contributions from all donors to UN consolidated appeals, 2005

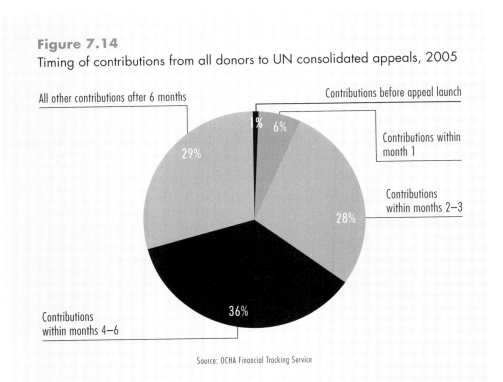

Source: OCHA Financial Tracking Service

International Federation
of Red Cross and Red Crescent Societies

Part 4: Improving the equity and timeliness of response

There have been a number of attempts to improve the equity of humanitarian response. The Good Humanitarian Donorship initiative has made equitable response a key priority. It was to report on its collective performance, using equity as a measure, in July 2006.

The European Commission's humanitarian aid department, ECHO, has recognized the need for a donor of last resort for forgotten emergencies and has developed a methodology for identifying such crises (see Chapter 1). In 2002, 16 per cent of ECHO's total budget of EUR 85 million (US$ 80 million) was dedicated to forgotten emergencies. In its 2006 aid strategy, ECHO classified Chechnya, Myanmar, the Saharawi refugees in Algeria, Nepal and the Kashmir crisis in India as forgotten emergencies.

Meanwhile, in March 2006, the UN launched the Central Emergency Response Fund (CERF) as one step towards reform of the UN system. The fund, which has requested US$ 500 million in voluntary support from donors, will provide rapid response funds within three to four days of a sudden-onset emergency. Furthermore, the CERF will target about one-third of its funds to forgotten crises.

Having funding available up front has several benefits. Crises that may have taken months to fund can now receive rapid start-up resources vital for mobilizing needs assessments and logistics pipelines. In addition, less high-profile disasters are now more likely to receive funding. Until the expanded CERF was introduced in 2006, agencies had to borrow to get immediate funding. Consequently, emergencies which were expected to be 'unpopular' lost out, since agencies would not borrow unless they were reasonably confident they would receive funding which would enable them to repay the loan.

The grant-based CERF mechanism should make a major difference in accessing timely funding for all emergency situations. However, as of June 2006, the CERF remained underfunded, with US$ 365 million in commitments and an additional US$ 56 million in uncommitted pledges. One possible explanation is that donors want to wait and see how the fund works before making financial commitments.

The International Federation of Red Cross and Red Crescent Societies (International Federation) has operated a similar kind of fund for over 20 years. Known as the Disaster Relief Emergency Fund (DREF), it provided over 10 million Swiss francs (US$ 8.5 million) of rapid response grants in 2005, half of which were for minor or forgotten emergencies (see Box 7.1).

The Disaster Relief Emergency Fund (DREF) was established in 1985 by the International Federation to provide initial start-up funds and essential finance to National Red Cross and Red Crescent Societies, allowing rapid response in the case of emergencies.

As well as kick-starting rapid emergency responses, DREF has increasingly been used to make funds available for responding to minor or neglected emergencies that would otherwise go unfunded. The fund also enables the International Federation to finance disaster preparedness and timely response and awareness-raising in the case of slow-onset disasters.

In 2005, DREF allocated 10.5 million Swiss francs (US$ 8.5 million), of which nearly half went on minor emergencies. The fund is replenished by donations to the International Federation's emergency appeals or by unearmarked funding from donors, which allows it to respond to minor emergencies.

Eighty per cent of disasters are managed at national level where no international appeal is launched to support them. Meanwhile, many slow-onset disasters remain unattractive to donors, even after an emergency appeal is launched. So in 2005, the International Federation decided to use DREF more ambitiously and proactively to support these minor and silent emergencies.

With the support of the Netherlands Red Cross and the Netherlands government, the International Federation increased the amount allocated to minor emergencies from 1.56 million Swiss francs (US$ 1.25 million) in 2004 to nearly 5 million Swiss francs (US$ 4 million) in 2005. Over the same period, the number of minor emergencies funded more than doubled from 27 to 61. Requests for minor emergency funding continued to rise during 2006.

Africa benefited most from DREF funding in 2005. The continent's National Societies generally have strong volunteer networks but lack finance to respond to disasters. DREF provides them with the money to mobilize volunteers and procure relief items, or replace supplies that have been distributed. The knowledge that the operation will be financed allows the National Society to act quickly.

In the Sahel and East Africa, DREF provided considerable support for National Societies to begin responding to food crises before major donors showed an interest in supporting them.

In the case of infectious diseases, rapid response and awareness-raising at community level are vital to prevent epidemics. In 2005, DREF made four minor emergency allocations to support rapid response to cholera outbreaks in Mozambique and West Africa, plus a significant allocation to help counter the outbreak of the Marburg virus in Angola.

In Asia, a minor emergencies grant enabled the recently formed Timor-Leste Red Cross to respond swiftly to acute food shortages arising from delayed rains and recurrent crop failure. In the Caribbean, DREF funding helped finance regional hurricane preparedness planning – which proved timely, as 2005 saw the worst hurricane season in recorded history.

In Lebanon, DREF resources helped ambulance services to continue operating when state support for the Lebanese Red Cross dried up during the political turmoil and bomb attacks that the country has suffered since October 2004. According to Knut Kasperson, the International Federation's head of delegation in Lebanon: "The Lebanese Red Cross has been able to carry out 450 to 500 life-saving missions per day. DREF ensured that the ambulances did not stop."

A review of DREF is being carried out in 2006. One question to be considered is whether the fund should be increased to allow more proactive support for countries and regions overlooked by donors. ■

While upfront funding is a key part of improving the adequacy of humanitarian response, ensuring equity in response depends on the capacity to compare needs and numbers of affected people across different crises.

In 2005 and early 2006, there were significant improvements in making needs assessments more comprehensive and the UN's Consolidated Appeals Process more rigorously prioritized. The Needs Analysis Framework (NAF) has been developed as a tool to help improve information on humanitarian needs in all emergencies. The NAF was piloted in five countries in 2005 – the Occupied Palestinian Territory, Democratic Republic of Congo, Côte d'Ivoire, Uganda and Burundi – and it is being integrated into all consolidated appeals in 2006. This should provide a more inclusive basis for the prioritization of needs and should thus contribute to more equitable response.

The key point about the CAP is that it is intended to contribute to efficient and equitable response by establishing a definitive statement of priority needs in each situation. In principle, this means that the needs identified 'inside the CAP' should be funded before other activities which are 'outside the CAP'.

However, as we have seen, priority needs within the CAP have only been about two-thirds funded in recent years, while, for a variety of reasons, a great deal of funding takes place outside the CAP. For example, bilateral government-to-government funding is not channelled through the CAP – nor is funding committed by a large number of NGOs. In addition, the often considerable resources available through the International Red Cross and Red Crescent Movement are recorded as outside the CAP.

Some donors and organizations bypass CAP processes for various reasons. Peter Rees, head of the International Federation's Operations Support Department, says: "The Federation is independent from the UN and does not appeal via a UN mechanism, such as the CAP. We do, however, regularly join the CHAP [Common Humanitarian Action Plan] process to ensure close coordination between UN, Red Cross/Red Crescent and NGO sectors."

Neglect of protracted crises and chronic vulnerability

Peter Rees points out that the CAP excludes all UN development funding. This means that statements of humanitarian needs – such as those presented in the CAP – fail to capture the full range of vulnerable people's needs. "The bigger question", says Rees, "is that humanitarian funding often comes as a result of a failed development approach or a failed political process." He argues that the apparent lack of dialogue between humanitarian and development sectors is "essentially non-strategic and inefficient".

When analysing the CAP data presented in this chapter, it is striking how neglected developmental crises become neglected humanitarian crises. Last year's slow-onset or chronic 'natural' disasters (e.g., locust plagues, drought, poverty and hunger in Niger; drought, poverty, disease and hunger in Malawi) attracted much lower levels of humanitarian aid per beneficiary than the quick-onset natural disasters (e.g., the tsunami and the South Asia earthquake). Both Niger's and Malawi's food crises have been recurring for some years now.

The persistent and recurrent nature of many humanitarian crises is driven as much by chronic poverty and vulnerability as it is by natural hazards. This is especially so in countries such as Niger, where the 2005 food crisis threatening 2.5 million people with starvation has been widely recognized as an acute manifestation of the chronic food insecurity which left 40 per cent of children routinely malnourished even before the situation was brought to the attention of the global media and humanitarian agencies.

Not only are such chronic crises poorly funded in terms of aid per targeted beneficiary, but the analysis of funding per sector reveals that programming to address more chronic issues, such as health, water and sanitation, agriculture and economic recovery, is neglected compared to quick, emergency food aid. Meanwhile, data on the timeliness of aid show that protracted, complex emergencies tend to attract funding far slower than flash appeals for sudden-onset natural disasters.

The chronically poor, vulnerable people, who are neglected when it comes to humanitarian response, are often the forgotten poor of development assistance – those who are hardest to reach and face the most obstacles to overcoming poverty and crisis.

Humanitarian interventions are focused on relieving humanitarian suffering rather than building long-term development. But looked at from the viewpoint of those in need, there is an increasing case for a closer integration of humanitarian and development response and for an integrated perspective which ensures equity, not only between humanitarian crises, but also between humanitarian crises and situations of chronic poverty and vulnerability.

Conclusions and recommendations

1. **Aid must be adequate as well as equitable** – to ensure there is enough money in the system to meet all basic humanitarian needs, not just fairer slices of a cake that is too small in the first place.

2. **Assessments of priority needs are pivotal** and work to improve their quality and comparability must continue. The ability to prioritize within an emergency and between emergencies is essential if the most urgent needs are to be funded first. This not only requires institutional change, but also discipline among donors and agencies so that funding flows to those priority needs.

International Federation
of Red Cross and Red Crescent Societies

3. **Needs assessments and the CAP must be more inclusive** of all implementation agencies if they are to make the most of their capacity to ensure an adequate and equitable response to all emergencies.

4. **Create a recognized minimum standard or benchmark of need** – a denominator applicable to all emergencies. This would enable an objective, comparable judgement of the point when funding was adequate to meet basic needs and, therefore, when any surplus resources could be transferred to needier situations. Currently, there is not even a standard definition of the numbers of people affected in different disasters.

5. **Consider annual targets for humanitarian aid**. The global response to disasters is financed by voluntary appeals. The humanitarian community could consider whether its goal is that all people affected by disasters should be entitled to a certain minimum level of humanitarian aid and, if so, whether the current appeal-based system can deliver the predictable resources necessary to achieve that.

6. **Ensure equity between humanitarian and development interventions** – not just equity between humanitarian crises – in order to address the needs of people suffering chronic vulnerability and extreme poverty. Donor policy should be driven by the perspective of affected individuals, not by the priorities of existing managerial departments.

This chapter was contributed by Development Initiatives (DI), drawing on the resources of the Global Humanitarian Assistance and Good Humanitarian Donorship project. DI welcomes corrections to any errors of fact or interpretation and additional information. Please contact di@devinit.org. Further data can be found at www.globalhumanitarianassistance.org. Box 7.1 was contributed by Elizabeth Soulié, the International Federation's Communications and Reporting Officer for the Operations Support Department.

Sources and further information

Coopération Internationale pour le Développement et la Solidarité (CIDSE). *Europe: A True Global Partner for Development? CIDSE Shadow Report on European Progress towards Millennium Development Goal 8.* CIDSE, April 2005.

Development Initiatives. *Global Humanitarian Assistance 2000.* Report commissioned by the Inter-Agency Standing Committee (IASC) from Development Initiatives. Geneva: IASC, 2000. Available at http://www.globalhumanitarianassistance.org/2000.htm

Development Initiatives. *Global Humanitarian Assistance 2003.* Report commissioned by the Humanitarian Financing Work Programme (HFWP) from Development Initiatives. Geneva: HFWP, 2003. Available at http://www.globalhumanitarianassistance.org/2003.htm

CHAPTER 7

Development Initiatives. *Global Humanitarian Assistance 2004–2005*. Report produced by Development Initiatives as part of the Global Humanitarian Assistance and Good Humanitarian Donorship project. Available at http://www.globalhumanitarianassistance.org

Development Initiatives. *What type of funding models best support funding according to need?* Resource document for Ottawa meeting on good humanitarian donorship. 2004. Available at http://www.reliefweb.int/ghd/GHD_Flexible_Funding_Models.pdf

Foy, C. and Helmich, H. (eds.). *Public Support for International Development*. Paris: OECD, 1996.

Fritz Institute. *Lessons from the Tsunami: Top Line Findings*. Fritz Institute, 2005. Available at http://www.fritzinstitute.org/PDFs/Programs/Findings_Sept2605.pdf

Organisation for Economic Co-operation and Development (OECD). *The Development Effectiveness Of Food Aid: Does Tying Matter?* OECD, 2006.

Oxfam International. *Predictable funding for humanitarian emergencies: a challenge to donors*. Oxfam briefing note. Oxfam International, October 2005.

United Nations Office for the Coordination of Humanitarian Affairs (OCHA). *Humanitarian Response Review*. Report commissioned by the United Nations Emergency Relief Coordinator and Under-Secretary-General for Humanitarian Affairs. OCHA, August 2005.

Web sites

Centre for Research on the Epidemiology of Disasters **http://www.cred.be**
Chronic Poverty Research Centre **http://www.chronicpoverty.org**
Consolidated Appeals Process, UN Office for the Coordination of Humanitarian Affairs **http://ochaonline.un.org/humanitarianappeal/**
Global Humanitarian Assistance **http://www.globalhumanitarianassistance.org**
Good Humanitarian Donorship **http://www.goodhumanitariandonorship.org**
Organisation for Economic Co-operation and Development, Development Co-operation Directorate **http://www.oecd.org/dac**
Organisation for Economic Co-operation and Development, Development Assistance Committee online statistics database **http://www.oecd.org/dac/stats/idsonline**
ReliefWeb Financial Tracking Service **http://www.reliefweb.int/fts**
Tsunami Evaluation Coalition Online Forum **http://www.tsunami-evaluation.org**
UN Office for the Coordination of Humanitarian Affairs Central Emergency Response Fund **http://ochaonline2.un.org/Default.aspx?tabid=7956**

---

[1] The DAC comprises the major group of donors who provide official development assistance (ODA): Australia, Austria, Belgium, Canada, Denmark, Finland, France, Germany, Greece, Ireland, Italy, Japan, Luxembourg, Netherlands, New Zealand, Norway, Portugal, Spain, Sweden, Switzerland, UK, USA and the European Commission. Humanitarian aid includes all funding from these governments to UN agencies, the International Red Cross and Red Crescent Movement, non-governmental organizations (NGOs) and direct expenditure classed as emergency and distress relief (including spending on refugees in donor countries for the first year of their residence).

International Federation of Red Cross and Red Crescent Societies

World Disasters Report

Disasters Report

Annex

2006

ANNEX

International Federation
of Red Cross and Red Crescent Societies

Disaster data

The death toll from natural and technological disasters during 2005 was 99,425 – above average for the decade, according to the Centre for Research on the Epidemiology of Disasters (CRED). Natural disasters dominated, causing 88,835 deaths, of which 84 per cent were due to October's South Asia earthquake.

The number of reported natural disasters was up 15 per cent from 2004, mainly due to a 50 per cent increase in floods. The number of technological disasters dropped 10 per cent compared with 2004, but the death toll of 10,590 was in line with the decade's average.

Last year, 161 million people were affected by natural disasters – one-third less than the decade's average of 250 million per year. During 2005, 27 disasters (10 floods, 9 windstorms, 7 droughts and the South Asia earthquake) affected more than 1 million people each. But none of these was on the scale of the floods which affected over 100 million people in Bangladesh, India and China in 2004.

The cost of damage inflicted by natural disasters last year was estimated at nearly US$ 160 billion – more than double the average per year for the decade. Hurricane Katrina accounted for three-quarters of this total.

Official development assistance (ODA) from members of the Development Assistance Committee (DAC) of the Organisation for Economic Co-operation and Development (OECD) grew to US$ 79.5 billion in 2004 (the latest year for which complete data are available). Although this was an increase in real terms of nearly 6 per cent compared with 2003, it equated to an average of just 0.26 per cent of all DAC donors' gross national income – well below the United Nations (UN) target of 0.7 per cent. In 2004, emergency/distress relief (not including the relief provided through multilateral institutions and non-governmental organizations) grew significantly to US$ 7.3 billion (see Figures 1–5).

EM-DAT: a specialized disaster database

Tables 1–13 on natural and technological disasters and their human impact over the last decade were drawn and documented from CRED's EM-DAT. Established in 1973 as a non-profit institution, CRED is based at the School of Public Health of the Catholic University of Louvain in Belgium and became a World Health Organization (WHO) collaborating centre in 1980. Although CRED's main focus is on public health, the centre also studies the socio-economic and long-term effects of large-scale disasters. In 2003, CRED initiated CE-DAT – a database for complex emergencies (see Box 1).

Reliable data on conflict-affected populations are notoriously difficult to obtain, but decision-makers are increasingly demanding a better evidence base for resource allocation. CE-DAT is an important initiative towards addressing this gap. Its approach is to compile and ana-lyse health and nutrition surveys undertaken in conflict and post-conflict situations.

The main objectives of CE-DAT are to:

- **Provide key nutritional, health and mortality indicators** for rational humanitarian aid decision-making;
- **Promote effectiveness of international policy** on response and prevention through evidence-based trend analysis and impact briefings; and
- **Support decision-making on humanitarian aid and relief operations** though an Internet-accessible, multi-sourced database on complex emergencies and their impact on the health status of human populations.

The following indicators are collected in CE-DAT:

- **Mortality rates.** Crude mortality, under-five mortality, infant mortality.
- **Malnutrition.** Acute malnutrition, chronic malnutrition, underweight, oedema and MUAC.
- **Vaccination coverage.** Measles, polio, DTP and tuberculosis.

Beyond compiling health indicators, CE-DAT also:

- **Specifies the populations.** The status of populations – whether internally displaced, resident or refugee – is included.
- **Identifies the location.** Data are broken down to the smallest administrative level boundary.
- **Provides methodologies.** Information is provided on how the data were collected, including sampling methods and lengths of recall periods.
- **States the sources.** All data are referenced to their original sources.
- **Collaborates with partners.** CRED collaborates actively with governmental and non-governmental agencies active in the field to improve the reliability of data on conflict-affected populations and its use for decision-making.

For further information, please go to http://www.cred.be/cedat/index.htm ■

Since 1988, with the sponsorship of the United States Agency for International Development's Office of Foreign Disaster Assistance (OFDA), CRED has maintained EM-DAT, a worldwide database on disasters. It contains essential core data on the occurrence and effects of more than 15,000 disasters in the world from 1900 to the present. The database is compiled from various sources, including UN agencies, non-governmental organizations, insurance companies, research institutes and press agencies.

Priority is given to data from UN agencies, followed by OFDA, governments and the International Federation. This prioritization is not a reflection of the quality or value of the data but the recognition that most reporting sources do not cover all disasters or may have political limitations that could affect the figures. The entries are constantly reviewed for redundancies, inconsistencies and the completion of missing data. CRED consolidates and updates data on a daily basis. A further check is made at monthly intervals. Revisions are made annually at the end of the calendar year.

The database's main objectives are to assist humanitarian action at both national and international levels; to rationalize decision-making for disaster preparedness; and to provide an objective basis for vulnerability assessment and priority setting.

Data definitions and methodology

CRED defines a disaster as "a situation or event, which overwhelms local capacity, necessitating a request to national or international level for external assistance (definition considered in EM-DAT); an unforeseen and often sudden event that causes great damage, destruction and human suffering".

For a disaster to be entered into the database, at least one of the following criteria must be fulfilled:
- Ten or more people reported killed
- 100 people or more reported affected
- Declaration of a state of emergency
- Call for international assistance

The number of people killed includes persons confirmed as dead and persons missing and presumed dead. People affected are those requiring immediate assistance during a period of emergency (i.e., requiring basic survival needs such as food, water, shelter, sanitation and immediate medical assistance). People reported injured or homeless are aggregated with those reported affected to produce a 'total number of people affected'.

The economic impact of a disaster usually consists of direct consequences on the local economy (e.g., damage to infrastructure, crops, housing) and indirect consequences (e.g., loss of revenues, unemployment, market destabilization). In EM-DAT, the registered figure corresponds to the damage value at the moment of the event and usually only to the direct damage, expressed in US dollars (2005 prices).

EM-DAT distinguishes two generic categories for disasters (natural and technological), divided into 15 main categories, themselves covering more than 50 sub-categories. For the production of the tables, natural disasters are split into two specific groups:
- **Hydrometeorological disasters:** avalanches/landslides, droughts/famines, extreme temperatures, floods, forest/scrub fires, windstorms and other disasters, such as insect infestations and wave surges.
- **Geophysical disasters:** earthquakes, tsunamis and volcanic eruptions.

ANNEX

The technological disasters comprise three groups:

- **Industrial accidents:** chemical spills, collapse of industrial infrastructure, explosions, fires, gas leaks, poisoning and radiation.
- **Transport accidents:** by air, rail, road or water means of transport.
- **Miscellaneous accidents:** collapse of domestic/non-industrial structures, explosions and fires.

In Tables 1–13, 'disasters' refer to disasters with a natural and technological trigger only, and do not include wars, conflict-related famines, diseases or epidemics.

The classification of countries as 'high', 'medium' or 'low human development' is based on the 2005 Human Development Index (HDI) of the United Nations Development Programme. For countries not appearing in the HDI, the World Bank's classification of economies by the countries' level of income is used ('high', 'middle' or 'low').

Caveats

Key problems with disaster data include the lack of standardized collection methodologies and definitions. The original information, collected from a variety of public sources, is not specifically gathered for statistical purposes. So, even when the compilation applies strict definitions for disaster events and parameters, the original suppliers of information may not. Moreover, data aren't always complete for each disaster. The quality of completion may vary according to the type of disaster (for example, the number of people affected by transport accidents is rarely reported) or its country of occurrence.

Data on deaths are usually available because they are an immediate proxy for the severity of the disaster. However, the numbers put forward immediately after a disaster may sometimes need to be seriously revised several months later.

Data on the numbers of people affected by a disaster can provide some of the most potentially useful figures, for planning both disaster preparedness and response, but they are sometimes poorly reported. Moreover, the definition of people affected remains open to interpretation, political or otherwise. Even in the absence of manipulation, data may be extrapolated from old census information, with assumptions being made about percentages of an area's population affected.

Data can also be skewed because of the rationale behind data gathering. Reinsurance companies, for instance, systematically gather data on disaster occurrence in order to assess insurance risk, but with a priority in areas of the world where disaster insurance is widespread. Their data may therefore miss out poor, disaster-affected regions where insurance is unaffordable or unavailable.

International Federation
of Red Cross and Red Crescent Societies

For natural disasters over the last decade, data on deaths are missing for one-tenth of reported disasters; data on people affected are missing for one-fifth of disasters; and data on economic damages are missing for 84 per cent of disasters. The figures should therefore be regarded as indicative. Relative changes and trends are more useful to look at than absolute, isolated figures.

Dates can be a source of ambiguity. For example, a declared date for a famine is both necessary and meaningless – a famine does not occur on a single day. In such cases, the date the appropriate body declares an official emergency has been used. Changes in national boundaries cause ambiguities in the data and may make long-term trend analysis more complicated.

Information systems have improved vastly in the last 25 years and statistical data are now more easily available, intensified by an increasing sensitivity to disaster occurrence and consequences. Nevertheless there are still discrepancies. An analysis of the quality and accuracy of disaster data, performed by CRED in 2002, showed that occasionally, for the same disaster, differences of more than 20 per cent may exist between the quantitative data reported by the three major databases – EM-DAT (CRED), NatCat (Munich Re) and Sigma (Swiss Re).

Despite efforts to verify and review data, the quality of disaster databases can only be as good as the reporting system. This, combined with the different aims of three major disaster databases (risk and economic risk analysis for the reinsurance companies and development agenda for CRED), may explain differences between data provided for the same disasters. However, in spite of these differences, the overall trends indicated by the three databases remain similar.

The lack of systematization and standardization of data collection is a major weakness when it comes to long-term planning. Fortunately, due to increased pressure for accountability from various sources, many donors and development agencies have started giving attention to data collection and its methodologies.

Part of the solution to this data problem lies in retrospective analysis. Data are most often publicly quoted and reported during a disaster event, but it is only long after the event, once the relief operation is over, that estimates of damage and death can be verified. Some data gatherers, like CRED, revisit the data; this accounts for retrospective annual disaster figures changing one, two and sometimes even three years after the event.

Improved data in EM-DAT

Last year, significant efforts were made to improve the EM-DAT information available to the public. These changes, made according to a systematic and strict methodology, affect the results in some tables and may modify some trends. The main areas of changes are:

- **Earthquakes.** A systematic review of earthquake data for the last ten years led to the introduction of 18 new disasters for the years 1996–1998. The inclusion of these events, plus the revision of already registered earthquakes, resulted in an increase of 8.19 million in the number of people reported affected for the years 1996–1999 and a decrease of 9.6 million in the number affected in 2001.
- **Floods.** An ongoing review of all registered data led to an increase of almost 7.5 million in the number of people reported affected by floods for the years 1996–2004.
- **Droughts/famines.** Improvements in this dataset (made in collaboration with the International Research Institute for Climate Prediction) included a review of over 800 historical drought disasters and 80 famines in EM-DAT, with dates and loss figures being reassigned as necessary. This led to an increase of 16 reported disasters and more than 47 million people affected for the years 2001–2004.
- **Economic loss/damage.** Information gaps and the lack of a single, consistent methodology led CRED to revise its dataset on economic data and consolidate its methodology on economic data entry. The revision led to an increase of more than US$ 70 billion (at 2005 prices) in the total amount of loss/damage reported for the years 1996–2004.

United States Committee for Refugees and Immigrants

The United States Committee for Refugees and Immigrants (USCRI) is the successor to the merged non-governmental organizations Immigration and Refugee Services of America and United States Committee for Refugees. USCRI resettles refugees, reports on the situation of refugees and asylum seekers abroad and encourages the public, policy-makers and the international community to respond appropriately and effectively to the needs of uprooted populations. Its antecedents go back to 1910.

USCRI travels to the scene of refugee emergencies to gather testimony from uprooted people, to assess their needs and to gauge governmental and international response. The committee conducts public briefings to present its findings and recommendations, testifies before the United States Congress, communicates concerns directly to governments and provides first-hand assessments to the media. USCRI publishes the annual (since 1961) *World Refugee Survey*, the monthly *Refugee Reports* and issue papers.

USCRI provided the data in Tables 14–16. The quality of the data in these tables is affected by the less-than-ideal conditions often associated with flight. Unsettled

International Federation
of Red Cross and Red Crescent Societies

conditions, the biases of governments and opposition groups and the need to use population estimates to plan for providing humanitarian assistance can each contribute to inaccurate estimates. The estimates reproduced in these tables are accurate as at May 2006.

Table 14 lists refugees and asylum seekers by country of origin, while Table 15 lists them by host country. Refugees are people who are outside their home country and are unable or unwilling to return to that country because they fear persecution or armed conflict. But most refugees never receive a formal status determination. Asylum seekers are people who claim and, prima facie, appear to be refugees. While not all asylum seekers are refugees, they are in need of international protection, at least until they are determined not to be refugees. USCRI also includes persons granted various subsidiary forms of protection if based on factors related to the refugee definition, as distinct from, for example, protection granted because of natural disaster.

Table 16 concerns internally displaced people (IDPs). Like refugees and asylum seekers, IDPs have fled their homes but remain in their home country. No universally accepted definition of IDPs exists. USCRI generally considers people who are uprooted within their country because of armed conflict or persecution – and thus would be refugees if they were to cross an international border – to be internally displaced. Others employ broader definitions, however, sometimes including people uprooted by natural or human-made disasters or other causes not directly related to human rights. IDPs often live in war-torn areas and are neither registered nor counted in any systematic way. Estimates of the size of IDP populations are frequently prone to great margins of error.

Philippe Hoyois, Senior Research Fellow with CRED, Regina Below, Manager of CRED's EM-DAT disaster database, and Debarati Guha-Sapir, Director of CRED, prepared the sections on natural and technological disasters, and official development assistance. For further information, please contact Centre for Research on the Epidemiology of Disasters (CRED), School of Public Health, Catholic University of Louvain, 30.94 Clos Chapelle-aux-Champs, B-1200 Brussels, Belgium. Tel: +32 2 764 3327 Fax: +32 2 764 3441 E-mail: cred@esp.ucl.ac.be Web: www.em-dat.net

The section on refugees, asylum seekers and IDPs was prepared by the US Committee for Refugees and Immigrants, 1717 Massachusetts Avenue NW, Suite 200, Washington DC 20036, USA (http://www.refugees.org). For questions regarding this section or data, please contact msmith@uscridc.org.

Figure 1

ODA net disbursements (US$ million, 2004 prices): 1995–2004

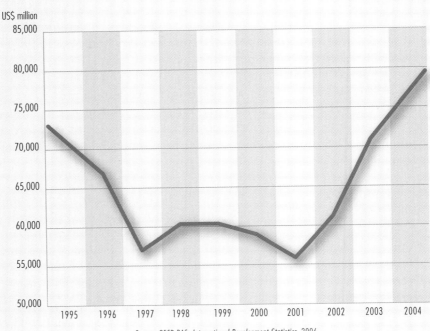

Source: OECD DAC: *International Development Statistics*, 2006

ODA from members of OECD's DAC grew to US$ 79.5 billion in 2004 (the latest year for which complete data are available), a global increase of 5.9 per cent compared with 2003, when taking account of both inflation and exchange rate movements.

The figure shows that 9.2 per cent more aid was given in 2004 compared with 1995 and that, compared with 2001, the year with the lowest figure for the decade considered, ODA increased by 42.2 per cent.

Since 2001, the annual average increase in ODA is 12.5 per cent.

These figures do not take into account non-DAC donors' development assistance of US$ 3.7 billion (2004 prices), of which 46.5 per cent was given by Saudi Arabia.

Also, voluntary contributions from the public via non-governmental organizations and private financial flows from migrants to their countries of origin are not considered.

International Federation
of Red Cross and Red Crescent Societies

Figure 2

ODA net disbursements in 2004 (US$ million, 2004 prices)

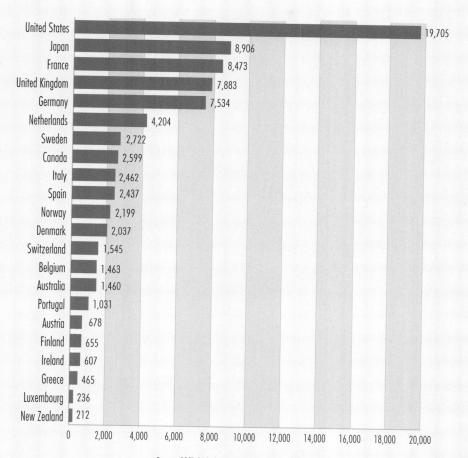

United States	19,705
Japan	8,906
France	8,473
United Kingdom	7,883
Germany	7,534
Netherlands	4,204
Sweden	2,722
Canada	2,599
Italy	2,462
Spain	2,437
Norway	2,199
Denmark	2,037
Switzerland	1,545
Belgium	1,463
Australia	1,460
Portugal	1,031
Austria	678
Finland	655
Ireland	607
Greece	465
Luxembourg	236
New Zealand	212

Source: OECD DAC: *International Development Statistics*, 2006

The five biggest donors of ODA in 2004 were the United States (25 per cent of all ODA), Japan and France (both 11 per cent), the United Kingdom (10 per cent) and Germany (9 per cent). Their combined total of US$ 52 billion (2004 prices) represents two-thirds of all ODA.

If the contributions of the 15 countries forming the European Union (before its enlargement) are aggregated, their ODA amounts to US$ 43 billion (2004 prices), representing 54 per cent of all ODA.

Figure 3
ODA: evolution of DAC contributions (US$ million, 2004 prices)

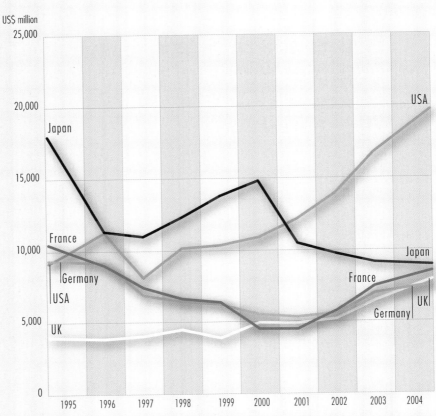

Source: OECD DAC: *International Development Statistics*, 2006

For the entire decade considered, the total contribution of the 15 countries forming the European Union (pre-enlargement) was US$ 339 billion (2004 prices), compared with US$ 118 billion for the United States and US$ 99 billion for Japan.

Compared with its lowest levels in 1997, the amount of United States' development assistance, expressed in 2004 prices, increased by a factor of 2.5 in 2004, while the contribution of EU countries increased by a factor of 1.3 over the same period.

Compared with 2003, the biggest individual increases (measured in 2004 prices), came from the United States (up US$ 3 billion), Portugal and the United Kingdom (both up US$ 600 million), France and Canada (both up US$ 300 million), in real terms.

Between 2003 and 2004, taking account of both inflation and exchange rate movements, Portugal increased its ODA by 188 per cent, Austria by 20 per cent, the United States by 18 per cent, Canada by 15 per cent and Greece by 13 per cent.

Japan was the only one of the big five donors to cut ODA in 2004, continuing a downward trend which has seen its development assistance fall by half in real terms since 1995.

Figure 4

ODA as percentage of DAC donors' GNI, 2004

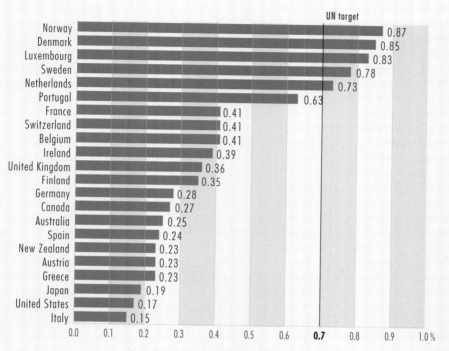

UN target

Norway	0.87
Denmark	0.85
Luxembourg	0.83
Sweden	0.78
Netherlands	0.73
Portugal	0.63
France	0.41
Switzerland	0.41
Belgium	0.41
Ireland	0.39
United Kingdom	0.36
Finland	0.35
Germany	0.28
Canada	0.27
Australia	0.25
Spain	0.24
New Zealand	0.23
Austria	0.23
Greece	0.23
Japan	0.19
United States	0.17
Italy	0.15

0.0   0.1   0.2   0.3   0.4   0.5   0.6   **0.7**   0.8   0.9   1.0 %

Source: OECD DAC: *International Development Statistics*, 2006

Expressed as a percentage of donor countries' gross national income (GNI), only five countries (Norway, Denmark, Luxembourg, Sweden and Netherlands) exceeded the UN's 0.7 per cent target for ODA during 2004.

Compared with 2003, the proportion of aid as a percentage of GNI in 2004 increased for ten countries (Denmark, Luxembourg, Portugal, Switzerland, United Kingdom, Canada, Spain, Austria, Greece and the United States). This increase was particularly significant in Portugal, with its contribution growing from 0.22 per cent of GNI to 0.63 per cent.

Compared with 2003, the proportion of aid as a percentage of GNI in 2004 decreased for six countries (Norway, Sweden, Netherlands, Belgium, Japan and Italy). This decrease was particularly significant in Belgium, with its contribution falling from 0.60 per cent of GNI to 0.41 per cent.

For six countries, the proportion of aid as a percentage of GNI remained equal to 2003 (France, Ireland, Finland, Germany, Australia and New Zealand).

Figure 5
Emergency/distress relief from DAC donors in 2004
(US$ million, 2004 prices)

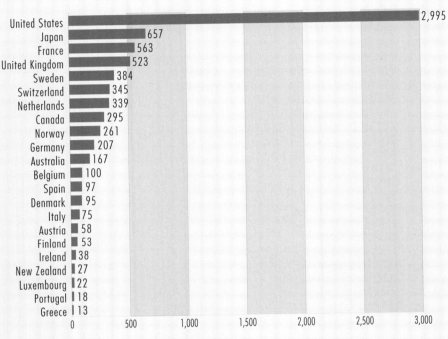

United States	2,995
Japan	657
France	563
United Kingdom	523
Sweden	384
Switzerland	345
Netherlands	339
Canada	295
Norway	261
Germany	207
Australia	167
Belgium	100
Spain	97
Denmark	95
Italy	75
Austria	58
Finland	53
Ireland	38
New Zealand	27
Luxembourg	22
Portugal	18
Greece	13

Source: OECD DAC: *International Development Statistics*, 2006

In 2004, bilateral emergency/distress relief (not including the relief provided through multilateral institutions and non-governmental organizations) grew from US$ 6.2 billion to US$ 7.3 billion (2004 prices).

This relief includes support for disaster preparedness and the cost of transporting and sustaining refugees in donor countries during the first 12 months of their stay (OECD DAC Statistical Reporting Directives, p.16).

Japan's bilateral emergency/distress relief of US$ 657 million in 2004 represented an increase of nearly 22 times its relief for 2003 (2004 prices). This significant increase is notably related to the Indian Ocean tsunami of December 2004. Portugal increased its relief 16 times over the same period. Meanwhile, the United States increased its relief by US$ 450 million (2004 prices) and accounted for 41 per cent of such relief in 2004.

Table 1 Total number of reported disasters[1], by continent and by year (1996 to 2005)

	1996	1997	1998	1999	2000	2001	2002	2003	2004	2005	Total
Africa	59	57	83	145	203	187	203	173	166	159	1,435
Americas	95	101	113	137	153	128	153	122	132	128	1,262
Asia	176	199	218	240	305	294	301	286	315	326	2,660
Europe	56	62	68	78	127	92	111	88	93	115	890
Oceania	17	15	17	15	13	18	18	20	21	16	170
High human development[2]	107	131	129	140	180	149	167	138	136	147	1,424
Medium human development	236	239	281	361	453	397	454	395	451	427	3,694
Low human development	60	64	89	114	168	173	165	156	140	170	1,299
Total	**403**	**434**	**499**	**615**	**801**	**719**	**786**	**689**	**727**	**744**	**6,417**

Source: EM-DAT, CRED, University of Louvain, Belgium

[1] In Tables 1–13, 'disasters' refer to those with a natural or technological trigger only, and do not include wars, conflict-related famines, diseases or epidemics.
[2] See note on UNDP's Human Development Index country status in the section on disaster definitions in the introduction to this annex.

With 744 disasters, 2005 was the third worst year of the decade.

Asia remains the most frequently hit continent in 2005, accounting for 44 per cent of the year's reported disasters.

Reported disasters in countries of low human development in 2005 were nearly one-third above the decade's average.

Countries of medium human development account for well over half of all reported disasters during the decade.

ANNEX

Table 2 Total number of people reported killed, by continent and by year (1996 to 2005)

	1996	1997	1998	1999	2000	2001	2002	2003	2004	2005	Total
Africa	3,444	4,079	6,931	2,649	5,839	4,437	7,520	6,179	4,240	2,913	48,231
Americas	2,565	3,073	21,856	33,985	2,055	3,437	2,088	2,151	8,269	4,767	84,246
Asia	69,584	71,220	82,262	75,862	12,137	29,246	13,180	38,796	238,042	90,748	721,077
Europe	1,203	1,177	1,434	19,451	1,590	2,195	1,701	46,889	1,182	951	77,773
Oceania	111	388	2,227	116	205	9	91	64	35	46	3,292
High human development[1]	2,171	2,530	3,129	5,460	2,261	2,145	1,910	47,447	1,311	2,754	71,118
Medium human development	17,020	18,274	42,380	70,105	13,927	33,307	15,015	42,812	241,640	17,550	512,030
Low human development	57,716	59,133	69,201	56,498	5,638	3,872	7,655	3,820	8,817	79,121	351,471
Total	**76,907**	**79,937**	**114,710**	**132,063**	**21,826**	**39,324**	**24,580**	**94,079**	**251,768**	**99,425**	**934,619**

Source: EM-DAT, CRED, University of Louvain, Belgium

[1] See note on UNDP's Human Development Index country status in the section on disaster definitions in the introduction to this annex.

In 2005, 91 per cent of people killed by disasters lived in Asia, above the decade's average of 77 per cent.

Countries of low human development accounted for 80 per cent of reported deaths in 2005, far above the decade's average of 38 per cent.

Over the past decade, reported deaths from global disasters were 84 per cent higher than deaths during 1986–1995. Numbers killed tripled in Oceania and more than doubled in the Americas over the same period.

The decade saw a number of major disasters: a famine in the Democratic People's Republic of Korea from 1995 to 1999 (at least 270,000 deaths); the Indian Ocean tsunami in 2004 (226,408 deaths); the South Asia earthquake in 2005 (74,647 deaths); a heatwave in Europe in 2003 (45,740 deaths); floods in Venezuela in 1999 (30,000 deaths); three other earthquakes – one in Iran in 2003 (Bam: 26,796 deaths), one in India in 2001 (Gujarat: 20,005 deaths) and one in Turkey in 1999 (Izmit: 17,127 deaths); and a hurricane in Central America in 1998 (Mitch: 18,791 deaths).

Table 3 Total number of people reported affected, by continent and by year (1996 to 2005) in thousands

	1996	1997	1998	1999	2000	2001	2002	2003	2004	2005	Total
Africa	4,277	7,736	10,150	14,345	26,088	18,542	47,921	25,896	28,323	18,790	202,068
Americas	1,868	2,700	16,468	7,856	889	11,375	1,902	3,800	4,268	8,025	59,152
Asia	211,439	56,953	316,191	191,621	225,034	131,490	585,290	232,167	136,595	133,873	2,220,652
Europe	274	549	3,401	6,311	2,911	787	1,443	1,547	538	527	18,285
Oceania	652	730	328	151	7	31	41	38	119	28	2,127
High human development[1]	2,113	1,834	2,166	8,615	1,089	7,352	1,915	989	887	6,818	33,778
Medium human development	207,635	58,162	337,453	199,083	223,474	133,396	585,465	236,509	144,348	125,589	2,251,114
Low human development	8,762	8,673	6,919	12,585	30,367	21,476	49,218	25,949	24,608	28,836	217,392
Total	**218,510**	**68,668**	**346,538**	**220,283**	**254,929**	**162,225**	**636,598**	**263,447**	**169,842**	**161,243**	**2,502,284**

Source: EM-DAT, CRED, University of Louvain, Belgium

[1] See note on UNDP's Human Development Index country status in the section on disaster definitions in the introduction to this annex.

Note: some totals may not match due to rounding.

On the basis of available data, an average of 250 million people were affected annually by disasters from 1996 to 2005 – almost 90 per cent of them in Asia.

Over the decade, 90 per cent of those affected lived in countries of medium human development, while 9 per cent lived in countries of low human development and just 1 per cent lived in countries of high human development.

During the decade, six disasters affected more than 100 million people: a drought in India in 2002; four floods in China in 1996, 1998, 1999 and 2003; and one windstorm in China in 2002.

Over the past decade, the number of people reported affected by disasters globally increased by one-third, compared with the decade 1986–1995. In the Americas, the number of people affected doubled over this period.

ANNEX

Table 4 Total amount of disaster estimated damage, by continent and by year (1996 to 2005) in millions of US dollars (2005 prices)

	1996	1997	1998	1999	2000	2001	2002	2003	2004	2005	Total
Africa	147	41	379	851	636	351	258	5,877	1,531	8	10,079
Americas	15,739	12,649	25,902	22,301	3,862	15,690	4,140	14,227	34,643	136,596	285,748
Asia	37,681	31,931	47,685	42,131	26,954	15,870	8,638	18,389	59,062	18,848	307,190
Europe	2,764	11,991	7,271	39,355	9,450	1,726	31,537	15,318	2,227	3,901	125,541
Oceania	1,165	301	406	1,050	608	398	424	638	578	199	5,768
High human development[1]	19,704	22,705	22,660	63,360	21,607	15,488	34,955	36,467	77,775	136,724	451,445
Medium human development	33,943	34,189	56,859	42,311	12,522	17,987	9,988	17,608	19,562	17,828	262,796
Low human development	3,849	20	2,124	17	7,382	561	54	374	702	5,001	20,085
Total	**57,496**	**56,914**	**81,643**	**105,689**	**41,511**	**34,036**	**44,997**	**54,449**	**98,040**	**159,552**	**734,325**

Source: EM-DAT, CRED, University of Louvain, Belgium

[1] See note on UNDP's Human Development Index country status in the section on disaster definitions in the introduction to this annex.

Note: some totals may not match due to rounding.

As mentioned in the introduction, damage assessment is frequently unreliable. Even for the existing data, the methodologies are not standardized and the financial coverage can vary significantly. Depending on where the disaster occurs and who reports it, estimations vary from zero to billions of US dollars. Damage is reported for 1.8 per cent of technological disasters and 27.5 per cent of natural disasters.

2005 was the costliest year of the decade, with disasters costing more than double the decade's average of US$ 73 billion per year. This was mainly due to Hurricane Katrina, which caused US$ 125 billion of damage (78 per cent of the total for 2005).

In 2005, nine other disasters caused damage estimated at more than US$ 1 billion: a typhoon in China; hurricanes in the USA and Cuba; two floods in China, two in India and one in Switzerland; and the South Asia earthquake.

Over the decade, 120 disasters caused US$ 1 billion or more of damage each. Countries of high human development accounted for 61 per cent of the decade's damage.

Table 5 Total number of reported disasters, by type of phenomenon and by year (1996 to 2005)

	1996	1997	1998	1999	2000	2001	2002	2003	2004	2005	Total
Avalanches/landslides	24	13	21	15	29	21	19	21	16	12	191
Droughts/famines	8	18	34	30	48	48	43	27	20	24	300
Earthquakes/tsunamis	13	22	30	33	31	25	36	40	43	24	297
Extreme temperatures	5	13	13	8	31	23	15	18	15	27	168
Floods	71	78	88	111	154	158	172	158	128	192	1,310
Forest/scrub fires	5	15	16	22	30	14	22	14	8	12	158
Volcanic eruptions	5	4	5	5	5	6	7	2	5	7	50
Windstorms	61	67	72	86	101	97	112	76	121	124	917
Other natural disasters[1]	1	3	1	2	4	2	0	0	12	0	25
Subtotal hydro-meteorological disasters	175	207	245	274	397	363	383	314	320	391	3,069
Subtotal geophysical disasters	18	26	34	38	36	31	43	42	48	31	347
Total natural disasters	**193**	**233**	**279**	**312**	**433**	**394**	**426**	**356**	**368**	**422**	**3,416**
Industrial accidents	35	35	43	37	51	54	48	52	81	69	505
Miscellaneous accidents	39	30	29	52	58	50	52	44	62	45	461
Transport accidents	136	136	148	214	259	221	260	237	216	208	2,035
Total technological disasters	**210**	**201**	**220**	**303**	**368**	**325**	**360**	**333**	**359**	**322**	**3,001**
Total	**403**	**434**	**499**	**615**	**801**	**719**	**786**	**689**	**727**	**744**	**6,417**

Source: EM-DAT, CRED, University of Louvain, Belgium

[1] Insect infestations and waves/surges.

In 2005, the three most frequent types of disaster were transport accidents (28 per cent), floods (26 per cent) and windstorms (17 per cent).

Over the past decade, 2005 saw the highest number of floods and windstorms.

Reported hydrometeorological disasters in 2005 were 27 per cent above the average for the decade, with high numbers of reported extreme temperatures (61 per cent above average), floods (47 per cent above average) and windstorms (35 per cent above average). The number of industrial accidents in 2005 was the second worst of the decade, while transport accidents have been decreasing since 2002.

Table 6 Total number of people reported killed, by type of phenomenon and by year (1996 to 2005)

	1996	1997	1998	1999	2000	2001	2002	2003	2004	2005	Total
Avalanches/landslides	1,155	801	981	351	1,023	692	1,149	706	357	649	7,864
Droughts/famines	54,000	54,520	57,875	54,029	370	199	533	21	13	161	221,721
Earthquakes/tsunamis	576	3,219	9,573	21,869	216	21,348	1,634	29,617	227,317	76,241	391,610
Extreme temperatures	300	619	3,225	771	922	1,653	3,369	48,228	239	923	60,249
Floods	7,187	6,971	9,691	34,367	6,429	4,662	4,122	3,716	6,957	6,135	90,237
Forest/scrub fires	45	32	119	70	47	33	6	47	14	47	460
Volcanic eruptions	4	53	n.a.	n.a.	n.a.	n.a.	200	n.a.	2	3	262
Windstorms	4,217	5,330	24,659	11,900	1,144	1,853	1,116	1,002	6,513	4,676	62,410
Other natural disasters[1]	20	400	n.a.	3	1	n.a.	ndr	ndr	27	ndr	451
Subtotal hydro-meteorological disasters	66,924	68,673	96,550	101,491	9,936	9,092	10,295	53,720	14,120	12,591	443,392
Subtotal geophysical disasters	580	3,272	9,573	21,869	216	21,348	1,834	29,617	227,319	76,244	391,872
Total natural disasters	**67,504**	**71,945**	**106,123**	**123,360**	**10,152**	**30,440**	**12,129**	**83,337**	**241,439**	**88,835**	**835,264**
Industrial accidents	674	1,055	1,942	740	1,770	1,270	1,112	1,444	1,797	2,158	13,962
Miscellaneous accidents	1,298	1,277	747	1,323	1,336	1,760	2,013	1,430	2,115	2,458	15,757
Transport accidents	7,431	5,660	5,898	6,640	8,568	5,854	9,326	7,868	6,417	5,974	69,636
Total technological disasters	**9,403**	**7,992**	**8,587**	**8,703**	**11,674**	**8,884**	**12,451**	**10,742**	**10,329**	**10,590**	**99,355**
Total	**76,907**	**79,937**	**114,710**	**132,063**	**21,826**	**39,324**	**24,580**	**94,079**	**251,768**	**99,425**	**934,619**

Source: EM-DAT, CRED, University of Louvain, Belgium

[1] Insect infestations and waves/surges.

Note: n.a. signifies no data available; ndr signifies no disaster reported. For more information, see section on caveats in introductory text.

Earthquakes accounted for 77 per cent of the total deaths reported for 2005, in a year when natural disasters claimed nearly 89,000 lives. The deadliest reported disasters of the decade were earthquakes and tsunamis (42 per cent), droughts/famines (24 per cent) and floods (10 per cent). Reported deaths from hydrometeorological disasters in 2005 were over three times lower than the decade's average of 44,000 deaths a year. Industrial and miscellaneous accidents peaked in 2005, with reported deaths over 50 per cent above the decade's average. However, the toll from all techno-logical disasters has remained fairly steady throughout the decade, averaging just under 10,000 deaths a year.

International Federation
of Red Cross and Red Crescent Societies

Table 7 Total number of people reported affected, by type of phenomenon and by year (1996 to 2005) in thousands

	1996	1997	1998	1999	2000	2001	2002	2003	2004	2005	Total
Avalanches/landslides	9	34	209	15	215	67	771	459	13	8	1,801
Droughts/famines	5,836	8,016	24,495	38,647	176,477	87,000	356,626	76,184	30,789	26,530	830,601
Earthquakes/tsunamis	5,490	1,227	3,678	6,856	2,479	9,711	851	4,194	3,147	3,928	41,562
Extreme temperatures	n.a.	615	36	725	28	213	104	1,840	2,140	2	5,703
Floods	179,496	44,957	291,542	149,740	64,998	34,461	167,408	169,113	116,990	74,285	1,292,989
Forest/scrub fires	6	53	167	19	39	6	26	184	21	7	527
Volcanic eruptions	7	7	8	34	119	78	278	25	53	332	940
Windstorms	27,630	13,594	26,286	23,905	10,511	30,635	110,464	10,782	16,383	56,062	326,252
Other natural disasters¹	n.a.	29	n.a.	1	17	n.a.	ndr	ndr	n.a.	ndr	48
Subtotal hydro-meteorological disasters	*212,977*	*67,297*	*342,736*	*213,053*	*252,284*	*152,382*	*635,400*	*258,561*	*166,336*	*156,895*	*2,457,921*
Subtotal geophysical disasters	*5,497*	*1,235*	*3,686*	*6,890*	*2,598*	*9,789*	*1,129*	*4,219*	*3,200*	*4,260*	*42,502*
Total natural disasters	**218,473**	**68,532**	**346,421**	**219,942**	**254,882**	**162,171**	**636,530**	**262,780**	**169,536**	**161,155**	**2,500,423**
Industrial accidents	15	113	63	324	17	19	2	647	156	16	1,372
Miscellaneous accidents	18	20	50	12	24	31	61	15	102	67	400
Transport accidents	3	3	4	5	7	3	6	5	48	6	89
Total technological disasters	**36**	**136**	**117**	**341**	**47**	**53**	**68**	**667**	**307**	**88**	**1,861**
Total	**218,510**	**68,668**	**346,538**	**220,283**	**254,929**	**162,225**	**636,598**	**263,447**	**169,842**	**161,243**	**2,502,284**

Source: EM-DAT, CRED, University of Louvain, Belgium

¹ Insect infestations and waves/surges.

Note: n.a. signifies no data available; ndr signifies no disaster reported. For more information, see section on caveats in introductory text.

Note: some totals may not match due to rounding.

Disasters which affected the most people in 2005 were floods (74 million people affected: 46 per cent of those affected by disasters) and windstorms (56 million people affected: 35 per cent of those affected by disasters).

For the third consecutive year, the number of people affected by droughts and famine decreased from a peak in 2002.

Over the decade, hydrometeorological disasters accounted for 98 per cent of all those affected by disasters, with floods affecting more than 50 per cent. Numbers affected by technological disasters in 2005 were less than half the decade's average.

ANNEX

Table 8 Total amount of disaster estimated damage, by type of phenomenon and by year (1996 to 2005) in millions of US dollars (2005 prices)

	1996	1997	1998	1999	2000	2001	2002	2003	2004	2005	Total
Avalanches/landslides	n.a.	20	1,066	n.a.	150	78	14	55	n.a.	n.a.	1,382
Droughts/famines	1,494	498	646	8,970	7,186	4,286	1,804	2,138	1,615	520	29,156
Earthquakes/tsunamis	713	6,032	3,267	41,096	428	7,947	1,702	9,292	37,625	5,080	113,181
Extreme temperatures	n.a.	3,655	4,431	1,172	141	221	0	6,423	0	155	16,197
Floods	35,755	15,936	47,737	17,097	21,218	3,996	28,362	15,551	8,343	14,439	208,434
Forest/scrub fires	2,144	20,692	1,534	575	1,201	99	143	2,755	3	40	29,186
Volcanic eruptions	21	10	n.a.	n.a.	2	16	10	n.a.	n.a.	n.a.	59
Windstorms	13,697	9,560	22,748	36,540	10,556	17,382	2,080	18,236	49,101	139,309	319,208
Other natural disasters[1]	n.a.	4	2	n.a.	136	n.a.	ndr	ndr	n.a.	ndr	142
Subtotal hydro-meteorological disasters	53,090	50,365	78,164	64,354	40,588	26,062	32,403	45,157	59,062	154,462	603,705
Subtotal geophysical disasters	733	6,042	3,267	41,096	430	7,963	1,712	9,292	37,625	5,080	113,240
Total natural disasters	53,824	56,406	81,431	105,450	41,017	34,025	34,115	54,449	96,687	159,542	716,946
Industrial accidents	1,501	464	154	4	n.a.	11	10,815	n.a.	931	n.a.	13,879
Miscellaneous accidents	1,914	31	22	3	493	n.a.	67	n.a.	n.a.	10	2,541
Transport accidents	257	13	35	233	n.a.	n.a.	n.a.	n.a.	422	n.a.	960
Total technological disasters	3,672	508	212	239	493	11	10,882	n.a.	1,353	10	17,380
Total	57,496	56,914	81,643	105,689	41,511	34,036	44,997	54,449	98,040	159,552	734,325

Source: EM-DAT, CRED, University of Louvain, Belgium

[1] Insect infestations and waves/surges.
Note: n.a. signifies no data available; ndr signifies no disaster reported. For more information, see section on caveats in introductory text.
Note: some totals may not match due to rounding.
Estimates of disaster damage must be treated with caution, as the financial value attached to infrastructure in developed countries is much higher than in developing countries.
While reporting is better for large disasters, the low reporting rates of direct damage make analysis difficult.
The costliest disasters of the decade were windstorms (43 per cent), floods (28 per cent) and earthquakes/tsunamis (15 per cent).
Hurricane Katrina, which cost US$ 125 billion, accounted for almost 40 per cent of all damage caused by windstorms over the decade.

International Federation
of Red Cross and Red Crescent Societies

Table 9 Total number of reported disasters, by type of phenomenon and by continent (1996 to 2005)

	Africa	Americas	Asia	Europe	Oceania	HHD[2]	MHD[2]	LHD[2]	Total
Avalanches/landslides	11	42	112	18	8	23	150	18	191
Droughts/famines	140	51	87	14	8	28	134	138	300
Earthquakes/tsunamis	20	45	171	52	9	50	214	33	297
Extreme temperatures	7	33	48	79	1	76	80	12	168
Floods	290	281	472	229	38	320	685	305	1,310
Forest/scrub fires	12	66	23	47	10	87	65	6	158
Volcanic eruptions	5	23	13	2	7	14	34	2	50
Windstorms	74	321	340	110	72	433	413	71	917
Other natural disasters[1]	13	2	7	1	2	2	13	10	25
Subtotal hydro-meteorological disasters	547	796	1,089	498	139	969	1,540	560	3,069
Subtotal geophysical disasters	25	68	184	54	16	64	248	35	347
Total natural disasters	**572**	**864**	**1,273**	**552**	**155**	**1,033**	**1,788**	**595**	**3,416**
Industrial accidents	49	39	361	56	0	56	395	54	505
Miscellaneous accidents	94	70	220	73	4	85	292	84	461
Transport accidents	720	289	806	209	11	250	1,219	566	2,035
Total technological disasters	**863**	**398**	**1,387**	**338**	**15**	**391**	**1,906**	**704**	**3,001**
Total	**1,435**	**1,262**	**2,660**	**890**	**170**	**1,424**	**3,694**	**1,299**	**6,417**

Source: EM-DAT, CRED, University of Louvain, Belgium

[1] Insect infestations and waves/surges.
[2] HHD stands for high human development, MHD for medium human development and LHD for low human development. See note on UNDP's Human Development Index country status in the section on disaster definitions in the introduction to this annex.

Floods were the most common natural disaster to hit Africa, Asia and Europe; windstorms were the most common disaster in the Americas and Oceania. More than half the decade's earthquakes and tsunamis occurred in Asia, while almost half the droughts/famines occurred in Africa and nearly half the extreme temperature events occurred in Europe. Droughts were most frequent in countries of medium and low human development. Windstorms and extreme temperatures were most common in countries of medium and high human development. Transport accidents were the most frequent, accounting for nearly one-third of all disasters reported over the decade.

ANNEX

Table 10 Total number of people reported killed, by type of phenomenon and by continent (1996 to 2005)

	Africa	Americas	Asia	Europe	Oceania	HHD[2]	MHD[2]	LHD[2]	Total
Avalanches/landslides	251	1,632	5,464	389	128	365	6,953	546	7,864
Droughts/famines	4,656	54	216,923	0	88	0	842	220,879	221,721
Earthquakes/tsunamis	3,313	2,861	364,651	18,584	2,201	2,625	306,845	82,140	391,610
Extreme temperatures	168	1,597	9,854	48,630	0	48,235	11,041	973	60,249
Floods	8,183	38,028	42,570	1,422	34	3,471	73,490	13,276	90,237
Forest/scrub fires	114	88	96	137	25	197	259	4	460
Volcanic eruptions	201	54	3	n.a.	4	52	10	200	262
Windstorms	1,535	28,110	31,900	610	255	5,813	51,411	5,186	62,410
Other natural disasters[1]	n.a.	3	448	n.a.	n.a.	n.a.	451	n.a.	451
Subtotal hydro-meteorological disasters	14,907	69,512	307,255	51,188	530	58,081	144,447	240,864	443,392
Subtotal geophysical disasters	3,514	2,915	364,654	18,584	2,205	2,677	306,855	82,340	391,872
Total natural disasters	**18,421**	**72,427**	**671,909**	**69,772**	**2,735**	**60,758**	**451,302**	**323,204**	**835,264**
Industrial accidents	2,785	277	10,056	844	ndr	360	10,631	2,971	13,962
Miscellaneous accidents	2,847	2,989	8,401	1,474	46	2,027	9,902	3,828	15,757
Transport accidents	24,178	8,553	30,711	5,683	511	7,973	40,195	21,468	69,636
Total technological disasters	**29,810**	**11,819**	**49,168**	**8,001**	**557**	**10,360**	**60,728**	**28,267**	**99,355**
Total	**48,231**	**84,246**	**721,077**	**77,773**	**3,292**	**71,118**	**512,030**	**351,471**	**934,619**

Source: EM-DAT, CRED, University of Louvain, Belgium

[1] Insect infestations and waves/surges.
[2] HHD stands for high human development, MHD for medium human development and LHD for low human development. See note on UNDP's Human Development Index country status in the section on disaster definitions in the introduction to this annex.
Note: n.a. signifies no data available; ndr signifies no disaster reported. For more information, see section on caveats in introductory text.
Over the decade, the biggest killers per continent (not including conflict- and disease-related deaths) were transport accidents in Africa (accounting for half the continent's deaths from disasters), floods in the Americas (45 per cent), earthquakes/tsunamis in Asia (51 per cent), extreme temperatures in Europe (63 per cent) and earthquakes/tsunamis in Oceania (67 per cent).
Analysing the figures by level of human development, HHD countries lost most lives to extreme temperatures (68 per cent), MHD countries to earthquakes/tsunamis (60 per cent) and LHD countries to droughts/famines (63 per cent).
90 per cent of deaths from technological disasters were in MHD and LHD countries.

Table 11 Total number of people reported affected, by type of phenomenon and by continent (1996 to 2005) in thousands

	Africa	Americas	Asia	Europe	Oceania	HHD[2]	MHD[2]	LHD[2]	Total
Avalanches/landslides	3	203	1,579	14	1	15	1,780	7	1,801
Droughts/famines	173,979	15,287	639,190	1,063	1,083	665	657,066	172,870	830,601
Earthquakes/tsunamis	361	3,757	33,392	4,016	36	833	36,301	4,429	41,562
Extreme temperatures	0	4,037	895	771	0	44	5,459	200	5,703
Floods	23,203	9,525	1,255,118	5,048	96	5,851	1,253,085	34,053	1,292,989
Forest/scrub fires	9	184	57	260	18	317	207	3	527
Volcanic eruptions	397	283	211	0	49	68	762	110	940
Windstorms	3,902	25,278	289,215	7,025	832	25,521	295,276	5,456	326,252
Other natural disasters[1]	n.a.	1	46	n.a.	n.a.	n.a.	19	29	48
Subtotal hydro-meteorological disasters	201,097	54,514	2,186,100	14,180	2,030	32,412	2,212,891	212,618	2,457,921
Subtotal geophysical disasters	759	4,040	33,603	4,016	85	901	37,062	4,539	42,502
Total natural disasters	201,856	58,554	2,219,703	18,196	2,114	33,313	2,249,953	217,157	2,500,423
Industrial accidents	10	576	716	71	ndr	440	928	5	1,372
Miscellaneous accidents	189	12	172	14	12	14	208	178	400
Transport accidents	13	9	62	4	n.a.	11	25	53	89
Total technological disasters	212	597	950	89	12	464	1,161	235	1,861
Total	202,068	59,152	2,220,652	18,285	2,127	33,778	2,251,114	217,393	2,502,284

Source: EM-DAT, CRED, University of Louvain, Belgium

[1] Insect infestations and waves/surges.
[2] HHD stands for high human development, MHD for medium human development and LHD for low human development. See note on UNDP's Human Development Index country status in the section on disaster definitions in the introduction to this annex.
Note: n.a. signifies no data available; ndr signifies no disaster reported. For more information, see section on caveats in introductory text.
Note: some totals may not match due to rounding.
Over the decade, the disasters which affected the most people per continent were: droughts/famines in Africa (accounting for 86 per cent of all disaster-affected Africans) and in Oceania (51 per cent); floods in Asia (57 per cent); and windstorms in the Americas (43 per cent) and Europe (38 per cent). Windstorms affected the most people in HHD countries (76 per cent), floods affected the most in MHD countries (56 per cent) and droughts/famines affected the most in LHD countries (80 per cent).
MHD countries accounted for 62 per cent of those affected by technological disasters.

ANNEX

Table 12 Total amount of disaster estimated damage, by type of phenomenon and by continent (1996 to 2005) in millions of US dollars (2005 prices)

	Africa	Americas	Asia	Europe	Oceania	HHD[2]	MHD[2]	LHD[2]	Total
Avalanches/landslides	n.a.	97	1,265	20	n.a.	20	1,362	n.a.	1,382
Droughts/famines	334	4,094	16,380	8,019	329	10,715	18,147	293	29,156
Earthquakes/tsunamis	5,824	7,689	70,060	29,609	n.a.	62,669	43,536	6,976	113,181
Extreme temperatures	1	5,620	3,650	6,706	221	12,418	3,779	n.a.	16,197
Floods	1,880	27,903	129,055	47,860	1,735	77,568	125,897	4,968	208,434
Forest/scrub fires	11	2,663	23,084	2,940	488	5,847	23,339	n.a.	29,186
Volcanic eruptions	10	22	3	24	n.a.	34	15	10	59
Windstorms	1,082	234,680	62,449	18,138	2,859	266,940	45,090	7,179	319,208
Other natural disasters[1]	6	n.a.	n.a.	n.a.	136	136	2	4	143
Subtotal hydro-meteorological disasters	3,314	275,057	235,883	83,684	5,768	373,644	217,617	12,445	603,705
Subtotal geophysical disasters	5,834	7,711	70,063	29,633	n.a.	62,703	43,551	6,986	113,240
Total natural disasters	**9,148**	**282,768**	**305,946**	**113,316**	**5,768**	**436,347**	**261,168**	**19,430**	**716,946**
Industrial accidents	838	1,245	696	11,100	ndr	12,345	1,316	218	13,879
Miscellaneous accidents	23	1,609	34	874	n.a.	2,429	107	5	2,541
Transport accidents	69	127	513	250	n.a.	324	204	432	960
Total technological disasters	**931**	**2,981**	**1,243**	**12,224**	**n.a.**	**15,097**	**1,627**	**655**	**17,380**
Total	**10,079**	**285,748**	**307,190**	**125,541**	**5,768**	**451,445**	**262,796**	**20,085**	**734,326**

Source: EM-DAT, CRED, University of Louvain, Belgium

[1] Insect infestations and waves/surges.

[2] HHD stands for high human development, MHD for medium human development and LHD for low human development. See note on UNDP's Human Development Index country status in the section on disaster definitions in the introduction to this annex.

Note: n.a. signifies no data available; ndr signifies no disaster reported. For more information, see section on caveats in introductory text.

Note: some totals may not match due to rounding.

Amounts of estimated damage must be approached with caution due to low reporting rates and methodological weaknesses.

Over the decade, floods proved costliest for Asia (accounting for 42 per cent of total reported damage) and Europe (38 per cent); windstorms proved costliest for the Americas (82 per cent) and Oceania (50 per cent); and earthquakes/tsunamis proved costliest for Africa (58 per cent).

In HHD countries, windstorms caused most damage (59 per cent), in MHD countries floods caused most damage (48 per cent) and in LHD countries, windstorms and earthquakes/tsunamis each caused around 35 per cent of all damage. LHD countries accounted for less than 3 per cent of the total global cost of disasters.

	Total number of people reported killed (1986–1995)	Total number of people reported affected (1986–1995)	Total number of people reported killed (1996–2005)	Total number of people reported affected (1996–2005)	Total number of people reported killed (2005)	Total number of people reported affected (2005)
Africa	**31,161**	**138,388,197**	**48,231**	**202,068,099**	**2,913**	**18,790,330**
Algeria	486	73,748	3,892	307,569	43	1,894
Angola	848	3,181,197	875	593,862	20	10,070
Benin	23	241,000	245	678,305	ndr	ndr
Botswana	28	1,436,507	3	143,736	n.a.	n.a.
Burkina Faso	38	2,899,824	95	110,220	ndr	ndr
Burundi	112	3,600	390	1,266,453	168	89,118
Cameroon	2,190	798,541	452	6,386	56	12
Canary Islands (ES)	ndr	ndr	136	869	36	17
Cape Verde	n.a.	6,306	18	40,000	ndr	ndr
Central African Republic	31	3,999	242	113,261	24	23,846
Chad	95	462,398	173	851,793	14	28
Comoros	24	50,200	282	284,300	26	284,000
Congo	663	16,500	119	118,663	19	3,500
Congo, DR of	824	28,009	2,682	268,477	286	5,664
Côte d'Ivoire	138	7,187	416	193	ndr	ndr
Djibouti	155	321,075	52	592,350	n.a.	47,000
Egypt	2,325	258,886	1,991	6,390	136	95
Equatorial Guinea	15	313	82	4,300	80	650
Eritrea[1]	61	1,615,725	128	6,580,043	56	30
Ethiopia[1]	956	37,361,788	1,118	78,324,181	242	242,460
Gabon	102	10,000	50	11	ndr	ndr
Gambia	100	n.a.	83	52,906	15	n.a.
Ghana	331	707,309	470	471,000	18	n.a.
Guinea	473	6,066	309	220,937	10	15
Guinea-Bissau	15	10,050	218	102,508	12	8
Kenya	1,456	3,900,294	1,454	16,372,805	141	2,536,308
Lesotho	40	601,500	1	772,251	ndr	ndr
Liberia	n.a.	1,002,000	70	5,000	ndr	ndr
Libyan AJ	290	121	200	79	ndr	ndr
Madagascar	663	2,274,434	1,074	4,883,115	109	78,910
Malawi	507	21,108,710	788	8,735,861	61	4,544,514
Mali	97	326,667	3,804	46,646	13	1,860
Mauritania	2,350	482,414	141	816,491	43	3,000
Mauritius	162	14,307	6	2,050	ndr	ndr
Morocco	1,009	38,203	1,520	375,669	46	36
Mozambique	5,977	6,364,211	1,450	9,088,781	22	1,447,837

	Total number of people reported killed (1986–1995)	Total number of people reported affected (1986–1995)	Total number of people reported killed (1996–2005)	Total number of people reported affected (1996–2005)	Total number of people reported killed (2005)	Total number of people reported affected (2005)
Namibia	20	413,200	21	1,054,548	ndr	ndr
Niger	250	2,771,992	135	7,318,599	n.a.	3,600,000
Nigeria	1,954	887,563	9,560	602,625	770	14,460
Reunion (FR)	79	10,261	2	3,700	ndr	ndr
Rwanda	355	81,678	268	1,313,445	ndr	ndr
Saint Helena (GB)	ndr	ndr	n.a.	300	ndr	ndr
Sao Tome and Principe	ndr	ndr	ndr	ndr	ndr	ndr
Senegal	131	32,925	1,601	1,224,981	n.a.	50,000
Seychelles	n.a.	n.a.	8	12,867	ndr	ndr
Sierra Leone	212	n.a.	869	215,025	20	15,000
Somalia	994	642,000	3,041	4,753,509	49	9,510
South Africa	2,229	5,120,497	1,695	4,207,658	101	376
Sudan	646	15,716,009	1,340	9,360,153	73	164,939
Swaziland	n.a.	525,000	52	1,393,209	n.a.	1,150
Tanzania	496	1,459,791	2,220	10,093,844	19	15,575
Togo	3	586,500	n.a.	95,405	ndr	ndr
Tunisia	109	154,716	383	27,134	ndr	ndr
Uganda	437	999,617	1,108	4,267,741	44	1,236,346
Zambia	429	3,773,204	486	16,816,259	123	4,362,040
Zimbabwe	233	19,600,155	413	7,069,636	18	62
Americas	**32,728**	**29,679,325**	**84,246**	**59,148,566**	**4,767**	**8,025,404**
Anguilla (GB)	ndr	ndr	n.a.	150	ndr	ndr
Antigua and Barbuda	4	76,732	3	24,559	ndr	ndr
Argentina	391	5,166,019	566	856,852	21	381
Aruba (NL)	ndr	ndr	ndr	ndr	ndr	ndr
Bahamas	4	1,700	3	12,000	n.a.	1,500
Barbados	n.a.	230	1	n.a.	ndr	ndr
Belize	n.a.	2,600	66	142,570	n.a.	n.a.
Bermuda	28	40	22	n.a.	ndr	ndr
Bolivia	200	868,856	915	759,481	n.a.	3,000
Brazil	3,211	5,210,267	2,213	12,843,410	115	41,986
Canada	262	64,206	411	76,698	4	5,900
Cayman Islands (GB)	ndr	ndr	1	300	ndr	ndr
Chile	753	491,993	208	639,152	61	29,105
Colombia	2,879	792,443	2,664	2,875,239	378	399,458
Costa Rica	121	400,708	154	869,863	20	4,072
Cuba	900	1,091,265	256	10,492,339	20	2,600,000
Dominica	1	3,711	14	990	ndr	ndr
Dominican Republic	380	1,216,020	1,645	1,107,711	148	2,466
Ecuador	5,888	483,561	799	414,263	ndr	ndr

	Total number of people reported killed (1986–1995)	Total number of people reported affected (1986–1995)	Total number of people reported killed (1996–2005)	Total number of people reported affected (1996–2005)	Total number of people reported killed (2005)	Total number of people reported affected (2005)
El Salvador	1,332	818,560	1,976	2,174,617	120	77,224
Falkland Islands (GB)	ndr	ndr	ndr	ndr	ndr	ndr
French Guiana (FR)	ndr	ndr	n.a.	70,000	ndr	ndr
Grenada	n.a.	1,000	40	61,045	1	835
Guadeloupe (FR)	5	11,084	25	153	ndr	ndr
Guatemala	432	125,025	2,616	837,404	1,542	476,647
Guyana	n.a.	481	44	919,974	34	274,774
Haiti	3,578	3,653,686	6,758	650,021	86	41,833
Honduras	854	217,106	14,967	3,898,964	61	104,669
Jamaica	125	1,431,712	36	388,022	6	10,396
Martinique (FR)	10	4,510	n.a.	600	ndr	ndr
Mexico	2,732	842,734	3,408	5,113,245	99	2,983,703
Montserrat (GB)	11	17,040	32	8,000	ndr	ndr
Netherlands Antilles (NL)	2	40,000	15	4	ndr	ndr
Nicaragua	388	712,285	3,490	1,552,973	7	7,170
Panama	174	54,939	49	71,833	3	7,000
Paraguay	n.a.	400,575	503	298,644	0	52,990
Peru	2,577	4,049,045	3,753	5,785,430	148	2,652
Puerto Rico (US)	160	100,599	167	23,453	ndr	ndr
St Kitts and Nevis	1	3,100	5	11,180	ndr	ndr
St Lucia	49	750	n.a.	375	ndr	ndr
St Pierre et Miquelon (FR)	ndr	ndr	ndr	ndr	ndr	ndr
St Vincent and the Grenadines	3	1,560	n.a.	1,634	n.a.	530
Suriname	169	13	10	n.a.	ndr	ndr
Trinidad and Tobago	11	1,030	3	2,377	n.a.	n.a.
Turks and Caicos Islands (GB)	n.a.	n.a.	43	200	ndr	ndr
United States	4,324	1,243,377	5,501	5,393,524	1,555	851,341
Uruguay	20	26,740	116	27,559	18	12
Venezuela	742	32,023	30,745	741,755	320	45,760
Virgin Islands (GB)	n.a.	10,000	n.a.	3	ndr	ndr
Virgin Islands (US)	7	10,000	3	n.a.	ndr	ndr
Asia	**400,265**	**1,690,068,149**	**721,077**	**2,220,652,039**	**90,748**	**133,872,598**
Afghanistan	3,680	417,059	10,274	7,016,889	650	42,570
Armenia[2]	91	1,300,798	16	319,156	ndr	ndr
Azerbaijan[2]	482	1,659,123	196	819,008	23	n.a.
Bahrain	10	n.a.	143	n.a.	ndr	ndr
Bangladesh	157,354	183,473,138	9,619	70,838,175	796	1,186,606

	Total number of people reported killed (1986–1995)	Total number of people reported affected (1986–1995)	Total number of people reported killed (1996–2005)	Total number of people reported affected (1996–2005)	Total number of people reported killed (2005)	Total number of people reported affected (2005)
Bhutan	39	65,600	200	1,000	ndr	ndr
Brunei Darussalam	ndr	ndr	ndr	ndr	ndr	ndr
Cambodia	637	3,429,000	615	13,527,614	29	600,000
China, PR of[3]	27,875	818,564,671	32,574	1,247,077,832	3,555	91,171,439
East Timor[4]	–	–	4	3,558	ndr	ndr
Georgia[2]	311	4,147	150	1,241,864	n.a.	2,500
Hong Kong (CN)[3]	316	12,673	87	4,637	n.a.	n.a.
India	42,026	561,472,995	85,001	686,724,143	5,405	28,262,805
Indonesia	7,641	5,139,970	174,738	4,626,139	1,697	152,848
Iran, Islamic Rep. of	42,848	1,878,767	34,260	64,264,807	1,098	130,329
Iraq	894	808,500	1,323	8,908	1,225	901
Israel	68	343	109	1,857	7	200
Japan	6,567	1,106,746	958	1,998,385	238	309,833
Jordan	66	18,369	114	330,274	ndr	ndr
Kazakhstan[2]	230	30,036	91	675,970	n.a.	25,000
Korea, DPR of	54,842	6,222,967	216,773	6,519,768	207	16,298
Korea, Rep. of	2,715	771,313	1,907	966,458	36	4,741
Kuwait	ndr	ndr	2	200	ndr	ndr
Kyrgyzstan[2]	232	195,306	203	13,536	3	2,050
Lao, PDR	66	3,150,862	159	1,680,005	ndr	ndr
Lebanon	70	105,575	48	17,555	ndr	ndr
Macau (CN)	n.a.	3,986	ndr	ndr	ndr	ndr
Malaysia	598	116,979	637	173,300	13	30,600
Maldives	n.a.	24,149	143	27,314	ndr	ndr
Mongolia	186	600,000	161	2,371,711	ndr	ndr
Myanmar	1,331	619,531	581	281,947	17	16
Nepal	3,335	1,272,951	3,367	1,471,803	243	31,674
Oman	ndr	ndr	104	104	ndr	ndr
Pakistan	7,239	22,233,550	79,634	18,480,367	74,568	10,396,730
Palestine (West Bank/Gaza)[5]	ndr	ndr	14	20	ndr	ndr
Philippines	24,141	42,991,053	6,006	17,196,335	116	213,066
Qatar	ndr	ndr	ndr	ndr	ndr	ndr
Saudi Arabia	2,034	n.a.	1,248	15,881	63	67
Singapore	27	237	n.a.	1,200	ndr	ndr
Sri Lanka	882	6,290,866	36,013	9,141,219	39	145,030
Syrian Arab Republic	46	n.a.	366	668,676	62	88
Taiwan (CN)	786	24,188	3,546	777,360	29	3,039
Tajikistan[2]	1,718	146,792	244	3,732,966	45	7,072
Thailand	3,973	11,735,586	9,737	25,280,191	103	255,226
Turkmenistan[2]	n.a.	420	51	n.a.	ndr	ndr

	Total number of people reported killed (1986–1995)	Total number of people reported affected (1986–1995)	Total number of people reported killed (1996–2005)	Total number of people reported affected (1996–2005)	Total number of people reported killed (2005)	Total number of people reported affected (2005)
United Arab Emirates	n.a.	100	183	41	ndr	ndr
Uzbekistan[2]	10	50,400	168	1,125,488	n.a.	1,500
Viet Nam	4,517	13,547,864	8,233	30,965,725	394	879,638
Yemen[6]	319	91,539	1,077	262,653	87	732
Yemen, Arab Rep.[6]	38	150,000				
Yemen, PDR[6]	25	340,000				
Europe	**43,207**	**17,139,944**	**77,773**	**18,285,498**	**951**	**526,781**
Albania	75	3,239,190	29	605,009	5	400,500
Andorra	ndr	ndr	ndr	ndr	ndr	ndr
Austria	38	130	261	71,294	4	900
Azores (PT)	172	n.a.	74	1,215	ndr	ndr
Belarus[2]	n.a.	40,000	92	23,499	ndr	ndr
Belgium	279	2,290	211	3,937	2	210
Bosnia and Herzegovina[7]	ndr	ndr	64	354,180	4	3,100
Bulgaria	71	8,179	49	13,940	32	12,200
Channel Islands (GB)	ndr	ndr	ndr	ndr	ndr	ndr
Croatia[7]	61	25	90	4,250	3	250
Cyprus	2	1,865	88	1,240	31	8
Czech Republic[8]	18	4	67	302,145	1	3
Czechoslovakia[8]	41	n.a.				
Denmark	55	100	13	2,072	4	n.a.
Estonia[2]	912	140	22	130	n.a.	100
Faroe Islands (DK)	ndr	ndr	ndr	ndr	ndr	ndr
Finland	ndr	ndr	35	448	n.a.	400
France	636	12,822	15,692	3,593,495	65	4,080
Germany[9]	143	132,195	5,616	447,621	4	617
Germany, Dem. Rep.[9]	92	n.a.				
Germany, Fed. Rep. of[9]	155	3,993				
Gibraltar (GB)	ndr	ndr	ndr	ndr	ndr	ndr
Greece	1,314	78,641	655	127,808	121	n.a.
Greenland (DK)	ndr	ndr	ndr	ndr	ndr	ndr
Holy See	–	–	ndr	ndr	ndr	ndr
Hungary	47	59	204	147,575	4	n.a.
Iceland	34	363	n.a.	199	ndr	ndr
Ireland	57	3,500	n.a.	1,000	n.a.	n.a.
Isle of Man (GB)	ndr	ndr	ndr	ndr	ndr	ndr
Italy	599	32,242	20,922	111,010	59	103
Latvia[2]	ndr	ndr	36	n.a.	n.a.	n.a.
Liechtenstein	ndr	ndr	ndr	ndr	ndr	ndr

	Total number of people reported killed (1986–1995)	Total number of people reported affected (1986–1995)	Total number of people reported killed (1996–2005)	Total number of people reported affected (1996–2005)	Total number of people reported killed (2005)	Total number of people reported affected (2005)
Lithuania[2]	6	780,000	62	n.a.	n.a.	n.a.
Luxembourg	ndr	ndr	20	n.a.	ndr	ndr
Macedonia, FYR of[7]	198	11,515	43	108,409	1	2,003
Malta	12	n.a.	325	6	26	2
Moldova[2]	50	50,580	10	2,610,957	n.a.	6,500
Monaco	ndr	ndr	ndr	ndr	ndr	ndr
Netherlands	135	262,063	1,317	5,303	11	16
Norway	275	4,000	251	2,142	n.a.	n.a.
Poland	318	294	1,085	244,753	164	3,640
Portugal	155	2,422	2,164	153,774	15	136
Romania	443	32,156	500	322,446	115	57,223
Russian Federation[2]	4,194	823,530	3,910	3,025,126	150	9,112
San Marino	ndr	ndr	ndr	ndr	ndr	ndr
Serbia and Montenegro[7]	11	6,011	132	82,800	2	2,750
Slovakia[8]	11	200	77	58,393	1	n.a.
Slovenia[7]	n.a.	n.a.	1	1,305	ndr	ndr
Soviet Union[2]	28,076	2,404,616				
Spain	399	6,018,838	734	56,519	29	1
Sweden	36	122	71	162	7	n.a.
Switzerland	53	7,205	127	4,305	18	2,500
Turkey	2,659	865,404	19,871	5,112,353	54	6,078
Ukraine[2]	144	2,109,079	610	387,867	13	8,349
United Kingdom	822	205,031	2,243	296,811	6	6,000
Yugoslavia[7]	409	1,140				
Oceania	**1,063**	**16,376,307**	**3,292**	**2,126,793**	**46**	**28,247**
American Samoa (US)	n.a.	n.a.	6	23,063	n.a.	n.a.
Australia	341	14,988,447	330	687,522	35	4,420
Cook Islands (NZ)	6	2,000	19	2,252	n.a.	608
Fiji	53	389,372	92	304,327	n.a.	n.a.
French Polynesia (FR)	10	n.a.	13	511	ndr	ndr
Guam (US)	1	6,115	233	22,064	ndr	ndr
Kiribati	ndr	ndr	n.a.	84,000	ndr	ndr
Marshall Islands	n.a.	6,000	ndr	ndr	ndr	ndr
Micronesia, Fed. States of	5	203	48	37,431	ndr	ndr
Nauru	ndr	ndr	ndr	ndr	ndr	ndr
New Caledonia (FR)	2	n.a.	2	1,100	ndr	ndr
New Zealand	19	13,472	28	9,040	n.a.	500
Niue (NZ)	n.a.	200	1	702	ndr	ndr

	Total number of people reported killed (1986–1995)	Total number of people reported affected (1986–1995)	Total number of people reported killed (1996–2005)	Total number of people reported affected (1996–2005)	Total number of people reported killed (2005)	Total number of people reported affected (2005)
Northern Mariana Islands (US)	ndr	ndr	ndr	ndr	ndr	ndr
Palau	ndr	ndr	1	12,004	ndr	ndr
Papua New Guinea	404	367,302	2,443	832,963	2	17,693
Samoa	21	283,000	10	n.a.	9	n.a.
Solomon Islands	139	239,024	n.a.	1,905	ndr	ndr
Tokelau (NZ)	n.a.	1,832	n.a.	26	n.a.	26
Tonga	1	3,103	n.a.	23,071	ndr	ndr
Tuvalu	n.a.	850	18	n.a.	ndr	ndr
Vanuatu	55	70,867	48	84,812	n.a.	5,000
Wallis and Futuna (FR)	6	4,520	ndr	ndr	ndr	ndr
Total	**508,424**	**1,891,651,922**	**934,619**	**2,502,280,995**	**99,425**	**161,243,360**

Source: EM-DAT, CRED, University of Louvain, Belgium

[1] Prior to 1993, Ethiopia was considered one country; after this date separate countries: Eritrea and Ethiopia.

[2] Prior to 1991, the Soviet Union was considered one country; after this date separate countries. The former western republics of the USSR (Belarus, Estonia, Latvia, Lithuania, Moldova, Russian Federation, Ukraine) are included in Europe; the former southern republics (Armenia, Azerbaijan, Georgia, Kazakhstan, Kyrgyzstan, Tajikistan, Turkmenistan, Uzbekistan) are included in Asia.

[3] Since July 1997, Hong Kong has been included in China.

[4] Since May 2002, East Timor has been an independent country.

[5] Since September 1993 and the Israel–PLO Declaration of Principles, the Gaza Strip and the West Bank have had a Palestinian government. Direct negotiations to determine the permanent status of these territories began in September 1999 but are far from a permanent agreement.

[6] Prior to May 1990, Yemen was divided into Arab and People's Democratic Republics; after this date it has been considered one country.

[7] Prior to 1992, Yugoslavia was considered one country; after this date separate countries: Bosnia and Herzegovina, Croatia, Serbia and Montenegro, Slovenia, FYR of Macedonia.

[8] Prior to 1993, Czechoslovakia was considered one country; after this date separate countries: Czech Republic and Slovakia.

[9] Prior to October 1990, Germany was divided into Federal and Democratic Republics; after this date it has been considered one country.

Note: n.a. signifies no data available; ndr signifies no disaster reported. For more information, see section on caveats in introductory text.

Note: some totals may not match due to rounding.

Over the last decade, the highest numbers of deaths per continent were reported in Nigeria (Africa), Venezuela (Americas), the Democratic People's Republic of Korea (Asia), Italy (Europe) and Papua New Guinea (Oceania).

The highest numbers of disaster-affected people per continent were reported in Ethiopia (Africa), Brazil (Americas), China (Asia), Turkey (Europe) and Papua New Guinea (Oceania).

Compared with 1986–1995, the past decade has seen disaster deaths rise by 84 per cent and the numbers affected by disasters rise by 32 per cent.

Table 14 Refugees and asylum seekers by country/territory of origin (1999 to 2005)

	1999	2000	2001	2002	2003	2004	2005
Africa	**3,072,800**	**3,254,300**	**2,923,000**	**2,907,700**	**3,102,100**	**3,209,300**	**3,196,900**
Algeria	5,000	–	10,000	–	–	–	900
Angola	339,300	400,000	445,000	402,000	312,000	219,700	213,500
Benin	–	–	–	–	–	–	100
Burkina Faso	–	–	–	–	–	–	100
Burundi	311,000	421,000	375,000	395,000	349,000	472,700	438,500
Cameroon	–	–	2,000	–	–	2,300	3,900
Central African Republic	–	–	22,000	14,000	41,000	29,700	43,700
Chad	13,000	53,000	35,000	–	3,000	53,000	49,900
Comoros	–	–	–	–	–	–	500
Congo, DR of	229,000	342,000	355,000	393,000	422,000	456,100	450,800
Congo	25,000	22,000	30,000	15,000	14,000	22,700	24,300
Côte d'Ivoire	–	–	–	22,000	51,000	44,900	25,300
Djibouti	1,000	1,000	–	–	–	–	100
Egypt	–	–	–	–	–	–	2,200
Equatorial Guinea	–	–	–	–	–	–	200
Eritrea	323,100	356,400	305,000	285,000	277,000	199,700	215,300
Ethiopia	53,300	36,200	13,000	15,500	14,500	46,800	63,900
Gambia	–	–	–	–	–	–	700
Ghana	10,000	10,000	10,000	10,000	10,000	10,000	10,000
Guinea	–	–	5,000	–	–	–	2,600
Guinea-Bissau	5,300	1,500	–	–	–	–	100
Kenya	5,000	–	–	–	–	10,100	11,400
Liberia	249,000	196,000	215,000	255,300	381,800	323,100	219,800
Madagascar	–	–	–	–	–	–	100
Malawi	–	–	–	–	–	2,900	3,800
Mali	2,000	–	–	–	–	4,000	3,300
Mauritania	45,000	45,000	50,000	40,000	20,000	28,600	29,300
Morocco	–	–	–	–	–	124,000	117,400
Mozambique	–	–	–	–	–	–	400
Namibia	1,000	–	–	–	–	–	1,200
Niger	–	–	–	–	–	–	100
Nigeria	–	–	10,000	15,000	17,000	25,700	22,800
Rwanda	27,000	52,000	60,000	36,000	40,000	45,900	102,500
Senegal	10,000	10,000	10,000	11,000	13,000	11,600	9,600
Sierra Leone	454,000	419,000	185,000	115,000	61,000	20,800	26,500
Somalia	415,600	370,000	300,000	282,900	263,300	311,600	328,000
South Africa	–	–	–	–	–	–	100
Sudan	423,200	392,200	440,000	471,000	595,000	697,500	670,900
Tanzania	–	–	–	–	–	4,100	5,400
Togo	3,000	2,000	–	–	4,000	4,200	44,100
Tunisia	–	–	–	–	–	–	100
Uganda	15,000	20,000	20,000	25,000	28,000	29,100	35,100

	1999	2000	2001	2002	2003	2004	2005
Western Sahara[1]	105,000	105,000	110,000	105,000	191,000	–	–
Zambia	–	–	–	–	–	–	500
Zimbabwe	–	–	–	–	2,500	8,500	17,900
East Asia and Pacific	**864,100**	**1,056,000**	**1,078,500**	**1,172,100**	**1,236,100**	**1,366,000**	**1,385,900**
Cambodia	15,100	16,400	16,000	16,000	16,000	15,000	16,400
China (Tibet)	130,000	130,000	151,000	160,900	139,900	155,300	156,300
East Timor	120,000	120,000	80,000	28,000	–	–	–
Fiji	–	–	–	–	–	–	300
Indonesia	8,000	6,150	5,500	5,100	23,400	23,500	44,300
Japan	–	–	–	–	–	–	100
Korea, DPR of	–	50,000	50,000	100,000	101,700	100,000	51,400
Korea, Rep. of	–	–	–	–	–	–	300
Lao PDR	13,900	400	–	–	15,000	12,700	15,700
Malaysia	–	–	–	–	–	–	200
Mongolia	–	–	–	–	–	–	400
Myanmar	240,100	380,250	450,000	509,100	584,800	688,500	727,100
Philippines	45,000	57,000	57,000	57,000	57,200	65,000	67,700
Thailand	–	–	–	–	–	–	200
Viet Nam	292,000	295,800	295,000	296,000	298,100	306,000	305,500
South and Central Asia	**2,906,750**	**3,832,700**	**4,961,500**	**3,878,600**	**2,839,500**	**2,461,700**	**2,725,700**
Afghanistan	2,561,050	3,520,350	4,500,000	3,532,900	2,533,200	2,070,500	2,192,100
Bangladesh	–	–	–	–	–	6,800	45,300
Bhutan	125,000	124,000	126,000	127,000	128,700	120,400	122,300
India	15,000	17,000	17,000	18,000	17,000	11,900	11,700
Kazakhstan	–	100	–	–	–	–	500
Kyrgyzstan	–	–	–	–	–	–	200
Nepal[2]	–	–	–	–	–	100,000	201,800
Pakistan	–	–	10,000	–	6,700	14,700	16,500
Sri Lanka	110,000	110,000	144,000	148,100	106,400	82,600	79,100
Tajikistan	62,500	59,750	55,000	52,600	47,500	54,800	54,200
Turkmenistan	–	–	–	–	–	–	100
Uzbekistan	33,200	1,500	–	–	–	–	1,900
Middle East	**3,987,050**	**5,426,500**	**4,428,000**	**3,244,500**	**3,220,200**	**3,366,600**	**3,898,800**
Iran	31,200	30,600	34,000	24,800	21,000	27,000	31,900
Iraq[3]	534,450	409,300	300,000	237,400	268,200	349,400	888,700
Israel	–	–	–	–	–	–	500
Jordan	–	–	–	–	–	–	500
Lebanon	–	4,400	–	1,200	–	3,900	700
Libyan AJ	–	–	–	–	–	300	100
Palestinian Territory, Occupied[4]	3,931,400	4,982,100	4,123,000	2,981,100	2,927,000	2,986,000	2,971,600
Syrian Arab Rep.		100	–		4,000	–	4,400
Yemen	–	–	–	–	–	–	400

	1999	2000	2001	2002	2003	2004	2005
Europe	**1,238,100**	**755,900**	**674,000**	**517,500**	**438,600**	**226,500**	**230,100**
Albania	–	–	–	–	–	3,300	2,900
Armenia	188,400	–	9,000	–	–	2,500	4,200
Azerbaijan	230,000	–	–	–	–	11,000	13,000
Belarus	–	–	–	–	–	–	1,300
Bosnia and Herzegovina	250,000	234,600	210,000	156,100	121,200	30,300	29,700
Bulgaria	–	–	–	–	–	–	1,100
Croatia	336,000	314,700	272,000	250,000	208,900	69,800	59,600
Czech Republic	–	–	–	–	–	–	100
Estonia	–	–	–	–	–	–	100
Georgia	2,800	22,400	21,000	11,400	6,600	20,000	23,100
Hungary	–	–	–	–	–	–	200
Latvia	–	–	–	–	–	–	100
Lithuania	–	–	–	–	–	–	200
Macedonia, FYR of	–	–	23,000	3,000	–	–	1,400
Moldova	–	–	–	–	–	–	1,500
Poland	–	–	–	–	–	–	500
Portugal	–	–	–	–	–	–	100
Romania	–	–	–	–	–	–	900
Russian Federation	12,350	22,700	18,000	27,900	25,600	39,400	34,000
Serbia and Montenegro	376,400	148,900	60,000	52,200	52,800	19,300	24,700
Slovenia	–	4,400	–	–	–	–	100
Turkey	11,800	12,600	43,000	16,900	17,600	26,600	25,700
Ukraine	–	–	10,000	–	5,900	4,300	5,500
United Kingdom	–	–	–	–	–	–	100
Americas and Caribbean	**393,800**	**366,750**	**428,000**	**454,200**	**319,000**	**339,800**	**324,000**
Argentina	–	–	–	–	–	–	300
Bolivia	–	–	–	–	–	–	100
Brazil	–	–	–	–	–	–	600
Colombia	–	2,300	23,000	42,900	230,700	261,000	257,900
Costa Rica	–	–	–	–	–	–	100
Cuba	850	1,200	3,000	31,500	26,500	25,100	16,700
Ecuador	–	–	–	–	–	–	200
El Salvador[5]	253,000	235,500	217,000	203,000	4,500	4,500	5,000
Grenada	–	–	–	–	–	–	100
Guatemala[5]	146,000	102,600	129,000	129,000	10,200	12,600	5,900
Guyana	–	–	–	–	–	–	500
Haiti	23,000	20,600	25,000	30,800	23,800	19,900	17,200
Honduras	–	–	–	–	–	–	1,300
Jamaica	–	–	–	–	–	–	300
Mexico	–	–	11,000	–	20,700	4,100	4,900
Nicaragua[5]	18,000	3,800	13,000	15,800	2,600	8,200	5,600

International Federation
of Red Cross and Red Crescent Societies

	1999	2000	2001	2002	2003	2004	2005
Peru	1,700	750	–	1,200	–	–	2,900
St Lucia	–	–	–	–	–	–	200
St Vincent and the Grenadines	–	–	–	–	–	–	400
Trinidad and Tobago	–	–	–	–	–	–	200
United States	–	–	–	–	–	–	200
Venezuela	–	–	–	–	–	4,400	3,400
Total	**12,511,350**	**14,692,150**	**14,493,000**	**12,174,600**	**11,163,500**	**10,969,900**	**11,761,400**

Source: US Committee for Refugees and Immigrants

Note: – indicates zero or near zero.

[1] This territory is now controlled by Morocco. Hence USCRI is listing Morocco as being the country of origin.

[2] New information has led USCRI to believe that the number of Nepalis in India who should be considered refugees is about 100,000 higher than last year. Some may be new outflows and others may have become refugees *sur place*.

[3] Higher numbers of Iraqi refugees have been added in Jordan and Syria. Reflecting on UNHCR's return advisory and the deteriorating situation in Iraq, USCRI considers that many beneficiaries of the temporary protection regime may have become refugees *sur place*. USCRI used the cohort that arrived after the war began as a rough proxy and only did so in countries where there was no meaningful opportunity for a full refugee status determination.

[4] See note 2, Table 15.

[5] The Nicaraguan Adjustment and Central American Relief Act of 1997 (NACARA) covers many long-pending Salvadorean and Guatemalan asylum applicants. Those who apply under NACARA are granted permanent residence at a rate of 96 per cent. Those denied can still pursue asylum pursuant to a federal court settlement. USCRI, therefore, considers that these populations have a durable solution and should no longer be counted as people in need of international protection.

The number of refugees worldwide rose to around 12 million in 2005 – although this is still nearly 3 million less than the high point in 2000. Almost half of the world's refugees in 2005 were Palestinians (nearly 3 million) and Afghans (2.2 million). There are also significant populations of refugees from Iraq (889,000), Myanmar (727,000) and Sudan (680,000).

Hundreds of thousands of Afghans went home from Pakistan and Iran in the largest repatriation of the year. However, even larger numbers of Afghans were revealed by a recent census in Pakistan and by a registration exercise in Iran, causing the total number of Afghan refugees to rise by 120,000 compared with 2004.

The largest repatriation in Africa was to Liberia. Nearly 73,000 returned from Guinea, more than 30,000 from Côte d'Ivoire and about 5,000 from Sierra Leone. Nearly 50,000 Burundians returned from Tanzania – although not always voluntarily – but this was offset somewhat by new flight to Rwanda and Uganda. Sudanese refugee numbers went down by around 30,000, largely due to repatriations from the Democratic Republic of Congo and Ethiopia, offset by new Sudanese refugees fleeing to Kenya and Chad. Over 28,000 Congolese (DRC) returned from Burundi along with 5,000 from Zambia, but this was offset by an additional 11,000 fleeing to Rwanda and 5,000 fleeing to Uganda.

The 56,000 increase in Rwandan refugees is largely attributable to a recount in the Democratic Republic of Congo, while 10,000 Rwandans fled to Burundi and over 6,000 to Uganda. Another dramatic outflow was of 40,000 Togolese, including more than 25,000 to Benin and 11,000 to Ghana.

The number of Myanmar refugees rose but this was mostly due to enhanced measurement in Malaysia and some increased registration in Thailand rather than any major new outflow. The effects of natural increase among Palestinians were offset by new information that many of those in Kuwait actually possessed Jordanian nationality.

Confidential but reliable sources indicate that, due to a combination of more aggressive enforcement in China and an improving food situation in North Korea, the number of North Koreans in China is about half what it was last year.

	1999	2000	2001	2002	2003	2004	2005
Africa	**3,147,000**	**3,346,000**	**3,002,000**	**3,030,000**	**3,245,500**	**3,293,500**	**3,176,100**
Algeria	84,000	85,000	85,000	85,000	170,000	102,000	94,500
Angola	15,000	12,000	12,000	12,000	13,000	14,900	14,900
Benin	3,000	4,000	5,000	6,000	5,000	5,900	32,000
Botswana	1,000	3,000	4,000	4,000	4,500	3,800	3,200
Burkina Faso	–	–	–	–	–	–	1,300
Burundi	2,000	6,000	28,000	41,000	42,000	60,700	40,600
Cameroon	10,000	45,000	32,000	17,000	25,000	65,000	58,900
Central African Rep.	55,000	54,000	49,000	50,000	51,000	30,600	26,500
Chad	20,000	20,000	15,000	16,000	156,000	260,000	275,500
Congo, DR of	235,000	276,000	305,000	274,000	241,000	200,700	204,500
Congo	40,000	126,000	102,000	118,000	91,000	71,700	69,600
Côte d'Ivoire	135,000	94,000	103,000	50,000	74,000	74,200	44,100
Djibouti	23,000	22,000	22,000	23,000	36,000	18,000	10,500
Egypt	47,000	57,000	75,000	78,000	69,000	85,800	86,700
Eritrea	2,000	1,000	2,000	3,000	4,000	4,700	6,000
Ethiopia	246,000	194,000	114,000	115,000	112,000	116,000	101,100
Gabon	15,000	15,000	20,000	20,000	19,000	19,100	13,400
Gambia	25,000	15,000	15,000	10,000	10,000	11,000	8,800
Ghana	12,000	13,000	12,000	41,000	48,000	48,100	59,000
Guinea	453,000	390,000	190,000	182,000	223,000	145,200	67,300
Guinea-Bissau	5,000	6,000	7,000	7,000	10,000	7,700	7,800
Kenya	254,000	233,000	243,000	221,000	219,000	269,300	314,600
Liberia	90,000	70,000	60,000	65,000	60,000	38,600	16,100
Libyan AJ	11,000	11,000	33,000	12,000	–	12,400	12,000
Malawi	–	–	6,000	13,000	12,000	7,000	9,600
Mali	7,000	7,000	9,000	4,000	7,000	12,300	13,100
Mauritania	25,000	25,000	25,000	25,000	26,500	30,600	30,600
Morocco	–	–	–	2,000	–	2,300	2,300
Mozambique	1,000	2,000	5,000	7,000	8,000	5,500	6,000
Namibia	8,000	20,000	31,000	26,000	15,000	16,900	14,300
Niger	2,000	1,000	1,000	–	–	–	300
Nigeria	7,000	10,000	7,000	7,000	10,000	9,500	9,400
Rwanda	36,000	29,000	35,000	32,000	37,000	36,100	49,500
Senegal	42,000	41,000	43,000	45,000	23,000	23,200	23,400
Sierra Leone	7,000	3,000	15,000	60,000	70,000	65,700	60,100
Somalia	–	–	–	–	–	3,000	2,900
South Africa	40,000	30,000	22,000	65,000	104,000	142,900	169,800
Sudan	363,000	385,000	307,000	287,000	280,000	225,900	231,700
Swaziland	–	–	1,000	1,000	–	–	1,000
Tanzania	413,000	543,000	498,000	516,000	480,000	602,300	549,100
Togo	10,000	11,000	11,000	11,000	12,000	11,700	9,700
Tunisia	–	–	–	–	–	–	100

	1999	2000	2001	2002	2003	2004	2005
Uganda	197,000	230,000	174,000	221,000	231,500	252,300	254,400
Zambia	205,000	255,000	270,000	247,000	239,000	174,000	155,900
Zimbabwe	1,000	2,000	9,000	10,000	8,000	6,900	14,000
East Asia and Pacific	**657,300**	**791,700**	**815,700**	**874,700**	**953,400**	**1,013,200**	**1,029,400**
Australia	17,000	16,700	21,800	25,000	22,800	14,600	14,800
Cambodia	100	50	1,000	300	100	–	200
China[1]	292,800	350,000	345,000	396,000	396,000	401,500	352,700
Hong Kong[1]	n.a.	n.a.	n.a.	–	–	–	–
Indonesia	120,000	120,800	81,300	28,700	300	–	100
Japan	400	3,800	6,400	6,500	7,900	6,100	2,600
Korea, Rep. of	–	350	600	–	1,700	2,200	2,100
Malaysia	45,400	57,400	57,500	59,000	75,700	101,200	152,700
Nauru	–	–	800	100	200	–	–
New Zealand	–	3,100	2,700	1,700	1,200	1,800	1,000
Papua New Guinea	8,000	6,000	5,400	5,200	7,800	7,800	10,000
Philippines	200	200	200	200	2,200	2,200	300
Thailand	158,400	217,300	277,000	336,000	421,500	460,800	477,500
Viet Nam	15,000	16,000	16,000	16,000	16,000	15,000	15,400
South and Central Asia	**1,689,000**	**2,655,600**	**2,702,800**	**2,188,600**	**1,872,900**	**1,724,600**	**1,953,600**
Bangladesh	53,100	121,600	122,000	122,200	119,900	150,000	150,100
India	292,000	290,000	345,800	332,300	316,900	393,300	515,100
Kazakhstan	14,800	20,000	19,500	20,600	15,300	15,800	7,300
Kyrgyzstan	10,900	11,000	9,700	8,300	8,200	4,200	3,100
Nepal	130,000	129,000	131,000	132,000	134,600	130,600	130,600
Pakistan	1,127,000	2,019,000	2,018,000	1,518,000	1,219,000	968,800	1,088,100
Sri Lanka	–	–	–	–	–	–	200
Tajikistan	4,700	12,400	4,600	3,500	3,200	3,700	2,600
Turkmenistan	18,500	14,200	14,000	13,700	14,100	13,300	12,000
Uzbekistan	38,000	38,400	38,000	38,000	41,700	44,900	44,500
Middle East	**5,849,000**	**6,035,300**	**6,830,200**	**5,290,300**	**4,353,100**	**4,288,100**	**4,855,400**
Gaza Strip	798,400	824,600	852,600	879,000	923,000	952,300	986,000
Iran	1,835,000	1,895,000	2,558,000	2,208,500	1,335,000	1,046,100	994,000
Iraq	129,400	127,700	128,100	134,700	131,500	96,600	63,400
Israel	400	4,700	4,700	2,100	1,000	4,900	1,500
Jordan[2]	1,518,000	1,580,000	1,643,900	155,000	163,700	168,300	609,500
Kuwait	52,000	52,000	50,000	65,000	65,000	51,800	14,300
Lebanon[2]	378,100	383,200	389,500	409,000	256,000	265,800	296,800
Qatar	–	–	–	–	–	–	100
Saudi Arabia	128,600	128,500	128,500	245,400	240,900	243,700	240,800
Syrian Arab Rep.[2]	379,200	389,000	397,600	482,400	497,000	701,700	866,300
United Arab Emirates	–	–	–	–	–	–	200
West Bank	569,700	583,000	607,800	627,500	665,000	682,700	699,800

	1999	2000	2001	2002	2003	2004	2005
Yemen	60,000	67,600	69,500	81,700	75,000	74,200	82,700
Europe	**1,909,100**	**1,153,300**	**972,800**	**877,400**	**884,500**	**610,500**	**530,200**
Albania	5,000	500	400	100	100	–	100
Armenia	240,000	–	11,000	11,000	11,000	11,200	11,300
Austria	16,600	6,100	10,800	30,900	17,600	19,300	17,300
Azerbaijan	222,000	3,600	7,000	11,400	10,300	9,800	3,300
Belarus	2,900	3,200	3,100	3,600	3,400	3,400	2,700
Belgium	42,000	46,400	41,000	30,300	33,000	24,500	14,100
Bosnia and Herzegovina	60,000	38,200	33,200	34,200	22,500	22,700	10,800
Bulgaria	2,800	3,000	2,900	1,200	800	5,200	5,200
Croatia	24,000	22,500	21,900	8,100	4,200	3,700	2,900
Cyprus	300	300	1,300	1,800	5,300	10,600	14,300
Czech Republic	1,800	4,800	10,600	6,300	3,900	2,700	1,300
Denmark	8,500	10,300	12,200	5,200	2,800	2,000	2,000
Finland	3,800	2,600	2,100	1,200	2,300	–	2,400
France	30,000	26,200	12,400	27,600	34,900	22,900	25,500
Georgia	5,200	7,600	7,900	4,200	3,900	2,600	2,500
Germany	285,000	180,000	116,000	104,000	90,800	83,300	64,200
Greece	7,500	800	6,500	1,800	5,200	10,200	11,300
Hungary	6,000	4,200	2,900	1,200	1,500	8,000	8,800
Iceland	100	50	–	–	–	–	300
Ireland	8,500	7,700	9,500	6,500	5,800	10,800	2,400
Italy	24,900	13,700	9,600	5,200	5,600	5,800	5,800
Liechtenstein	–	–	–	–	–	–	200
Lithuania	100	150	300	200	100	–	600
Macedonia, FYR of	17,400	9,000	3,600	2,700	2,300	2,200	2,200
Malta	–	–	–	–	200	–	2,400
Moldova	–	–	300	300	100	–	200
Netherlands	40,000	29,600	31,000	17,200	14,600	12,800	14,400
Norway	9,500	8,600	13,200	5,900	11,000	8,900	4,300
Poland	1,300	2,300	1,800	300	1,500	8,700	6,200
Portugal	1,700	1,600	50	–	–	–	400
Romania	900	2,100	200	100	200	2,400	2,300
Russian Federation	104,300	36,200	28,200	17,400	161,300	150,000	149,200
Serbia and Montenegro	476,000	484,200	400,000	353,000	291,100	76,500	78,600
Slovak Republic	400	400	3,100	4,500	4,700	3,300	3,100
Slovenia	5,000	12,000	2,700	400	100	–	200
Spain	4,500	1,100	1,000	200	200	–	1,600
Sweden	20,200	18,500	18,500	24,900	25,600	19,400	19,400
Switzerland	104,000	62,600	57,900	44,200	38,300	31,200	10,500
Turkey	9,100	9,900	12,600	10,000	9,500	7,800	7,300
Ukraine	5,800	5,500	6,000	3,600	3,100	6,400	4,000
United Kingdom	112,000	87,800	69,800	79,200	55,700	22,200	14,600

International Federation
of Red Cross and Red Crescent Societies

	1999	2000	2001	2002	2003	2004	2005
Americas and the Caribbean	**737,000**	**562,100**	**597,000**	**756,500**	**543,500**	**535,600**	**475,000**
Argentina	3,300	1,000	3,100	2,700	2,300	3,900	3,900
Bahamas	100	100	100	–	–	–	–
Belize	3,000	1,700	–	1,000	900	–	700
Bolivia	400	–	400	400	500	–	500
Brazil	2,300	2,700	4,050	3,700	3,900	3,800	3,700
Canada	53,000	54,400	70,000	78,400	70,200	54,800	39,500
Chile	300	300	550	400	500	–	900
Colombia	250	250	200	200	200	–	200
Costa Rica	22,900	7,300	10,600	12,800	13,600	10,600	12,200
Cuba	1,000	1,000	1,000	1,000	800	–	700
Dominican Republic	650	500	500	300	500	–	1,000
Ecuador	350	1,600	4,300	9,100	16,500	45,100	47,400
El Salvador	–	–	–	–	200	–	–
Guatemala	750	700	700	700	800	–	400
Jamaica	50	50	–	–	–	–	–
Mexico	8,500	6,500	6,200	4,000	2,900	4,500	3,400
Nicaragua	500	300	–	–	300	–	200
Panama	600	1,300	1,500	1,700	2,000	–	2,200
Paraguay	–	–	50	–	–	–	–
Peru	700	750	750	900	800	–	1,200
United States[3]	638,000	481,500	492,500	638,000	244,200	232,800	176,700
Uruguay	150	50	100	100	100	–	100
Venezuela	200	100	400	1,100	182,300	180,100	180,100
Total	**13,988,000**	**14,543,700**	**14,921,000**	**12,337,500**	**11,852,900**	**11,465,500**	**12,019,700**

Source: US Committee for Refugees and Immigrants

Note: – indicates zero or near zero; n.a. not available, or reported estimates unreliable.
[1] As of 1997, figures for Hong Kong are included in total for China.
[2] In the light of persistent protection gaps, USCR concluded in 2003 that the inclusion clause of Article 1D of the UN Refugee Convention brings Palestinian refugees under the Convention's application. Accordingly, USCR changed its statistical approach in 2003 by applying the Convention's definition of refugee status – including its cessation – to this population rather than UNRWA's registration criteria as before. The numbers in Lebanon were adjusted to reflect the acquisition of citizenship in Lebanon and other countries.
[3] Includes asylum applications pending in the United States; USCRI estimates the number of individuals represented per case.

In 2005, Pakistan continued to host more refugees (over 1 million) than any other country in the world, while Iran hosted nearly 1 million refugees. The Middle East hosted 4.8 million refugees, while Africa hosted over 3 million. By contrast, Europe hosted 530,000 refugees and the Americas and Caribbean hosted 475,000.

USCRI adjusted the number of Burundians in Tanzania upwards to reflect new analysis of the durability of protection for more than 100,000 'long-stayers' and made the same calculations for 40,000 Chadians in Cameroon. USCRI adjusted the number of Western Saharan refugees in Algeria downwards by 67,000 to reflect new data. A joint UNHCR–host government re-registration exercise reduced the count of former Yugoslav refugees in Serbia and Montenegro by more than 200,000 as many had been found to have naturalized, returned or resettled, some earlier than 2004. USCRI also reduced the count of Eritreans in Sudan, although the number is still believed to be substantially more than UNHCR's figures.

Erratum: The figure of 20,600 refugees, recorded in WDR 2005 as hosted by New Zealand in 2004, was incorrect. The figure should have read 1,800 and has been corrected in this year's tables.

	1999	2000	2001	2002	2003	2004	2005
Africa[1]	**10,355,000**	**10,527,000**	**10,935,000**	**15,230,000**	**13,099,000**	**12,163,000**	**11,921,300**
Algeria	100,000	100,000	100,000	100,000	100,000	400,000	400,000
Angola	1,500,000	2,000,000	2,000,000	2,000,000	1,000,000	60,000	61,700
Burundi	800,000	600,000	600,000	400,000	400,000	145,000	117,000
Central African Republic	–	–	5,000	10,000	200,000	200,000	200,000
Congo, DR	800,000	1,500,000	50,000	2,000,000	3,200,000	2,330,000	1,664,000
Congo	500,000	30,000	2,000,000	100,000	60,000	48,000	48,000
Côte d'Ivoire	–	2,000	5,000	500,000	500,000	500,000	500,000
Eritrea	250,000	310,000	90,000	75,000	75,000	59,000	50,500
Ethiopia	300,000	250,000	100,000	90,000	90,000	132,000	150,000
Guinea	–	60,000	100,000	20,000	20,000	82,000	82,000
Guinea-Bissau	50,000	–	–	–	–	–	–
Kenya	100,000	100,000	200,000	230,000	230,000	360,000	381,900
Liberia	50,000	20,000	80,000	100,000	500,000	464,000	48,000
Nigeria	5,000	–	50,000	50,000	57,000	200,000	200,000
Rwanda	600,000	150,000	–	–	–	–	–
Senegal	–	5,000	5,000	5,000	17,000	–	–
Sierra Leone	500,000	700,000	600,000	–	–	3,000	–
Somalia	350,000	300,000	400,000	350,000	350,000	400,000	370,000
Sudan	4,000,000	4,000,000	4,000,000	4,000,000	4,800,000	5,300,000	5,335,000
Togo	–	–	–	–	–	–	3,000
Uganda	450,000	400,000	500,000	600,000	1,400,000	1,330,000	1,740,500
Zimbabwe	–	–	50,000	100,000	100,000	150,000	569,700
East Asia and Pacific	**1,577,000**	**1,670,000**	**2,266,000**	**1,349,000**	**1,400,000**	**1,160,000**	**992,000**
East Timor	300,000	–	–	–	–	–	–
Indonesia	440,000	800,000	1,400,000	600,000	600,000	500,000	342,000
Korea, DPR of	–	100,000	100,000	100,000	50,000	50,000	50,000
Myanmar	600,000	600,000	600,000	600,000	600,000	550,000	540,000
Papua New Guinea	5,000	–	1,000	–	–	–	–
Philippines	200,000	140,000	135,000	45,000	150,000	60,000	60,000
Solomon Islands	32,000	30,000	30,000	4,000	–	–	–
Europe	**3,993,000**	**3,539,000**	**2,785,000**	**2,560,000**	**2,455,800**	**2,226,500**	**2,013,700**
Armenia	–	–	50,000	50,000	50,000	50,000	8,000
Azerbaijan	568,000	575,000	572,000	576,000	571,000	528,000	558,400
Bosnia and Herzegovina	830,000	518,000	439,000	368,000	327,200	309,200	183,400
Croatia	50,000	34,000	23,000	17,000	12,600	12,600	4,900
Cyprus	265,000	265,000	265,000	265,000	265,000	150,000	150,000
Georgia	280,000	272,000	264,000	262,000	260,000	260,000	240,000
Macedonia, FYR of	–	–	21,000	9,000	–	2,700	800
Russian Federation	800,000	800,000	474,000	371,000	368,000	339,000	265,000

	1999	2000	2001	2002	2003	2004	2005
Serbia and Montenegro	600,000	475,000	277,000	262,000	252,000	225,000	247,400
Turkey[1]	600,000	600,000	400,000	380,000	350,000	350,000	355,800
Americas and Caribbean	**1,886,000**	**2,176,000**	**2,465,000**	**2,518,000**	**2,742,000**	**2,912,000**	**2,970,000**
Colombia	1,800,000	2,100,000	2,450,000	2,500,000	2,730,000	2,900,000	2,900,000
Haiti	–	–	–	6,000			
Mexico	16,000	16,000	15,000	12,000	12,000	12,000	10,000
Peru	70,000	60,000	–	–	–	–	60,000
Middle East[1]	**1,917,000**	**1,700,000**	**1,670,000**	**2,646,000**	**2,346,000**	**1,648,000**	**1,792,000**
Palestinian Territory, Occupied	17,000	–	20,000	26,000	–	–	–
Iraq	900,000	700,000	700,000	1,100,000	800,000	1,000,000	1,300,000
Israel	200,000	200,000	200,000	250,000	276,000	10,000	9,000
Jordan	–	–	–	800,000	800,000	168,000	160,000
Lebanon	350,000	350,000	250,000	300,000	300,000	300,000	250,000
Syrian Arab Rep.	450,000	450,000	500,000	170,000	170,000	170,000	73,000
South and Central Asia	**1,617,000**	**1,542,000**	**2,402,000**	**2,023,000**	**1,511,000**	**1,205,000**	**1,282,800**
Afghanistan[1]	500,000	375,000	1,000,000	700,000	200,000	167,000	153,200
Bangladesh	50,000	60,000	100,000	60,000	61,000	65,000	65,000
India	507,000	507,000	500,000	600,000	650,000	500,000	600,000
Nepal[1]	–	–	–	100,000	100,000	100,000	100,000
Pakistan[1]	–	–	2,000	–	–	17,000	20,000
Sri Lanka	560,000	600,000	800,000	563,000	500,000	353,000	341,200
Uzbekistan	–	–	–	–	–	3,000	3,400
Total	**21,345,000**	**21,154,000**	**22,523,000**	**26,326,000**	**23,553,800**	**21,314,500**	**20,971,800**

Source: US Committee for Refugees and Immigrants

Note: – indicates zero or near zero; n.a. not available, or reported estimates unreliable.

[1] Estimates of the size of internally displaced populations are frequently subject to great margins of error and are often imprecise, particularly in these countries and regions.

According to USCRI, estimated numbers of global internally displaced people (IDPs) remained at around 21 million in 2005, albeit less than the 26 million peak in 2002. Africa accounted for well over half of all IDPs, with 5.3 million in Sudan, 1.7 million in Uganda and 1.6 million in the Democratic Republic of Congo (DRC). Other significant populations of IDPs included Colombia (2.9 million) and Iraq (1.3 million).

In early 2006, the Internal Displacement Monitoring Centre (IDMC) of the Norwegian Refugee Council put the figure of IDPs in December 2005 at 23.7 million, including 3.7 million in Colombia. IDMC reported that conflict newly uprooted over 2 million people during 2005, although nearly 4 million others were able to return home, especially in the DRC, Southern Sudan and Liberia. However, these returns were often not sustainable.

According to IDMC, continued violence in eastern provinces of the DRC displaced at least half a million people during 2005, while in Zimbabwe the government evicted 570,000 people from their homes in urban slums. Ongoing fighting in Colombia displaced over 200,000 more people. In Iraq, military operations caused the often temporary displacement of an estimated 200,000 people. In Sudan's Darfur region, brutal attacks on civilians led to the displacement of tens of thousands. Civil wars generated roughly half of all IDP situations, while at least 16 governments or occupation authorities directly or indirectly displaced people in 2005, according to IDMC. The organization added that in a quarter of IDP situations, governments restricted international humanitarian access to affected people.

Index

INDEX

INDEX

International Federation
of Red Cross and Red Crescent Societies

sanitation 9, 33, 58, 158, 159, 183-185, 190, 197

Saudi Arabia 170, 222, 231

Save the Children 102, 112, 114, 115

Scotland 11, 167

seismology 85
see also earthquakes
see also Richter scale

Selassie, Haile 29

Senegal 117, 119, 120, 128, 129, 220, 226, 230, 234

septicaemia 95

Serbia 121, 224, 225, 228, 232, 233, 235

settlements 77, 82, 154

sexually transmitted infections 44, 105
see also HIV/AIDS

shanty towns 72

shelter 15, 33, 81, 151, 183, 184, 197

Shirkat Gah women's collective 148
see also women's grass-roots organizations

Sicily 119, 123, 126, 127
see also Italy

Sierra Leone 177, 220, 226, 229, 230, 234

skilled birth attendants (SBAs) 93

social exclusion 74

social violence 72, 74

social vulnerability 34, 35, 37, 38, 76, 141

Somalia 8, 11, 14, 17, 25, 26, 31, 32, 39, 41, 117, 167, 220, 226, 230, 234

South Asia 8, 11, 14, 17-19, 27, 30, 107, 114, 137, 162, 163, 171, 180, 182, 190, 195, 208, 210

South Asia earthquake 8, 11, 14, 18, 19, 27, 30, 163, 171, 182, 190, 195, 208, 210

Southern Africa 48

Soviet Union 168, 225

Spain 4, 117, 120, 121, 124-126, 128, 131, 133, 136, 138, 192, 224, 232
see also Canary Islands
see also Ceuta
see also Fuerteventura
see also Melilla
see also Tenerife

Spanish Red Cross 119, 121, 124, 128, 129, 139

Spindler, William 124, 130

Sri Lanka 106, 141, 147, 150, 154, 155, 156, 159, 161, 162, 222, 227, 231, 235
see also Ampara

stakeholders 64, 157

stress 147, 148

stunted 68, 98

Suárez, María 90

sub-Saharan Africa 13, 60, 63, 94, 121, 182

subsidy programme 52, 60
see also area-based subsidy

Sudan 11, 17, 18, 20, 31, 32, 39, 165, 172, 178, 180, 220, 226, 229, 230, 233, 234, 235
see also Darfur

surgery 98, 99, 104, 110, 146

survivor 155

Swiss Re 22, 199

Switzerland 2, 121, 192, 210, 224, 232

Tajikistan 177, 225, 227, 231

Tamil Nadu 143, 158, 162
see also India

technological disaster(s) 22, 195, 198, 201, 210, 212, 213, 216, 217
see also disaster(s)
see also natural disaster(s)

village(s) 9, 25, 46, 48, 49, 51, 52, 67, 69, 73, 74, 77, 93, 95-99, 101, 103, 106, 111, 112, 124, 149-155, 158, 159

village development committee 99

village health assistant 101

village health post(s) 99, 101, 111

violent deaths 74

volcano 70, 84

volunteer(s) 15, 67, 81, 84, 100, 107, 112, 121, 125, 129, 136, 151, 153, 159, 160, 188

vulnerability 4, 14, 20-23, 31, 34-38, 48, 50, 56, 59, 61, 64, 67-72, 75, 76, 79, 81, 83, 86, 89, 104, 127, 141, 145, 157, 160, 189, 190, 191, 197

Vulnerability Assessment Committee (VAC) 50, 51, 58

vulnerability reduction 35

vulnerable housing 88

Wahlstrom, Margareta 27, 31, 33

Washington Post, The 24, 40, 128

water 9, 11, 15, 25, 33, 35, 37, 47, 53, 58, 60, 62, 67, 86, 122, 128, 129, 135, 142, 145, 146, 153, 158, 159, 183-185, 190, 197, 198

water supply 159

West Africa 11, 17, 28, 33, 117, 125, 126, 175, 180, 188

western donor(s) 21, 30, 165

Western Sahara 11, 117, 119, 121, 128

wetlands 142

widow(s) 84, 97, 151

windstorm(s) 4, 70, 87, 159, 195, 197, 209, 211-218

women 4, 9, 12, 27, 30, 33, 35, 46, 49, 53, 54, 73-77, 79, 83, 84, 88, 89, 93, 95, 97-100, 102-114, 124, 137, 141-151, 154-157, 160-163

Women's Coalition for Disaster Management 159

women's grass-roots organizations 159

World Bank 21, 34, 58, 65, 68, 73, 75, 83, 90, 98, 157, 161, 162, 167, 178, 180, 198

World Blood Donor Day 100

World Conference on Disaster Reduction (WCDR) 34

World Disasters Report 2, 25, 27, 38, 106, 122, 141, 161, 162, 185

World Food Programme (WFP) 28, 58, 96

World Health Organization (WHO) 95, 195

Yemen 68, 117, 120, 223, 225, 227, 232

youth education 84
     see also education

Zimbabwe 30, 63, 177, 220, 227, 231, 234, 235